THE PSYCHOLOGY
OF JUDGMENT
AND DECISION MAKING

THE PSYCHOLOGY
OF JUDGMENT
AND DECISION MAKING

SCOTT PLOUS

Wesleyan University

McGraw-Hill, Inc.
New York St. Louis San Francisco Auckland Bogotá
Caracas Lisbon London Madrid Mexico City Milan
Montreal New Delhi San Juan Singapore
Sydney Tokyo Toronto

This book is printed on acid-free paper.

THE PSYCHOLOGY OF JUDGMENT
AND DECISION MAKING

Credits appear on pages 293–294, and on this page by reference.

20 DOC/DOC 0 9 8 7 6 5

ISBN 0-07-050477-6

This book was set in New Aster by The Clarinda Company.
The editors were Christopher Rogers and James R. Belser;
the designer was Rafael Hernandez;
the production supervisor was Annette Mayeski.
The cover painting was by Paul Rogers.
R. R. Donnelley & Sons Company was printer and binder.

Library of Congress Cataloging-in-Publication Data

Plous, Scott.
    The psychology of judgment and decision making / Scott Plous.
        p.   cm.
    Includes bibliographical references and index.
    ISBN 0-07-050477-6
    1. Decision-making.   2. Judgment.   I. Title.
BF448.P56   1993
153.8′3—dc20   92-38542

ABOUT THE AUTHOR

Photo by Paul Romé

Scott Plous is an assistant professor of psychology at Wesleyan University. He graduated *Summa cum Laude* from the University of Minnesota and received his Ph.D. in psychology at Stanford University. Following graduate school, he completed two years of postdoctoral study in political psychology at Stanford and held a two-year visiting professorship at the University of Illinois in Champaign/ Urbana.

Plous has been the recipient of several honors and awards, including a MacArthur Foundation Fellowship in International Peace and Cooperation, the Gordon Allport Intergroup Relations Prize, the IAAP Young Psychologist Award, and the Slusser Peace Essay Prize. He teaches courses in judgment and decision making, social psychology, statistics, and research methods, and he has published more than 20 articles in journals and magazines such as *Psychology Today*, *Psychological Science*, the *Journal of Consulting and Clinical Psychology*, the *Journal of Conflict Resolution*, and the *Journal of Applied Social Psychology*.

Although Plous is best known for his research on the psychology of the nuclear arms race, his recent work has focused on ethical issues concerning animals and the environment. In 1991, he published the first large-scale opinion survey of animal rights activists, and he is currently editing an issue of the *Journal of Social Issues* on the role of animals in human society. In addition to academic life, Plous has served as a political or business consultant on numerous projects, and many of his experiences consulting have laid the foundation for this book.

To P.G.Z. and K.M.,
Who Believed
When Others Did Not.

CONTENTS

FOREWORD

To discover where the *action* is in psychology, look to social psychology. In recent years, the field of social psychology has emerged as central in psychology's quest to understand human thought, feeling, and behavior. Thus, we see the inclusion-by-hyphenation of social psychology across diverse fields of psychology, such as social-cognitive, social-developmental, social-learning, and social-personality, to name but a few recent amalgamations.

Social psychologists have tackled many of society's most intractable problems. In their role as the last generalists in psychology, nothing of individual and societal concern is alien to social psychological investigators—from psychophysiology to peace psychology, from students' attributions for failure to preventive education for AIDS. The new political and economic upheavals taking place throughout Europe and Asia, with the collapse of Soviet-style communism, are spurring social psychologists to develop new ways of introducing democracy and freedom of choice into the social lives of peoples long dominated by authoritarian rule. Indeed, since the days when George Miller, former president of the American Psychological Association, called upon psychologists to "give psychology back to the people," social psychologists have been at the forefront.

The **McGraw-Hill Series in Social Psychology** is a celebration of the contributions made by some of the most distinguished researchers, theorists, and practitioners of our craft. Each author in our series shares the vision of combining rigorous scholarship with the educator's goal of communicating that information to the widest possible audience of teachers, researchers, students, and interested laypersons. The series is designed to cover the entire range of social psychology, with titles reflecting both broad and more narrowly focused areas of specialization. Instructors may use any of these books as supplements to a basic text, or use a combination of them to delve into selected topics in greater depth.

ABOUT THIS BOOK

Just as cognitive psychologists have advanced the frontiers of decision research by exposing several limitations of traditional "rational-actor" models of decision making, social psychologists have enriched this area of knowledge by expanding its boundaries in many directions. In this new and original integration of the entire field, Scott Plous shows us how a social perspective on judgment and decision making can offer practical suggestions on how to deal with many common problems in daily life. Not only has Plous created an easily grasped overview of a vast research literature; his book includes a number of novel insights, valuable new terms, and intriguing conclusions.

What I believe readers will find most delightful here is the remarkable blend of high-level scholarship and Plous's concern for effectively communicating complex ideas to the broadest possible audience—from undergraduates, to professionals in business and health, to national public opinion leaders. This book is filled with pedagogical gems, new formulas for enriching old ideas, unique exercises in critical thinking that instruct while they capture the imagination, and provocative juxtapositions of usually unrelated topics. Rarely has a first book by a young scholar offered so much to so many on such a vital topic.

Philip Zimbardo

PREFACE

Today, Americans can choose from more than 25,000 products at the supermarket. They can read any of 11,000 magazines or periodicals. And they can flip channels between more than 50 television stations (Williams, 1990, February 14). In short, they are faced with a bewildering array of choices.

How do people make decisions? How do they sift through the information without drowning in a sea of alternatives? And what are the factors that lead them in a certain direction?

This book offers some tentative answers. It is a book intended for nonspecialists who would like an introduction to psychological research on judgment and decision making. The focus is on experimental findings rather than psychological theory, surprising conclusions rather than intuitions, and descriptive prose rather than mathematics. It is, in brief, a book designed to entertain and challenge as much as to inform and instruct.

The book is divided into six sections. The first two sections cover several building blocks of judgment and decision making: perception, memory, context, and question format. In the third and fourth sections, historical models of decision making are contrasted with recent models that take into account various biases in judgment. The fifth section examines judgments made by and about groups, and the sixth section discusses common traps in judgment and decision making. Each chapter is intended as a relatively "free standing" review of the topic it covers; thus, readers can skip or rearrange chapters with ease.

An unusual feature of this book is the Reader Survey preceding Chapter 1. The Reader Survey is made up of questions that are reproduced or adapted from many of the studies discussed in later chapters. Once you complete the survey, you will be able to compare your answers with the responses people gave in the original studies. Sometimes your answers will match theirs, sometimes they will not. In either event, though, you will have a written record of what your own style of judgment and decision making was before reading this book. Because your answers to the Reader Survey will be discussed throughout the book, it is very important that you complete the survey *before* reading any of the chapters.

A NOTE ON PSYCHOLOGICAL EXPERIMENTATION

To readers unfamiliar with psychology, some of the terminology and experimental procedures discussed in this book may seem callous or insensitive. For example, experimental participants are referred to impersonally as "subjects." Also, a number of experimental procedures initially deceive participants about the true purpose of the study, and the final results of some studies portray human decision makers as seriously biased or flawed in some way.

These concerns are important and deserve some comment.

First, the reason for using an impersonal term such as *subject* is that it often allows for greater clarity than generic terms such as *person* or *individual,* and it is less awkward than terms such as *participant* or *volunteer.* The word *subject*—which is standard in psychology and is used throughout this book—does not mean that psychologists treat experimental participants as though they are inanimate objects. In fact, the actual *subject* of most psychological research is not the experimental participant per se—it is the participant's *behavior.*

Second, there are several reasons why deception is sometimes used in psychological research. In many cases, subjects are given vague or misleading "cover stories" so that they are not influenced by the true purpose of the experiment. For example, subjects in an experiment on group dynamics might be told initially that the experiment is about "learning and memory" to keep them from paying too much attention to their division into groups. In other cases, deception is used to give the appearance of a situation that would otherwise be impossible to create. For instance, subjects in an experiment on creativity might be randomly assigned to receive positive or negative feedback about their solutions to a problem. If subjects were accurately informed in advance that they would be receiving randomly assigned feedback, the feedback would not be viewed as meaningful.

Although there are good reasons to oppose the use of deception in research (Warwick, 1975, February), it is important to note that the American Psychological Association (1989) has established a set of ethical guidelines designed to protect subjects in the event that deception is used. These guidelines mandate that subjects be told enough about the experiment to give their informed consent, that deception be used only as a last resort, that subjects be protected from harm or significant discomfort, that subjects be allowed to discontinue participation at any time, that information about individual subjects be treated as confidential, and that any use of deception be explained after the experiment is over. Most universities require investigators to adhere strictly to these guidelines.

Finally, there are several reasons for concentrating on biases and flaws more than successes. The most mundane reason for emphasizing such research is that there is simply more of it (Kahneman, 1991). Academic journals prefer to publish research findings that run counter to ordinary intuitions, and, as a consequence, more research has been published on failures in decision making than on successes. In this respect, professional journals are similar to newspapers and magazines: They place a premium on news that is surprising or intriguing. According to one estimate (Christensen-Szalanski & Beach, 1984), journal articles cite studies of flawed reasoning roughly six times more often than studies of successful reasoning. Because this book is intended as an introduction to research on judgment and decision making, it naturally reflects the wider priorities of the research community.

There is a more important reason for focusing on shortcomings, however. Failures in judgment and decision making are usually more informative than successes—even (and especially) when successes are the rule. The attention this book devotes to biases and errors is not meant to imply that people are generally poor decision makers; rather, it suggests that failures in judgment and decision making often reveal how these processes work, just as failures in an automobile often reveal how a car works. As Richard Nisbett and Lee Ross (1980, p. xii) explain, this approach is based on "the same premise that leads many of our colleagues to study perceptual illusions or thinking disorders—the belief that the nature of cognitive structures and processes can be revealed by the defects which they produce."

And of course, an emphasis on error has the additional advantage of yielding results that are easy to apply. Once you recognize that a certain situation typically leads to biases or errors, you can often sidestep it or take remedial actions. To facilitate this process, I have included everyday examples from medicine, law, business, education, nuclear arms control (my own specialization), and other fields. Indeed, many of the results in this book are general enough that I offer the following pledge to readers not yet familiar with research on judgment and decision making: *by judiciously applying the results described in this book, you should be better able to avoid decision biases, errors, and traps, and you will better understand the decisions made by other people.*

ACKNOWLEDGMENTS

I wish to thank the following people for their comments on earlier drafts of this book: Joel Brockner, Baruch Fischhoff, Nancy Gallagher, Beth Loftus, Duncan Luce, Dave Myers, Heather Nash, Jim Plous, Paul Slovic, Janet Sniezek, Mark Snyder, Amos Tversky, Willem Wagenaar, Elke Weber, and Phil Zimbardo.

I am also indebted to Tamra Williams and Heather Nash for their library assistance, and to Steven Lebergott for running what is arguably the best Interlibrary Loan Service in the United States.

It was a pleasure working with Chris Rogers, Laura Lynch, Nomi Sofer, Jim Belser, and other members of the editorial staff at McGraw-Hill.

And for all that coffee, for innumerable discussions late into the night, for love and encouragement and cheerful help every step of the way, I thank Diane Ersepke.

Scott Plous

THE PSYCHOLOGY
OF JUDGMENT
AND DECISION MAKING

READER SURVEY

It is very important that you complete this survey BEFORE reading ahead. That way, you won't fall prey to hindsight biases, or the "I-knew-it-all-along effect" (discussed in Chapter 3). If you prefer not to write in the book, just jot down your answers on a piece of paper and use the paper as a bookmark.

(1) Linda is 31 years old, single, outspoken, and very bright. She majored in philosophy. As a student, she was deeply concerned with issues of discrimination and social justice, and also participated in antinuclear demonstrations. Please check off the most likely alternative:

☑ Linda is a bank teller.
❏ Linda is a bank teller and is active in the feminist movement.

(2) If you were faced with the following choice, which alternative would you choose?

❏ A 100 percent chance of losing $50
☑ A 25 percent chance of losing $200, and a 75 percent chance of losing nothing

(3) John is envious, stubborn, critical, impulsive, industrious, and intelligent. In general, how emotional do you think John is? (Circle *one* number)

Not emotional at all 1 2 ③ 4 5 6 7 8 9 Extremely emotional

(4) Jim is intelligent, skillful, industrious, warm, determined, practical, and cautious. Please circle the other traits you think Jim is most likely to have.

Circle one trait in each pair:

Generous	——	Ungenerous
Unhappy	——	Happy
Irritable	——	Good-natured
Humorous	——	Humorless

(5) Here's a question for college students only: Compared to other students of your sex and age, what are the chances that the following events will happen to you? (Check the *one* answer that comes closest to your view for each event.)

(5a) *Will develop a drinking problem:*

- ❏ 60+ percent more likely
- ❏ 40 percent more likely
- ❏ 20 percent more likely
- ❏ No more or less likely
- ❏ 20 percent less likely
- ☑ 40 percent less likely
- ❏ 60+ percent less likely

(5b) *Will own your own home:*

- ❏ 60+ percent more likely
- ☑ 40 percent more likely
- ❏ 20 percent more likely
- ❏ No more or less likely
- ❏ 20 percent less likely
- ❏ 40 percent less likely
- ❏ 60+ percent less likely

(5c) *Will receive a postgraduate starting salary above $15,000:*

- ❏ 60+ percent more likely
- ❏ 40 percent more likely
- ❏ 20 percent more likely
- ☑ No more or less likely
- ❏ 20 percent less likely
- ❏ 40 percent less likely
- ❏ 60+ percent less likely

(5d) *Will have a heart attack before the age of 40:*

- ❏ 60+ percent more likely
- ❏ 40 percent more likely
- ❏ 20 percent more likely
- ❏ No more or less likely
- ☑ 20 percent less likely
- ❏ 40 percent less likely
- ❏ 60+ percent less likely

(6) As the president of an airline company, you have invested $10 million of the company's money into a research project. The purpose was to build a plane that would not be detected by conventional radar, in other words, a

radar-blank plane. When the project is 90 percent completed, another firm begins marketing a plane that cannot be detected by radar. Also, it is apparent that their plane is much faster and far more economical than the plane your company is building. The question is: Should you invest the last 10 percent of the research funds to finish your radar-blank plane?

- ❑ NO—It makes no sense to continue spending money on the project.
- ☑ YES—As long as $10 million is already invested, I might as well finish the project.

(7) Which is a more likely cause of death in the United States — being killed by falling airplane parts or by a shark?

- ☑ Falling airplane parts
- ❑ Shark

(8) For each pair, circle the cause of death that is most common in the United States:

Diabetes/(Homicide)
(Tornado)/Lightning
(Car Accidents)/Stomach Cancer

(9) Consider the following historical scenario: "The government of a country not far from Superpower A, after discussing certain changes in its party system, began broadening its trade with Superpower B. To reverse these changes in government and trade, Superpower A sent its troops into the country and militarily backed the original government."

(9a) Which country is Superpower A?

- ❑ Soviet Union
- ☑ United States

(9b) How confident are you of your answer? (Circle one number.)

Not confident at all (1) 2 3 4 5 6 7 8 9 Very confident

(10) Here's another scenario: "In the 1960s Superpower A sponsored a surprise invasion of a small country near its border, with the purpose of overthrowing the regime in power at the time. The invasion failed, and most of the original invading forces were killed or imprisoned."

(10a) Which country is Superpower A?

- ☑ Soviet Union
- ❑ United States

(10b) How confident are you of your answer? (Circle *one* number.)

Not confident at all   1 ② 3 4 5 6 7 8 9   Very confident

(11) Place a check mark beside the alternative that seems most likely to occur within the next ten years:

☑ An all-out nuclear war between the United States and Russia

☐ An all-out nuclear war between the United States and Russia in which neither country intends to use nuclear weapons, but both sides are drawn into the conflict by the actions of a country such as Iraq, Libya, Israel, or Pakistan

(12) A piece of paper is folded in half. It is folded in half again, and again. . . . After 100 folds, how thick will it be?

(12a) My best guess is that the paper will be _____ 1cm _____ thick.

(12b) I am 90 percent sure that the correct answer lies between _____ .5 – 4cm _____ and _____ 1 cm _____ .

(13) Including February 29, there are 366 possible birthdays in a year. Consequently, a group would need to contain 367 members in order to be absolutely sure that at least two people shared the same birthday. How many people are necessary in order to be 50 percent certain?

The group would need _____ 133 _____ members.

(14) Suppose a study of 250 neurology patients finds the following frequencies of dizziness and brain tumors:

		BRAIN TUMOR	
		Present	**Absent**
	Present	160	40
Dizziness			
	Absent	40	10

(14a) Which cells of the table are needed in order to determine whether dizziness is associated with brain tumors in this sample of people? (Check all that apply.)

☑ Upper left
☑ Lower left
☐ Upper right
☐ Lower right

(14b) According to the data in the table, is dizziness associated with brain tumors?

      ☑ Yes   ❏ No   ❏ Not sure

(15) The mean IQ of the population of eighth graders in a city is *known* to be 100. You have selected a random sample of 50 children for a study of educational achievements. The first child tested has an IQ of 150. What do you expect the mean IQ to be for the whole sample?

ANSWER: 100

(16) On the whole, do you see yourself as a sexist person? (Check *one*.)

      ❏ Yes   ☑ No   ❏ Not sure

(17) If all the human blood in the world were poured into a cube-shaped tank, how wide would the tank be?

The tank would be ___1 mile___ wide.

(18) If you had to guess, which of the following interpretations of a Rorschach inkblot are most predictive of male homosexuality? (If you haven't heard of the Rorschach inkblot test, just skip this question.) Rank the following interpretations from 1 (most predictive of homosexuality) to 6 (least predictive of homosexuality).

  __1__ Human figures of indeterminate sex
  __2__ Human figures with both male and female features
  __4__ Buttocks or anus
  __3__ Genitals
  __6__ A contorted, monstrous figure
  __5__ Female clothing

(19) "Memory can be likened to a storage chest in the brain into which we deposit material and from which we can withdraw it later if needed. Occasionally, something gets lost from the `chest,' and then we say we have forgotten."

Would you say this is a reasonably accurate description of how memory works?

      ☑ Yes   ❏ No   ❏ Not sure

(20) A man bought a horse for $60 and sold it for $70. Then he bought it back for $80 and again sold it for $90. How much money did he make in the horse business?

The man ended up with a final profit of $ _20_ .

(21a) Absinthe is:

- ☑ A liqueur
- ❏ A precious stone

(21b) What is the probability that your answer is correct?
(Circle *one* number.)

.50   .55   .60   .65   .70   .75   .80   .85   .90   (.95)   1.00

(22) Without actually calculating, give a quick (five-second) estimate of the following product:

$8 \times 7 \times 6 \times 5 \times 4 \times 3 \times 2 \times 1 =$ _1784_

(23) Suppose you consider the possibility of insuring some property against damage, e.g., fire or theft. After examining the risks and the premium you find that you have no clear preference between the options of purchasing insurance or leaving the property uninsured.

It is then called to your attention that the insurance company offers a new program called *probabilistic insurance*. In this program you pay half of the regular premium. In case of damage, there is a 50 percent chance that you pay the other half of the premium and the insurance company covers all the losses; and there is a 50 percent chance that you get back your insurance payment and suffer all the losses.

For example, if an accident occurs on an odd day of the month, you pay the other half of the regular premium and your losses are covered; but if the accident occurs on an even day of the month, your insurance payment is refunded and your losses are not covered.

Recall that the premium for full coverage is such that you find this insurance barely worth its cost.

Under these circumstances, would you purchase probabilistic insurance?

- ❏ Yes
- ☑ No

(24) Suppose you performed well on a variety of tests over a range of occasions, but other people taking the same tests did not do very well. What would you conclude? (Check the *one* answer that comes closest to your view.)

- ☐ Explanation A: The tests were probably easy.
- ☐ Explanation B: The other people were probably low in ability.
- ☑ Explanation C: I am either good at taking tests or must have known the material well.

In a few pages, you will be asked some questions about the following sentences. Please read them carefully now and continue with the Reader Survey:

- The ants ate the sweet jelly which was on the table.
- The ants were in the kitchen.
- The ants ate the sweet jelly.
- The ants in the kitchen ate the jelly which was on the table.
- The jelly was on the table.
- The ants in the kitchen ate the jelly.

(25) If you were faced with the following choice, which alternative would you choose?

- ☑ A sure gain of $240
- ☐ A 25 percent chance to gain $1000, and 75 percent chance to gain nothing

(26) If you were faced with the following choice, which alternative would you choose?

- ☐ A sure loss of $750
- ☑ A 75 percent chance to lose $1000, and 25 percent chance to lose nothing

(27) What do you think is the most important problem facing this country today?

The most important problem is: _Pollution_ _____

(28a) If you were given a choice, which of the following gambles would you prefer?

- ☐ $1,000,000 for sure
- ☑ A 10 percent chance of getting $2,500,000, an 89 percent chance of getting $1,000,000, and a 1 percent chance of getting $0

(28b) If you were given a choice, which of the following gambles would you prefer?

- ❏ An 11 percent chance of getting $1,000,000, and an 89 percent chance of getting $0
- ☑ A 10 percent chance of getting $2,500,000, and a 90 percent chance of getting $0

(29) Imagine two urns filled with millions of poker chips. In the first urn, 70 percent of the chips are red and 30 percent are blue. In the second urn, 70 percent are blue and 30 percent are red. Suppose one of the urns is chosen randomly and a dozen chips are drawn from it: eight red chips and four blue chips. What are the chances that the chips came from the urn with mostly red chips? (Give your answer as a percentage.)

Answer: ___40___ percent

(30) How much money would you pay to play a game in which an unbiased coin is tossed until it lands on Tails, and at the end of the game you are paid $(\$2.00)^K$ where K equals the number of tosses until Tails appears? In other words, you would be paid $2.00 if Tails comes up on the first toss, $4.00 if Tails comes up on the second toss, $8.00 if Tails comes up on the third toss, and in general:

Tosses until Tails:	1	2	3	4	5	⋯	K
Payoff in Dollars:	2	4	8	16	32	⋯	2^K

I would pay $___2___ to play this game.

(31) Suppose an unbiased coin is flipped three times, and each time the coin lands on Heads. If you had to bet $100 on the next toss, what side would you choose?

- ❏ Heads
- ☑ Tails
- ❏ No preference

(32) Compare Lines 1, 2, and 3 with Line A below. Which line is equal in length to Line A? (Check *one* answer.)

A   1   2   3

☐ Line A is equal in length to Line 1.
☐ Line A is equal in length to Line 2.
☑ Line A is equal in length to Line 3.

(33) How many times does the letter f appear in the following sentence?

These functional fuses have been developed after years of scientific investigation of electric phenomena, combined with the fruit of long experience on the part of the two investigators who have come forward with them for our meetings today.

The letter f appears _____6_____ times.

(34) Without looking back at the list, please indicate whether the following sentences were included in the set of sentences you read earlier. After each answer, indicate your degree of confidence using a 1 to 5 scale in which 1 = "very low" and 5 = "very high."

(34a) "The ants ate the jelly which was on the table."

☑ This sentence appeared before.
❑ This sentence did not appear before.

My confidence rating is: ____4____

(34b) "The ants in the kitchen ate the sweet jelly which was on the table."

❑ This sentence appeared before.
☑ This sentence did not appear before.

My confidence rating is: ____3____

(34c) "The ants ate the sweet jelly."

☑ This sentence appeared before.
❑ This sentence did not appear before.

My confidence rating is: ____4____

(35) Suppose that scores on a high school academic achievement test are moderately related to college grade point averages (GPAs). Given the percentiles below, what GPA would you predict for a student who scored 725 on the achievement test?

Student Percentile	Achievement Test	GPA
Top 10%	> 750	> 3.7
Top 20%	> 700	> 3.5
Top 30%	> 650	> 3.2
Top 40%	> 600	> 2.9
Top 50%	> 500	> 2.5

I would predict a grade point average of ___3.6___.

(36) Does the act of voting for a candidate change your opinion about whether the candidate will win the election?

      ☑ Yes   ❑ No   ❑ Not sure

(37) Consider the two structures, A and B, which are displayed below.

Structure A:

X X X X X X X X X
X X X X X X X X X
X X X X X X X X X

Structure B:

X X
X X
X X
X X
X X
X X
X X
X X
X X

A *path* is a line that connects an X in the top row of a structure to an X in the bottom row by passing through one (and only one) X in each row. In other words, a path connects three X's in Structure A (one in each of the three rows) and nine X's in Structure B (one in each of the nine rows). One example of a path is drawn in each structure above.

(37a) In which of the two structures are there more paths?

     ❑ Structure A   ☑ Structure B

(37b) Approximately how many paths are in Structure A?   <u>100</u>

(37c) Approximately how many paths are in Structure B?   <u>150</u>

(38) Which of the following sequences of X's and O's seems more like it was generated by a random process (e.g., flipping a coin)?

    ❑ XOXXXOOOOXOXXOOOXXXOX

    ☑ XOXOXOOOXXOXOXOOXXXOX

(39) Suppose each of the cards below has a number on one side and a letter on the other, and someone tells you: "If a card has a vowel on one side, then it has an even number on the other side." Which of the cards would you need to turn over in order to decide whether the person is lying?

I would need to turn over the following cards

(check all that apply):

☑ E
☐ 4
☐ K
☑ 7

SECTION I

PERCEPTION, MEMORY, AND CONTEXT

There is no such thing as context-free decision making. All judgments and decisions rest on the way we see and interpret the world. Accordingly, this first section discusses the way that judgments and decisions are influenced by selective perception, pressures toward cognitive consistency, biases in memory, and changes in context.

CHAPTER 1

SELECTIVE PERCEPTION

*"We do not first see, then define,
we define first and then see."*

—Walter Lippmann (cited in Snyder & Uranowitz, 1978)

Look in front of you. Now look at your hands. Look at the cover of this book. How much of what you see is determined by your expectations?

If you are like most people, your perceptions are heavily influenced by what you expect to see. Even when something is right before your eyes, it is hard to view it without preconceived notions. You may feel that you are looking at things in a completely unbiased way, but as will become clear, it is nearly impossible for people to avoid biases in perception. Instead, people selectively perceive what they expect and hope to see.

CALLING A SPADE A SPADE

One of the earliest and best known experiments on selective perception was published by Jerome Bruner and Leo Postman (1949). Bruner and Postman presented people with a series of five playing cards on a tachistoscope (a machine that can display pictures for very brief intervals), varying the exposure time from ten milliseconds up to one second. The cards they showed these people were similar to the cards on the cover of this book. Take a moment now to note what these cards are.

Did you notice anything strange about the cards? Most people who casually view the cover of this book never realize that one of the cards is actually a *black* three of hearts! Bruner and Postman found that it took people more than four times longer to recognize a trick card than a normal card, and they found that most reactions to the incongruity could be categorized as one of four types: dominance, compromise, disruption, or recognition.

A *dominance* reaction consisted mainly in what Bruner and Postman called "perceptual denial." For example, faced with a black three of hearts, people were very sure that the card was a normal three of hearts or a normal three of spades. In the first case, form is dominant and color is assimilated to prior expectations, and in the second case, color

15

is dominant and form is assimilated. In Bruner and Postman's experiment, 27 of 28 subjects (or 96 percent of the people) showed dominance reactions at some point.

Another reaction people had was to *compromise*. For instance, some of Bruner and Postman's subjects reported a red six of spades as either a purple six of spades or a purple six of hearts. Others thought that a black four of hearts was a "greyish" four of spades, or that a red six of clubs was "the six of clubs illuminated by red light" (remember, experimental subjects were shown the cards on a tachistoscope). Half of Bruner and Postman's subjects showed compromise responses to red cards, and 11 percent showed compromise responses to black cards.

A third way that people reacted to the incongruity was with *disruption*. When responses were disrupted, people had trouble forming a perception of any sort. Disruption was rare, but when it happened, the results were dramatic. For example, one experimental subject exclaimed: "I don't know what the hell it is now, not even for sure whether it's a playing card." Likewise, another subject said: "I can't make the suit out, whatever it is. It didn't even look like a card that time. I don't know what color it is now or whether it's a spade or heart. I'm not even sure now what a spade looks like! My God!"

The final reaction was, of course, one of *recognition*. Yet even when subjects recognized that something was wrong, they sometimes misperceived the incongruity. Before realizing precisely what was wrong, six of Bruner and Postman's subjects began to sense that something was strange about how the symbols were positioned on the card. For example, a subject who was shown a red six of spades thought the symbols were reversed, and a subject who was shown a black four of hearts declared that the spades were "turned the wrong way."

These results show that expectations can strongly influence perceptions. In the words of Bruner and Postman (p. 222): "Perceptual organization is powerfully determined by expectations built upon past commerce with the environment." When people have enough experience with a particular situation, they often see what they expect to see.

Item #33 of the Reader Survey contains another illustration of how prior experience can interfere with accurate perceptions. In that question, you were asked to count how many times the letter f appeared in the following sentence:

> These functional fuses have been developed after years of scientific investigation of electric phenomena, combined with the fruit of long experience on the part of the two investigators who have come forward with them for our meetings today.

Most native English speakers underestimate the number of times the letter f appears (Block & Yuker, 1989). The correct answer is 11 (including four times in which f appears in the word *of*). Because experienced

speakers pronounce the word *of* with a "v" sound, they have more difficulty detecting these occurrences of the letter f than do inexperienced
speakers, and as a result, past experience actually lowers performance.

POTENT EXPECTATIONS

Imagine you are a male college student participating in a study at the
Rutgers Alcohol Research Laboratory. Your job, you are told, is to drink
a vodka and tonic, wait twenty minutes for the alcohol to enter your
bloodstream, and speak with a female assistant of the experimenter in
an attempt to make as favorable an impression as possible. The experimenter then mixes a vodka and tonic in proportion to your body weight,
hands you the glass, and leaves you in a private room to consume the
drink.

After you have finished the drink, a female assistant enters the room,
sits down, and looks you straight in the eye. You begin to talk to her.
How nervous are you? How fast is your heart beating?

When G. Terrence Wilson and David Abrams (1977) conducted this
experiment, they found that subjects who thought they had been given a
vodka and tonic showed much smaller increases in heart rate than subjects who thought they had been given tonic water alone—regardless of
whether subjects had actually ingested alcohol. Heart rates were not significantly affected by whether subjects had been given alcohol to drink;
they were affected by whether subjects *believed* they had been given
alcohol to drink. Expectations proved more important than changes in
blood chemistry.

David McMillen, Stephen Smith, and Elisabeth Wells-Parker (1989)
took these results one step further. Using an experimental technique
similar to the one used by Wilson and Abrams, these researchers randomly assigned college students to drink either alcoholic beverages or
nonalcoholic beverages. Some of the students had been previously identified as high "sensation seekers" who liked to take risks, and others had
been identified as low "sensation seekers." Then, half an hour after
drinking their beverages, the students played a video game in which
they drove along a roadway and had the opportunity to pass other cars
by using an accelerator pedal. Students were told to drive the simulated
car as they would drive a real car.

McMillen and his colleagues found that high sensation seekers who
believed they had consumed alcohol—whether or not they actually
had—changed lanes and passed cars significantly more often than high
sensation seekers who, rightly or wrongly, did not have this belief. In
contrast, low sensation seekers who thought they had consumed alcohol
were more cautious than low sensation seekers who thought they had
not. Equally strong expectancy effects have been found among frequent
users of marijuana (Jones, 1971).

In these experiments and the experiment of Bruner and Postman, people's perceptions were strongly influenced by their prior beliefs and expectations. Psychologists refer to such influences as "cognitive" factors. Yet perception is affected not only by what people *expect* to see; it is also colored by what they *want* to see. Factors that deal with hopes, desires, and emotional attachments are known as "motivational" factors. The remaining sections of this chapter discuss instances of selective perception in which motivational factors are intertwined with cognitive factors.

WHEN THE GOING GETS ROUGH

On November 23, 1951, the Dartmouth and Princeton football teams went head to head in Princeton University's Palmer Stadium. Shortly after the kickoff, it became clear that the game was going to be a rough one. Princeton's star player, who had just appeared on the cover of *Time* magazine, left the game with a broken nose. Soon thereafter, a Dartmouth player was taken off the field with a broken leg. By the end of the game—which Princeton won—both sides had racked up a sizable number of penalties.

Following the game, tempers flared and bitter accusations were traded. Partisans on both sides wrote scathing editorials. For example, four days after the game, a writer for the *Daily Princetonian* (Princeton's student newspaper) declared: "This observer has never seen quite such a disgusting exhibition of so-called 'sport.' Both teams were guilty but the blame must be laid primarily on Dartmouth's doorstep. Princeton, obviously the better team, had no reason to rough up Dartmouth." On the same day, the *Dartmouth* (Dartmouth's undergraduate newspaper) charged that Princeton's coach had instilled a "see-what-they-did-go-get-them attitude" in his players. Throughout the ensuing week, Dartmouth and Princeton students continued to fiercely debate what had happened and who was responsible.

Into that turmoil stepped Albert Hastorf (a social psychologist then at Dartmouth) and Hadley Cantril (a Princeton survey researcher). Capitalizing on the controversy, Hastorf and Cantril (1954) conducted what is now a classic study of selective perception.

They began by asking 163 Dartmouth students and 161 Princeton students the following question, among others: "From what you saw in the game or the movies, or from what you have read, which team do you feel started the rough play?" Not surprisingly, Hastorf and Cantril found a large discrepancy between common Dartmouth and Princeton reactions. Of the Dartmouth students, 53 percent asserted that both sides started it, and only 36 percent said that Dartmouth started it. In contrast, 86 percent of the Princeton students felt that Dartmouth had started it, and only 11 percent said that both sides were initiators.

This difference of opinion led Hastorf and Cantril to wonder whether Dartmouth and Princeton students were actually *seeing* different games, or whether they were observing the same game but simply interpreting the evidence differently. To explore this question, they asked a new group of students at each school to watch a film of the game and to record any infractions they noticed. Students from both schools watched the very same film, and they used the same rating system to record any observed infractions.

As you can see in Figure 1.1, the results showed a great deal of selective perception. Dartmouth students observed nearly the same number of infractions on both sides (4.3 for their side and 4.4 for Princeton), whereas Princeton students saw the Dartmouth team commit more than twice as many infractions as the Princeton team (9.8 compared with 4.2 for themselves). In fact, there was such a discrepancy in perceptions that when Princeton sent a copy of the film to several Dartmouth alumni for a group showing, one Dartmouth alumnus who previewed the film could not see any of the Dartmouth infractions and, in confusion, sent Princeton a telegram asking for the rest of the film!

Based on these differences in perception, Hastorf and Cantril (1954, pp. 132–133) concluded that: "It seems clear that the 'game' actually was many different games. . . . It is inaccurate and misleading to say that

FIGURE 1.1

An example of selective perception. *(Taken from Hastorf and Cantril, 1954.)*

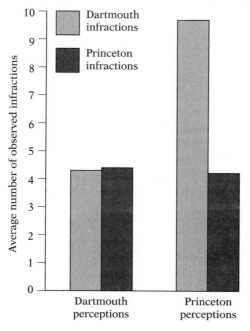

different people have different 'attitudes' concerning the same 'thing.' For the 'thing' simply is *not* the same for different people whether the 'thing' is a football game, a presidential candidate, Communism, or spinach." In 1981, John Loy and Donald Andrews carefully replicated Hastorf and Cantril's study, and they came to much the same conclusion.

THE HOSTILE MEDIA EFFECT

Many years after the Dartmouth-Princeton study, Robert Vallone, Lee Ross, and Mark Lepper (1985) speculated that this kind of selective perception might lead political partisans on each side of an issue to view mass media coverage as biased against their side. Vallone, Ross, and Lepper called this phenomenon the "hostile media effect," and they first studied it in the context of the 1980 presidential election between Jimmy Carter and Ronald Reagan. Three days before the election, they asked 160 registered voters to indicate whether media coverage of the candidates had been biased, and if so, to indicate the direction of the bias. What they found is that approximately one-third of the respondents felt that media coverage had been biased, and in roughly 90 percent of these cases, respondents felt that the media had been biased against the candidate they supported.

Intrigued by these initial findings, Vallone, Ross, and Lepper (1985) conducted a second study in which 68 "pro-Israeli" college students, 27 "pro-Arab" students, and 49 "generally mixed" or "neutral" students watched the same set of televised news segments covering the tragic Beirut massacre (in 1982, a series of Arab-Israeli conflicts had resulted in the massacre of Arab civilians in the refugee camps at Sabra and Chatilla, Lebanon). The news segments were drawn from six different evening and late-night news programs broadcast nationally in the United States over a ten-day period.

In support of the hostile media effect, Vallone, Ross, and Lepper found that each side saw the news coverage as biased in favor of the other side. Pro-Arab students thought the news segments were generally biased in favor of Israel, pro-Israeli students thought the segments were biased against Israel, and neutral students gave opinions that fell between the two groups. Moreover, pro-Arab students felt that the news programs had excused Israel "when they would have blamed some other country," whereas pro-Israeli students felt the programs blamed Israel "when they would have excused some other country."

As in the case of the Dartmouth-Princeton game, Vallone, Ross, and Lepper found that these disagreements were not simply differences of opinion; they were differences in *perception*. For example, pro-Arab and pro-Israeli students differed in their perceptions of the number of favorable and unfavorable references that had been made to Israel during the news programs. On the average, pro-Arab students reported that 42 percent of the references to Israel had been favorable and only 26 percent had been unfavorable. Pro-Israeli students, on the other hand, recalled 57 percent of the references to Israel as having been *un*favorable and only 16 percent as having been favorable. Furthermore, pro-Israeli students thought that most neutral viewers would become more negative toward Israel as a result of watching the news clips, whereas pro-Arab students thought that most would not.

Vallone, Ross, and Lepper concluded that partisans tend to view media coverage of controversial events as unfairly biased and hostile to the position they advocate. They also speculated that similar biases in perception might arise in the context of mediation, arbitration, or other situations in which two sides are heavily committed to prior positions. This speculation makes good sense. As we will see in Chapter 2, when people become committed to a particular cause or a course of action, their perceptions often change in order to remain consistent with this commitment.

CONCLUSION

Perceptions are, by their very nature, selective. Even the simple identification of a playing card—or the perception of one's own intoxication— depends critically on cognitive and motivational factors. Consequently, before making an important judgment or decision, it often pays to pause and ask a few key questions: Am I motivated to see things a certain way? What expectations did I bring into the situation? Would I see things differently without these expectations and motives? Have I consulted with others who don't share my expectations and motives? By asking such questions, decision makers can expose many of the cognitive and motivational factors that lead to biases in perception.

CHAPTER 2

COGNITIVE DISSONANCE

Soon after the first studies of selective perception, Leon Festinger (1957) proposed the theory of "cognitive dissonance." Since the 1950s, dissonance theory has generated hundreds of experiments, many of them among the most clever and entertaining in psychology. To understand the theory of cognitive dissonance and see how dissonance can influence judgment and decision making, consider a story told by Nathan Ausubel (1948; see also Deci, 1975, pp. 157–158).

A PARABLE OF COGNITIVE DISSONANCE

There was once a Jewish tailor who had the temerity to open his shop on the main street of an anti-semitic town. To drive him out of town, a gang of youths visited the shop each day, standing in the entrance and shouting, "Jew! Jew!"

After several sleepless nights, the tailor finally devised a plan. The next time that the gang came to threaten him, the tailor announced that anyone who called him a Jew would get a dime. He then handed dimes to each member of the gang.

Delighted with their new incentive, members of the gang returned the next day, shouting "Jew! Jew!", and the tailor, smiling, gave each one a nickel (explaining that he could only afford a nickel that day). The gang left satisfied because, after all, a nickel was a nickel.

Then, on the following day, the tailor gave out only pennies to each gang member, again explaining that he could afford no more money than that. Well, a penny was not much of an incentive, and members of the gang began to protest.

When the tailor replied that they could take it or leave it, they decided to leave it, shouting that the tailor was crazy if he thought that they would call him a Jew for only a penny!

WHY THE CHANGE?

Why would members of the gang harass the tailor for free but not for a penny? According to the theory of cognitive dissonance, people are usually motivated to reduce or avoid psychological inconsistencies. When the tailor announced that he was *happy* to be called a Jew, and when he changed the gang's motivation from anti-semitism to monetary reward, he made it inconsistent (or "dissonance-arousing") for gang members to please him without financial compensation. In the absence of a sufficiently large payment, members of the gang could no longer justify behaving at variance with their objective (which was to upset the tailor, not to make him happy).

BOREDOM CAN BE FUN

The same principle was demonstrated by Leon Festinger and Merrill Carlsmith (1959) in one of the most famous studies in all of social psychology. Sixty male undergraduates at Stanford University were randomly assigned to one of three experimental conditions. In the *$1.00* condition, participants were required to perform tedious laboratory tasks for an hour, after which they were paid $1.00 to tell a waiting student that the tasks were interesting and enjoyable. In the *$20.00* condition, students were paid $20.00 to do the same thing. And in the *control* condition, participants simply engaged in the tedious tasks.

What were the tasks? First, students spent half an hour using one hand to put 12 spools onto a tray, unload the tray, refill the tray, unload the tray again, and so on. Then, after thirty minutes were up, they spent the remainder of the hour using one hand to turn each of 48 pegs on a pegboard—one-quarter turn at a time! Each participant was seen individually, and the experimenter simply sat by, stopwatch in hand, busily making notes on a sheet of paper.

Once the student had finished his tasks, the experimenter leaned back in his chair and said:

> I'd like to explain what this has been all about so you'll have some idea of why you were doing this. . . . There are actually two groups in the experiment. In one, the group you were in, we bring the subject in and give him essentially no introduction to the experiment. . . . But in the other group, we have a student that we've hired that works for us regularly, and what I do is take him into the next room where the subject is waiting—the same room you were waiting in before—and I introduce him as if he had just finished being a subject in the experiment. . . . The fellow who works for us then, in conversation with the next subject, makes these points: . . . It was very enjoyable, I had a lot of fun, I enjoyed myself, it was very interesting. . . .

Following this explanation, the experimenter asked subjects in the control condition to rate how enjoyable the tasks had been. In the $1.00 and $20.00 conditions, however, the experimenter continued with his explanation:

The fellow who normally does this for us couldn't do it today—he just phoned in, and something or other came up for him—so we've been looking around for someone that we could hire to do it for us. You see, we've got another subject waiting [looks at watch] who is supposed to be in that other condition. . . . If you would be willing to do this for us, we'd like to hire you to do it now and then be on call in the future, if something like this should ever happen again. We can pay you a dollar [or twenty dollars, depending on condition] for doing this for us, that is, for doing it now and then being on call. Do you think you could do that for us?

All $1.00 and $20.00 subjects agreed to be hired, and after they told the waiting person how enjoyable the tasks were, they were asked, among other things, to evaluate the tasks. What Festinger and Carlsmith (1959) found was that subjects in the $1.00 condition rated the tasks as significantly more enjoyable than did subjects in the other two conditions.

Festinger and Carlsmith argued that subjects who were paid only $1.00 to lie to another person experienced "cognitive dissonance." According to Festinger (1957), people experience cognitive dissonance when they simultaneously hold two thoughts that are psychologically inconsistent (i.e., thoughts that feel contradictory or incompatible in some way). In this instance, the dissonant cognitions were:

1. The task was extremely boring.
2. For only $1.00, I (an honest person) just told someone that the task was interesting and enjoyable.

When taken together, these statements imply that subjects in the $1.00 condition had lied for no good reason (subjects in the $20.00 condition, on the other hand, had agreed to be "hired" for what they apparently considered to be a very good reason: $20.00).

Festinger (1957) proposed that people try whenever possible to reduce cognitive dissonance. He regarded dissonance as a "negative drive state" (an aversive condition), and he presented cognitive dissonance theory as a motivational theory (despite the word "cognitive"). According to the theory, subjects in the experiment should be motivated to reduce the inconsistency between the two thoughts listed above.

Of course, there wasn't much subjects could do about the second thought. The fact was that subjects *did* tell another person that the task was enjoyable, and they did it for only $1.00 (and they certainly weren't going to change their view of themselves as honest and decent people). On the other hand, the tediousness of the task afforded subjects some room to maneuver. Tediousness, you might say, is in the eye of the beholder.

Thus, Festinger and Carlsmith (1959) concluded that subjects in the

$1.00 condition later evaluated the task as relatively enjoyable so as to reduce the dissonance caused by telling another person that the task was interesting and enjoyable. In contrast, subjects in the $20.00 condition saw the experimental tasks for what they were: crushingly dull. Subjects in that condition had no need to reduce dissonance, because they already had a good explanation for their behavior—they were paid $20.00.

SELF-PERCEPTION THEORY

The story does not end here, because there is another way to account for what Festinger and Carlsmith found. In the mid-1960s, psychologist Daryl Bem proposed that cognitive dissonance findings could be explained by what he called "self-perception theory." According to self-perception theory, dissonance findings have nothing to do with a negative drive state called dissonance; instead, they have to do with how people infer their beliefs from watching themselves behave.

Bem's self-perception theory is based on two main premises:

1. People discover their own attitudes, emotions, and other internal states partly by watching themselves behave in various situations.
2. To the extent that internal cues are weak, ambiguous, or uninterpretable, people are in much the same position as an outside observer when making these inferences.

A self-perception theorist would explain Festinger and Carlsmith's results by arguing that subjects who saw themselves speak highly of the task for only $1.00 inferred that they must have enjoyed the task (just as an outside observer would infer). On the other hand, subjects in the $20.00 condition inferred that their behavior was nothing more than a response to being offered a large financial incentive—again, as an outside observer would. The difference between self-perception theory and dissonance theory is that self-perception theory explains classical dissonance findings in terms of how people infer the causes of their behavior, whereas cognitive dissonance theory explains these findings in terms of a natural motivation to reduce inner conflict, or dissonance. According to Bem, subjects in the Festinger and Carlsmith (1959) study could have experienced no tension whatsoever and still given the same pattern of results.

A great deal of research has been conducted comparing these theories (cf. Bem, 1972), but it is still an open question as to which theory is more accurate or more useful in explaining "dissonance phenomena." For many years, researchers on each side of the issue attempted to design a definitive experiment in support of their favored theory, but each round of experimentation served only to provoke another set of experiments from the other side. In the final analysis, it probably makes sense to assume that *both* theories are valid in a variety of situations (but following psychological tradition, I will use dissonance terminology as a shorthand for findings that can be explained equally well by self-perception theory).

As the next sections demonstrate, cognitive dissonance influences a wide range of judgments and decisions. Most dissonance-arousing situations fall into one of two general categories: predecisional or postdecisional. In the first type of situation, dissonance (or the prospect of dissonance) influences the decisions people make. In the second kind of situation, dissonance (or its prospect) follows a choice that has already been made, and the avoidance or reduction of this dissonance has an effect on later behavior.

AN EXAMPLE OF PREDECISIONAL DISSONANCE

A father and his son are out driving. They are involved in an accident. The father is killed, and the son is in critical condition. The son is rushed to the hospital and prepared for the operation. The doctor comes in, sees the patient, and exclaims, "I can't operate; it's my son!"

Is this scenario possible? Most people would say it is not. They would reason that the patient cannot be the doctor's son if the patient's father has been killed. At least, they would reason this way until it occurred to them that the surgeon might be the patient's *mother.*

If this possibility had not dawned on you, and if you consider yourself to be relatively nonsexist, there is a good chance you are experiencing dissonance right now (see Item #16 of the Reader Survey for a self-rating of sexism). Moreover, according to the theory of cognitive dissonance, you should be motivated to reduce that dissonance by behaving in a more nonsexist way than ever.

In 1980, Jim Sherman and Larry Gorkin used the female surgeon story to test this hypothesis. Sherman and Gorkin randomly assigned college students to one of three conditions in an experiment on "the relationship between attitudes toward social issues and the ability to solve logical problems." In the *sex-role* condition, students were given five minutes to figure out how the story of the female surgeon made sense. In the *non-sex-role* condition, students were given five minutes to solve an equally difficult problem concerning dots and lines. And in the *control* condition, students were not given a problem to solve. In the sex-role and non-sex-role conditions, the experimenter provided the correct solution after five minutes had passed (roughly 80 percent of the subjects were not able to solve the assigned problem within five minutes).

Next, subjects were told that the experiment was over, and they were presented with booklets for another experimenter's study about legal decisions (the students had been told previously that they would be participating in "a couple of unrelated research projects"). Subjects were informed that the principal investigator of the other study was in South Bend, Indiana, and that they should put the completed booklets in envelopes addressed to South Bend, seal the envelopes, and drop them in a nearby mailbox. Then subjects were left alone to complete the booklet on legal decisions.

In reality, the experiment on legal decisions was nothing more than a way to collect information on sexism without subjects detecting a connection to the first part of the experiment. Subjects read about an affirmative action case in which a woman claimed that she had been turned down for a university faculty position because of her gender. Then they indicated what they thought the verdict should be, how justified they thought the university was in hiring a man rather than the woman, and how they felt about affirmative action in general.

Sherman and Gorkin (1980) found that, compared with subjects in the control group and subjects who were presented with the problem concerning dots and lines, subjects who had failed to solve the female surgeon problem were more likely to find the university guilty of sexual discrimination, less likely to see the university as justified in hiring a male for the job, and more supportive of affirmative action policies in general. In other words, after displaying traditional sex-role stereotypes, students tried to reduce their dissonance by acting more "liberated" (or, in terms of self-perception theory, trying to show themselves that they were not sexist). This method of dissonance reduction, called "bolstering," has also been used successfully to promote energy conservation. S. J. Kantola, G. J. Syme, and N. A. Campbell (1984) found that heavy users of electricity cut their consumption significantly when they were informed of their heavy use and reminded of an earlier conservation endorsement they had made.

OTHER EXAMPLES OF PREDECISIONAL DISSONANCE

Predecisional dissonance can also influence consumer behavior, as shown by Anthony Doob and his colleagues (1969). These researchers matched 12 pairs of discount stores in terms of gross sales, and they randomly assigned each member of a pair to introduce a house brand of mouthwash at either $0.25 per bottle or $0.39 per bottle. Then, after nine days, the store selling the mouthwash at $0.25 raised the price to $0.39 (equal to the price at the other store). The same procedure was followed with toothpaste, aluminum foil, light bulbs, and cookies (and, in general, the results for these items paralleled the results using mouthwash).

What Doob et al. (1969) found was that, consistent with cognitive dissonance theory, stores that introduced the mouthwash at a higher price tended to sell more bottles. In 10 of 12 pairs, the store that introduced the mouthwash at $0.39 later sold more mouthwash than did the store that initially offered the mouthwash for $0.25.

Doob and his associates explained this finding in terms of customer "adaptation levels" and the need to avoid dissonance. They wrote: "When mouthwash is put on sale at $0.25, customers who buy it at that price or notice what the price is may tend to think of the product in terms of $0.25. They say to themselves that this is a $0.25 bottle of mouthwash. When, in subsequent weeks, the price increases to $0.39, these customers will tend to see it as overpriced, and are not inclined to buy it at this much higher price" (p. 350). Furthermore, according to dissonance theory, the more people pay for something, the more they should see value in it and feel pressure to continue buying it. This principle is true not only with purchases, but with any commitment of resources or effort toward a goal (for another example, see Aronson & Mills, 1959). The net result is similar to that found with many of the behavioral traps discussed in Chapter 21.

EXAMPLES OF POSTDECISIONAL DISSONANCE

Postdecisional dissonance is dissonance that follows a decision rather than precedes it. In the mid-1960s, Robert Knox and James Inkster studied postdecisional dissonance by approaching 141 horse bettors at Exhibition Park Race Track in Vancouver, Canada: 72 people who had just finished placing a $2.00 bet within the past thirty seconds, and 69 people who were about to place a $2.00 bet in the next thirty seconds. Knox and Inkster reasoned that people who had just committed themselves to a course of action (by betting $2.00) would reduce postdecisional dissonance by believing more strongly than ever that they had picked a winner.

To test this hypothesis, Knox and Inkster (1968) asked people to rate their horse's chances of winning on a 7-point scale in which 1 indicated that the chances were "slight" and 7 indicated that the chances were "excellent." What they found was that people who were about to place a bet rated the chance that their horse would win at an average of 3.48 (which corresponded to a "fair chance of winning"), whereas people who had just finished betting gave an average rating of 4.81 (which corresponded to a "good chance of winning"). Their hypothesis was confirmed—after making a $2.00 commitment, people became more confident that their bet would pay off.

This finding raises an interesting question: Does voting for a candidate increase your confidence that the candidate will win the election?

(See Item #36 of the Reader Survey for your answer.) In 1976, Oded Frenkel and Anthony Doob published a study exploring this question.

Frenkel and Doob used the same basic procedure as Knox and Inkster (1968); they approached people immediately before and immediately after they voted. In one experiment they surveyed voters in a Canadian provincial election, and in another they queried voters in a Canadian federal election. In keeping with the results of Knox and Inkster, Frenkel and Doob (1976, p. 347) found that: "In both elections, voters were more likely to believe that their candidate was the best one and had the best chance to win after they had voted than before they voted."

CONCLUSION

As the opening story of the Jewish tailor shows, cognitive dissonance theory can be a formidable weapon in the hands of a master. Research on cognitive dissonance is not only bountiful and entertaining, it is directly applicable to many situations. For example, retail stores often explicitly label introductory offers so as to avoid the kind of adaptation effects found by Doob et al. (1969). Similarly, many political campaigns solicit small commitments in order to create postdecisional dissonance (this strategy is sometimes known as the "foot-in-the-door technique"). In the remainder of this book, we will discuss several other applications and findings from cognitive dissonance theory.

One of the leading authorities on dissonance research is Elliot Aronson, a student of Festinger and an investigator in many of the early dissonance experiments (for readers interested in learning more about the theory of cognitive dissonance, a good place to begin is with Aronson, 1969, 1972). It is therefore appropriate to conclude this chapter with a statement by Aronson (1972, p. 108) on the implications of cognitive dissonance theory:

> If a modern Machiavelli were advising a contemporary ruler, he might suggest the following strategies based upon the theory and data on the consequences of decisions:
>
> 1. If you want someone to form more positive attitudes toward an object, get him to commit himself to own that object
> 2. If you want someone to soften his moral attitude toward some misdeed, tempt him so that he performs that deed; conversely, if you want someone to harden his moral attitudes toward a misdeed, tempt him—but not enough to induce him to commit the deed*

---

*The masculine pronouns in this statement refer to people of both genders. Before 1977 (when the American Psychological Association adopted guidelines for nonsexist language), this literary practice was common in psychology.

It is well known that changes in attitude can lead to changes in behavior, but research on cognitive dissonance shows that changes in attitude can also *follow* changes in behavior. According to the theory of cognitive dissonance, the pressure to feel consistent will often lead people to bring their beliefs in line with their behavior. In Chapter 3, we will see that, in many cases, people also distort or forget what their initial beliefs were.

CHAPTER 3

MEMORY AND HINDSIGHT BIASES

> "To-day isn't any other day, you know."
> "I don't understand you," said Alice. "It's
> dreadfully confusing!"
> "That's the effect of living backwards," the Queen said kindly:
> "it always makes one a little giddy at first—"
> "Living backwards!" Alice repeated in great astonishment.
> "I never heard of such a thing!"
> "—but there's one great advantage in it, that one's memory
> works both ways. . . . It's a poor sort of memory that only works backwards,"
> the Queen remarked.
>
> —Lewis Carroll, *Through the Looking-Glass*

Take a moment to reflect on whether the following statement is true or false: "Memory can be likened to a storage chest in the brain, into which we deposit material and from which we can withdraw it later if needed. Occasionally, something gets lost from the 'chest,' and then we say we have forgotten."

What do you think—true or false? (See Item #19 of the Reader Survey for your answer.) Roughly 85 percent of the college students in a study by P. A. Lamal (1979, October) agreed with this statement, yet something is terribly wrong with the way it characterizes memory (aside from the question of whether material is ever truly lost from memory). Memories are *not* like copies of our past experiences on deposit in a memory bank. Instead, they are constructed at the time of withdrawal (Loftus, 1980; Myers, 1990). The "materials" used in this split-second reconstruction are logical inferences that fill in missing detail, associated memories that blend in with the original memory, and other relevant information. To verify that memory is reconstructive, try an exercise suggested by Myers (1990): Close your eyes and recall a scene in which you experienced something pleasurable. Don't read any further until you have finished replaying your experience.

Did you see yourself in the scene? Most people do. But if you saw yourself, then you must have reconstructed the scene (unless, of course, you were looking at yourself during the original experience).

31

SHATTERED MEMORIES

One of the best demonstrations that memory is reconstructive was provided in two experiments by Beth Loftus and John Palmer (1974). In the first experiment, 45 students were asked to view seven different film clips depicting a traffic accident. The clips ranged from five to thirty seconds in length and were borrowed from longer driver's education films.

After each film clip, students answered a series of questions, including one on how fast the cars had been traveling. One-fifth of the students answered the question: "About how fast were the cars going when they contacted each other?" Equal numbers of the remaining students answered the same question, except that the word "contacted" was replaced with "hit," "bumped," "collided," or "smashed."

As you can see in Table 3.1, students who were asked how fast the cars were going when they "smashed" gave a mean estimate that was 9 miles faster than the average estimate given by students who were asked how fast the cars were going when they "contacted" each other. Thus, Loftus and Palmer concluded that the form of a question—even when changed by only one word—can markedly affect how people reconstruct their memory of an event.

If anything, results from the second experiment were even more dramatic. This time, Loftus and Palmer had 150 students watch a one-minute film that included a four-second, multiple-car crash. Fifty students were asked: "About how fast were the cars going when they smashed into each other?" Another 50 students were asked: "About how fast were the cars going when they hit each other?" And the last 50 students were not asked to judge car speed. Then the students returned one week later and, without viewing the film again, answered a series of questions. The key question Loftus and Palmer were interested in was whether students remembered having seen any shattered glass during the car crash.

Loftus and Palmer found that asking students how fast the cars were going when they "smashed" not only led to faster estimates, but that one

TABLE 3.1
HOW FAST WERE THE CARS GOING WHEN THEY . . .

Verb	Mean Speed
Smashed	40.8
Collided	39.3
Bumped	38.1
Hit	34.0
Contacted	31.8

Note: These are average speed estimates from Experiment 1 of a study by Elizabeth Loftus and John Palmer (1974).

TABLE 3.2
DID YOU SEE ANY BROKEN GLASS?

Response	EXPERIMENTAL CONDITION		
	"Smashed"	"Hit"	Control Group
Yes	16	7	6
No	34	43	44

Note: This is the distribution of "yes" and "no" answers found in Experiment 2 of a study by Elizabeth Loftus and John Palmer (1974). Fifty subjects were assigned to each of the three experimental conditions.

week later, a greater proportion of the students remembered the accident as having involved broken glass. The results, which show statistically reliable differences among the experimental conditions, are shown in Table 3.2. What is interesting about these results is that the accident never involved broken glass—subjects who estimated the speed of smashing cars reconstructed the accident so that it involved broken glass!   < false memories >

SWEET REMEMBRANCES

As the experiments by Loftus and Palmer show, memories are not fixed in storage. In 1971, John Bransford and Jeffrey Franks further showed that memories are not stored separately from one another. Bransford and Franks (1971) initially presented college students with a list of sentences about an event. For example, one of the lists—reprinted on page 7 of the Reader Survey—went like this:

- The ants ate the sweet jelly which was on the table.
- The ants were in the kitchen.
- The ants ate the sweet jelly.
- The ants in the kitchen ate the jelly which was on the table.
- The jelly was on the table.
- The ants in the kitchen ate the jelly.

Then, after five minutes or so, students were presented with another list of sentences and asked to indicate which sentences were in the first list. They were also asked to rate their confidence in each answer on a scale from 1 to 5. Item #34 in the Reader Survey contains a second list of sentences, along with blanks for confidence ratings as to whether these sentences appeared in the original list.

As it happens, the only sentence that appeared in the first set was Item #34c: "The ants ate the sweet jelly." If you are similar to most people in the study by Bransford and Franks, you were moderately confident (2 to 4 on the confidence scale) that this sentence had appeared before.

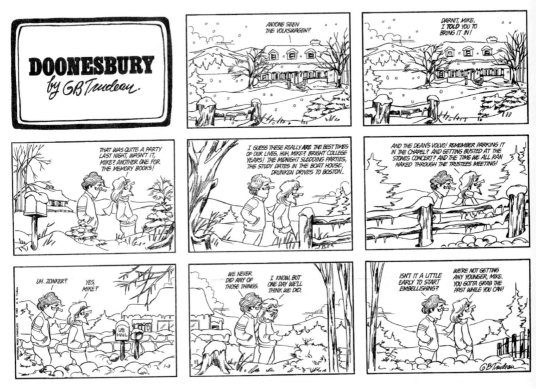

FIGURE 3.1

Reconstructive memory. (Doonesbury copyright 1992 G. B. Trudeau. Reprinted with permission of Universal Press Syndicates. All rights reserved.)

More interesting is your response to Item #34b: "The ants in the kitchen ate the sweet jelly which was on the table." Even though this sentence did not appear in the first set, students in the study by Bransford and Franks tended to be very confident that they had seen it before. Were you? *No.*

What is significant about the sentence in Item #34b is that it contains combinations of relations that are not contained in any individual sentence from the first set. The original sentences never explicitly stated that the jelly in the kitchen was sweet, or that the ants in the kitchen ate the sweet jelly. The sentence in Item #34b can only be derived by combining separate sentences from the first set.

Thus, people do not simply memorize sentences; they construct and memorize a general scenario. Once one piece of information is integrated with others, it is sometimes difficult to remember which information was new and which was already known.

I KNEW IT ALL ALONG → Hindsight Bias

People also have difficulty telling how they are affected by information about an outcome. For example, if they learn about the results of a psychological experiment, they tend to regard the findings as having been fairly predictable all along—or at least more predictable than they would have judged before learning of the results (one of the reasons why this book has a Reader Survey!). Moreover, if people are asked to behave as though they know nothing about the outcome of an experiment, they still respond more like people who know about the results than people who do not. That is, if they are asked to estimate in retrospect how likely they once thought the results were to occur, they assign higher probabilities than do people predicting the experimental outcome in advance.

This tendency is known as "hindsight bias," or the "I-knew-it-all-along" effect. Hindsight bias is the tendency to view what has already happened as relatively inevitable and obvious—without realizing that retrospective knowledge of the outcome is influencing one's judgments. Hindsight biases have been documented in elections (Leary, 1982; Synodinos, 1986), medical diagnoses (Arkes, Wortmann, Saville, & Harkness, 1981), pregnancy tests (Pennington, Rutter, McKenna, & Morley, 1980), buying decisions (Walster, 1967), games (Leary, 1981), and a number of other areas. They have also been shown using a variety of experimental techniques, response instructions, and groups of people (for reviews of hindsight bias and related effects, see Campbell & Tesser, 1983; Christensen-Szalanski & Willham, 1991; Hawkins & Hastie, 1990; Verplanken & Pieters, 1988).

One of the first studies on hindsight bias was published in 1975 by Baruch Fischhoff and Ruth Beyth. The main events Fischhoff and Beyth (1975) used in their study were President Nixon's trips to China and the Soviet Union in 1972. In the first phase of the experiment, several groups of Israeli students were asked to estimate the probability of 15 different outcomes for either the China trip or the Soviet trip—*before* the trip took place. For example, students who were asked about the China trip estimated the chances that the United States would establish a diplomatic mission in Peking, that President Nixon would meet Mao at least once, that President Nixon would announce the trip a success, and so forth. Similarly, students who were asked about Nixon's trip to the Soviet Union estimated outcomes such as the establishment of a joint space program, or the arrest of Soviet Jews trying to speak with Nixon.

In the second phase of the study—two weeks to six months after the trip had taken place—students were asked to recall what their earlier predictions had been. For instance, students who had answered questions about the China trip were told the following:

> As you remember, about two weeks ago, on the eve of President Nixon's trip to China, you completed a questionnaire by providing probabilities for the occurrence of a number of possible outcomes of the trip. We are presently interested in the relation between the quality of people's predictions and their ability to remember their predictions. For this reason, we would like to have you fill out once again the same questionnaire which you completed two weeks ago, giving the *same probabilities which you gave then.* If you cannot remember the probability which you then assigned, give the probability which you would have given to each of the various outcomes on the eve of President Nixon's trip to China.

Students were also asked to indicate whether, as far as they knew, each outcome had in fact occurred. Fischhoff and Beyth wanted to see if students would remember their predictions as having been more accurate than they actually were.

In general, this is just what Fischhoff and Beyth (1975) found. Three-quarters of the students tended to remember having assigned higher probabilities than they actually had to outcomes that they thought had occurred, and the majority of students remembered having assigned lower probabilities to outcomes they believed had not occurred. Hindsight biases were particularly strong when the initial predictions preceded the recall task by several months. When three to six months separated the prediction and recall tasks, 84 percent of the students showed hindsight biases—after learning the outcome of Nixon's trips, they viewed the outcome as having been more predictable than it actually was.

REDUCING HINDSIGHT BIAS

In 1977, Paul Slovic and Baruch Fischhoff published a study that showed how to reduce hindsight biases when learning the results of research (the feeling of having known the results all along). Slovic and Fischhoff found that hindsight biases diminished when people stopped to consider reasons why the results might have turned out differently.

Subjects in this research read four brief descriptions of studies drawn from biology, psychology, and meteorology. *Foresight* subjects were told that the four studies would be conducted soon, and *hindsight* subjects were told that the studies had already been conducted. After reading about each study, all subjects then estimated the probability of replicating an outcome obtained on the first experimental trial (each trial always had two possible outcomes). In other words, hindsight subjects were told that a particular outcome had already been observed, and foresight subjects were asked to *suppose* the outcome occurred.

Slovic and Fischhoff (1977) found that compared with foresight subjects, hindsight subjects gave higher probability estimates that all future trials would replicate the first one. This difference was substantially reduced, however, when hindsight subjects were asked to consider reasons why *either* experimental outcome might have occurred. Hindsight bias was still present in this case, but to a much lesser degree.

Thus, the moral of the story is as follows: If you want to reduce hindsight biases, you should explicitly consider how past events might have turned out differently. If you only consider the reasons why something turned out as it did, you run a good risk of overestimating how inevitable that outcome was and how likely similar outcomes are in the future. In fact, Fischhoff (1977) has found that informing people about hindsight bias and encouraging them to avoid it is not enough to remove the bias. To avoid the ravages of hindsight bias, it is important to consider how an alternative outcome might have occurred.

CONCLUSION

In his book *Memory*, Ian Hunter (1964) tells the story of two British psychologists who secretly recorded a discussion that took place after a meeting of the Cambridge Psychological Society. Two weeks later, the psychologists contacted all the participants and asked them to write down everything they could remember about the discussion. When these accounts were checked against the original recording, it turned out that respondents typically omitted more than 90 percent of the specific points that had been discussed. Moreover, of the points that were recalled, nearly half were substantially incorrect. Respondents remembered comments that were never made, they transformed casual remarks into lengthy orations, and they converted implicit meanings into explicit comments.

This story highlights the value of keeping accurate records. Even the most sophisticated decision maker is susceptible to biases in memory, and there is no better way to avoid these biases than maintaining careful notes and records of past events (e.g., meetings, important conversations, and agreements). As the research in this chapter shows, memory is, by its very nature, reconstructive and highly dependent upon contextual factors. Chapter 4 further explores the effects of context on judgment and decision making.

CHAPTER 4

CONTEXT DEPENDENCE

As the previous three chapters imply, the effect of a stimulus is "context-dependent." That is, decision makers do not perceive and remember material in isolation; they interpret new information in light of past experience and the context in which the material occurs. In one situation, a stimulus (for example, a personality trait) may be perceived one way, and in another situation, the "same" stimulus may be seen very differently. Many perceptual illusions exploit the principle of context dependence (see Figure 4.1). In the area of judgment and decision making, four of the best illustrations of context dependence are the contrast effect, the primacy effect, the recency effect, and the halo effect.

THE CONTRAST EFFECT

Here is a simple experiment you can perform on yourself (or on your friends). All you need is three large bowls of water. Fill the first bowl with hot water, the second bowl with tepid water, and the third bowl with ice water. Next, submerge one hand in the hot bowl and one in the cold bowl, and keep them there for thirty seconds. Once your hands have adjusted to the water temperature, place the "hot" hand in the bowl of tepid water and, after five seconds, join it with the "cold" hand.

If you are like most people, you will feel a very strange sensation. The hand that was formerly in hot water will be telling you that the tepid water is cold, and the hand that was in cold water will be telling you that the tepid water is hot. In fact, if you try this experiment on a friend and keep the temperature of the tepid water a secret, she or he will probably not be able to tell what temperature the tepid water is. Each hand will be exhibiting a "contrast effect," but the two effects will be in opposite directions!

Many early studies in psychology concerned perceptual judgments such as temperature discrimination, color discrimination, and weight estimation. Consequently, contrast effects were among the first psychological phenomena to be reliably demonstrated in the laboratory. For example, Muzafer Sherif, Daniel Taub, and Carl Hovland (1958) published an influential article on contrast effects in judgments of weight. Sherif, Taub, and Hovland found that when subjects initially lifted a heavy weight, they subsequently rated relatively light weights as lighter than they actually were.

FIGURE 4.1

To see some effects of context on visual perception, hold this page up to a bright light source. Most people report that the edges of the square bend inward and that the parallel lines no longer look parallel. *(Adapted from Block and Yuker, 1989.)*

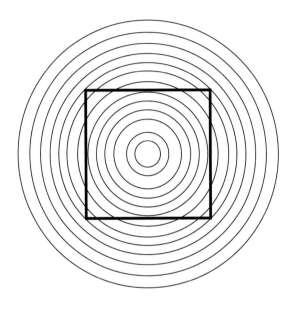

FIGURE 4.1 (continued)

One of the most interesting studies of the contrast effect was published by Stanley Coren and Joel Miller (1974). Coren and Miller noted that a 5-foot 10-inch sports announcer looks very short when interviewing a team of basketball players, but looks very tall when interviewing race horse jockeys. At the same time, the apparent size of the announcer does not shrink when the announcer is standing beside a large race horse—or, for that matter, a stadium.

From this observation, Coren and Miller speculated that the contrast effect only occurs when the contrasted stimuli are similar to one another. To test this hypothesis, they presented a dozen volunteers with each of the clusters shown in Figure 4.2. The cluster in the upper left quadrant is an example of the famous Ebbinghaus illusion. In the Ebbinghaus illusion, the center circle appears larger when it is surrounded by smaller circles than when it is contrasted with larger circles.

Coren and Miller found, however, that the Ebbinghaus illusion diminished as the surrounding shapes became less like circles (as judged by the experimental volunteers). The illusion was weaker with hexagons than circles, weaker still with triangles, and weakest of all using irregular polygons. By comparing the quadrants in Figure 4.2, you can see that even simple judgments of size depend critically upon context.

FIGURE 4.2

Stanley Coren and Joel Miller explored the contrast effect using four variants of the Ebbinghaus illusion. The upper left quadrant contains a typical example of the standard Ebbinghaus illusion. (Coren and Miller, 1974. Reprinted with permission.)

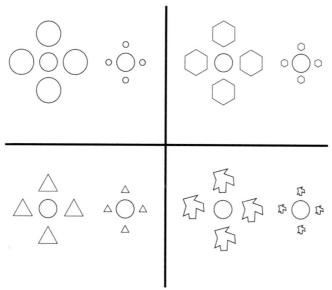

THE PRIMACY EFFECT

A classic study of context dependence was published by Solomon Asch (1946). Although Asch is best known for his research on conformity (discussed in Chapter 17), he also pioneered the study of "impression formation." In most of his research on impression formation, Asch asked subjects to give their impressions of a hypothetical person who had certain traits. His 1946 article reviewed 10 different experiments using this paradigm, but for now, we will consider just one.

In this experiment, Asch asked subjects for their impressions of someone with the traits listed in Item #3 of the Reader Survey. Half of the subjects were asked about someone who was *envious, stubborn, critical, impulsive, industrious, and intelligent.* The other half were asked about someone with the very same characteristics, except that the characteristics were presented in the opposite order: *intelligent, industrious, impulsive, critical, stubborn, and envious.*

What Asch found was that the characteristics appearing early in each series influenced impressions more strongly than the characteristics appearing later. This pattern is known as a "primacy effect." If you responded to Item #3 by rating John's emotionality as very high, a primacy effect may have occurred—the emotional traits *envious* and *stubborn* may have affected your impressions more than they would have if they had appeared later in the list.

Would *envious* and *stubborn* still produce a primacy effect if *intelligent* preceded them as the first word? According to a study by Norman Anderson (1965), they probably would. Anderson found that the primacy effect is not merely a product of the first entry in a series. Instead, it is a general relationship between the position an entry occupies and the effect it has on judgments. First impressions are the most important impressions, but second and third impressions still show a significant primacy effect.

THE RECENCY EFFECT

The primacy effect occurs not only when people form impressions of each other, but in a great many situations involving the evaluation of sequential information. For example, a primacy effect sometimes occurs when people are exposed to opposite sides of a controversial issue. In many cases, people are more influenced by the first presentation of an issue than by subsequent presentations.

This is not always the case, however. In some instances, the final presentation has more influence than the first presentation. Such a pattern is known as the "recency effect." The recency effect often occurs when people are able to remember the last presentation more clearly than the first one.

An interesting question arises as to which effect is the strongest. For example, suppose you are participating in a public debate, and suppose further that you are offered the choice of speaking first or last. What should you choose? If you speak first, you might be able to take advantage of a primacy effect, but if you speak last, you might capitalize on a recency effect. Which choice is best?

This question was investigated by Norman Miller and Donald Campbell (1959). Miller and Campbell edited the transcript of a court trial concerning damages allegedly incurred as a result of a defective vaporizer. The proceedings were rearranged so that all the material for the plaintiff appeared in one block of text, and all the material for the defendant appeared in another block. In other words, the "pro" communication included testimony from witnesses called by the plaintiff, the cross-examination of witnesses for the defense by the plaintiff's lawyer, and the opening and closing speeches by the plaintiff's lawyer. The "con" communication included testimony from witnesses for the defense, the cross-examination by the defense, and the opening and closing speeches by the counsel for the defense.

After Miller and Campbell edited the transcripts, they recorded the proceedings with different people reading the parts of different characters (lawyers, witnesses, and so forth). Each recording lasted about forty-five minutes, and the communications were presented in one of eight different ways (see Figure 4.3 for an overview). In some conditions, subjects rendered judgments immediately after hearing back-to-back communications (pro-con or con-pro), and in other conditions, a one-week delay separated various phases of the experiment.

FIGURE 4.3

Norman Miller and Donald Campbell (1959) investigated primacy and recency effects by comparing the impact of communications in the eight experimental conditions shown below.

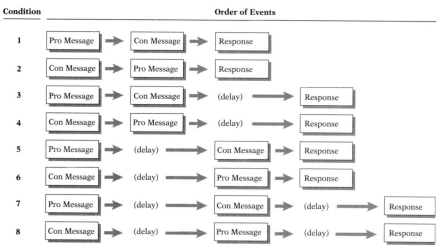

What Miller and Campbell found was a primacy effect in some cases and a recency effect in others—that is, they found that in some conditions people were more persuaded by the first communication, and in others, they were more persuaded by the second communication (regardless of whether the communication was pro or con). When subjects were asked about the court case one week after hearing back-to-back presentations (Conditions 3 and 4), a primacy effect occurred. On the other hand, when the communications were separated by a week and subjects were asked about the case immediately after the second communication (Conditions 5 and 6), a recency effect occurred. The first two conditions and the last two conditions did not result in significant primacy or recency effects.

Miller and Campbell (1959) also found evidence that recency effects were a function of differences in recall. As measured by a multiple-choice test, subjects in Condition 5 tended to recall more factual material about the con communication than about the pro communication, and subjects in Condition 6 tended to recall more factual material about the pro communication than about the con communication.

So to answer the original question: If you are offered the choice of speaking first or last in a public debate, you should speak first if the other side will follow you immediately and there will be a delay between the debate and people's responses to it. For example, if you are debating an issue that will be voted on in a week, then you should choose to speak first. On the other hand, if some time will separate the two communications, and if people will be asked to act immediately after the second presentation, you should capitalize on the recency effect and choose to go last.

Stephen Hoch (1984) found essentially the same results in several experiments on how people make predictions. Hoch asked people to generate reasons why a future event might occur ("pro-reasons") and reasons why the same event might not occur ("con-reasons"). For some events people listed pro-reasons first, and for others they listed con-reasons first. Hoch found a strong primacy effect when people generated both sets of reasons back-to-back, but a recency effect when people worked on a three-minute task between listing pro- and con-reasons. These findings are consistent with age-old selling techniques in which customers are encouraged to list the reasons for making a purchase (pro-reasons) and list the reasons against making a purchase (con-reasons). If the two sets of reasons are generated back-to-back, customers may unwittingly fall prey to primacy effects (Gross, 1964).

HALO EFFECTS

Contrast, primacy, and recency effects show that the same stimulus can have a different effect depending on its context and order of presentation. Another example of context dependence is the "halo" effect, so named by Edward Thorndike back in 1920. Thorndike found that when army superiors were asked to evaluate their officers in terms of intelligence, physique, leadership, and character, the ratings were often highly correlated. According to Thorndike, a flight commander who had supervised the work of aviation cadets showed a correlation of .51 between his ratings of their intelligence and their physique, .58 between their intelligence and their leadership ability, and .64 between their intelligence and their character.[*] Thorndike also found positive correlations among various teacher evaluations that were used to determine salaries and promotions. In one case, for example, general merit as a teacher correlated strongly with ratings of general appearance, health, promptness, intellect, and integrity and sincerity. In another case, ratings of a teacher's voice correlated strongly with ratings of intelligence and "interest in community affairs."

In his original article on the halo effect, Thorndike (1920, pp. 28–29) concluded that "even a very capable foreman, employer, teacher, or department head is unable to treat an individual as a compound of separate qualities and to assign a magnitude to each of these in independence of the others." Nowadays, we know that Thorndike's findings were partly due to technical aspects of how the rating scales were constructed, but his general idea has stood the test of time. Even when ratings are solicited using sophisticated measurement techniques, a halo effect often results (Cooper, 1981; Feldman, 1986).

Since the time of Thorndike's observations, many different halo effects have been documented. For example, research on "beauty halo effects" has shown that, relative to average-looking or unattractive people, physically attractive people are seen as happier, higher in occupational status, more likely to get married, and more desirable in terms of personality (Dion, Berscheid, & Walster, 1972). David Landy and Harold Sigall (1974) also found that essays were rated as higher in quality when they were attributed to a physically attractive author rather than an average-looking or unattractive author.

As in the case of the contrast effect, many pioneering experiments on the halo effect were performed by Asch (1946). For instance, in one experiment, Asch asked roughly half the subjects to form an impression of someone who was intelligent, skillful, industrious, warm, determined, practical, and cautious. Similarly, he asked the other subjects to form an impression of someone who was intelligent, skillful, industrious,

---

*Correlation coefficients usually vary between +1.00 and –1.00. Positive correlations mean that one variable increases as the other increases, negative correlations mean that one variable decreases as the other increases, and a correlation of 0.00 means that the variables are not related in either direction. Thus, in Thorndike's case, high ratings of intelligence were associated with high ratings of other desirable characteristics.

cold, determined, practical, and cautious. Thus, both groups of subjects heard the same description, except that the person was described as warm in the first instance and cold in the second.

Subjects were then presented with pairs of traits (mostly opposites) and were asked to indicate which trait was most consistent with the impression they had formed of the person. The pairs included traits such as generous/ungenerous, unhappy/happy, irritable/good-natured, and humorous/humorless. In keeping with the earlier findings of Thorndike, Asch found that the inclusion of a central characteristic such as warm or cold influenced subjects' overall impression of the person—that is, subjects created a "halo." For example, 75 to 95 percent of the subjects who formed an impression of the warm person thought that such a person would also be generous, happy, good-natured, and humorous (you can compare yourself to these subjects by checking your answer to Item #4 of the Reader Survey). In contrast, only 5 to 35 percent of the subjects who formed an impression of the cold person thought that such a person would have these traits.

These results are not simply a by-product of using simple paper-and-pencil tasks. Harold Kelley (1950) published a study that explored the halo effect using real people instead of lists of traits, and he found much the same halo effect that Asch had observed several years earlier. Students who were led to expect a warm instructor saw the instructor not only as relatively considerate, good-natured, and sociable, but as more popular, humorous, and humane. Moreover, there was a marginal tendency for students to interact more with the instructor when they believed he was warm. Fifty-six percent of the "warm" subjects entered into the class discussion, compared with only 32 percent of the "cold" subjects. These results suggest that the halo effect operates in social interactions and may influence subsequent behavior.

As with the contrast, primacy, and recency effects, the halo effect illustrates that the way people react to a stimulus is context-dependent. Indeed, there is no such thing as a stimulus without a context. Contextual factors strongly influence how people respond—whether the stimulus is a geometric shape, a personality trait, a legal argument, or spinach.

CONCLUSION

Context effects are so common they sometimes seem invisible. In fact, it is hard to imagine a world in which perceptions are *not* context-dependent. What would such a world look like? What would it mean to talk about context-free judgment?

As a student in one of my seminars pointed out, context effects raise profound questions about the nature of social relationships. For example, the contrast effect suggests that it is impossible to "know a person" in any absolute sense. When you judge the honesty of a friend, this judgment is relative and depends to some extent on the honesty of other people you know. According to the contrast effect, you will see your friend as more honest if other people you know deceive you—even if the behavior of your friend remains the same. The judgment you make of a friend's honesty may *seem* unrelated to the honesty of other people, but as the research in this chapter shows, social judgments often depend in part on context.

Even happiness is context-dependent. Philip Brickman, Dan Coates, and Ronnie Janoff-Bulman (1978) found this to be the case in a study of Illinois State Lottery winners. Compared with a geographically matched control group of nonwinners, lottery winners reported feeling less pleasure from a variety of daily activities, including watching television, talking with friends, eating breakfast, buying clothes, and so forth. Brickman, Coates, and Janoff-Bulman argued that this difference was partly the result of a contrast effect in which ordinary activities were compared with the thrill of winning a lottery.

Persuasion professionals have long recognized the power of context effects. For instance, real estate agents sometimes exploit the contrast effect by showing buyers a run-down or overpriced property before the home that is under serious consideration. Political candidates often capitalize on the halo effect by painting a picture of wide-ranging ability from one or two previous successes. And advertisers take painstaking care to create appealing contexts for the products they promote.

Of course, the effects of context are not limitless. A pathological liar will not seem honest regardless of how much other people lie, and an incompetent politician can only exploit the halo effect so far. A background of concentric circles can make the edges of a square seem curved, but it cannot make a square into a circle. Nonetheless, any comprehensive analysis of judgment and decision making must take context effects into account. Indeed, some authors have suggested that laboratory demonstrations of context effects *underestimate* the effects of context in daily life (Hershey & Schoemaker, 1980).

HOW QUESTIONS AFFECT ANSWERS

Section I showed how the context of a stimulus shapes the way it is perceived. The present section extends this theme by considering how the format of a problem can influence the way people respond to it. Chapters 5 and 6 focus on the following two questions: (1) How much do judgments and decisions depend on the way a problem is worded? (2) What are some specific ways in which the wording of a question or problem influences the answer?

CHAPTER 5

PLASTICITY

Just as every stimulus has a context, so has every question. This chapter takes a look at how the context and wording of questions can influence judgment and decision making.

In some cases, offering the same choice in two different contexts can lead to very different answers. For example, suppose you were faced with the following choice:

> **Alternative A:** A 100 percent chance of losing $50
> **Alternative B:** A 25 percent chance of losing $200, and a 75 percent chance of losing nothing

Which alternative would you choose? (see Item #2 of the Reader Survey for your answer). If you are like 80 percent of the people asked by Paul Slovic, Baruch Fischhoff, and Sarah Lichtenstein (1982b), you prefer Alternative B. Most people are "risk seeking" when it comes to losses; that is, they prefer to risk a relatively large loss (in this case, $200) rather than suffer a sure loss with the same expected value (a 25 percent chance of losing $200 has the same expected value as a sure loss of $50 because both alternatives yield the same expected return over the long run).

A moment's reflection will reveal that something is wrong here, though. If people were always risk seeking when it came to losses, then insurance companies would be out of business. The insurance industry is based on people's willingness to pay a sure loss (a "premium") in order to avoid a larger but uncertain loss. Do people behave differently when sure losses are dressed in the language of insurance? How would people choose between Alternative A and Alternative B if a sure loss of $50 were presented as an *insurance premium* that protected against the potential of losing $200?

Slovic, Fischhoff, and Lichtenstein found that in this case, 65 percent of their respondents preferred the sure loss of $50. Perhaps because insurance premiums highlight the potential for large losses, or perhaps because they invoke a social norm to act prudently, people prefer to pay a premium rather than risk a larger loss. In any event, it is clear that the very same choice leads to a different preference when it is cast in terms

51

TABLE 5.1
WHICH ALTERNATIVE DO YOU PREFER?

RISKY ALTERNATIVE			Gamble Context, % Preferring	Insurance Context, % Preferring
Probability	Loss, $	Sure Loss, $	Sure Loss	Sure Loss
.001	10,000	10	54	81
.01	10,000	100	46	66
.01	100,000	1000	37	76
.10	10,000	1000	29	59

Note: As the two far right columns in this table show, 20 to 40 percent more people prefer a sure loss in the context of an insurance premium than in the context of a pure gamble. This data comes from a study by John Hershey and Paul Schoemaker (1980).

of insurance. When a sure loss is presented as an insurance premium, most people become "risk averse" rather than risk seeking; they prefer a sure loss to the risk of losing a larger amount.

Slovic, Fischhoff, and Lichtenstein (1982b) found a similar reversal of preferences when people were given a choice between paying $5 or facing a 1 in 1000 chance of losing $5000. Although only two people out of every five preferred to pay $5 in the context of a simple preference, roughly two out of three preferred the sure loss when it was presented as an insurance premium. The same effect has also been documented across a range of situations by John Hershey and Paul Schoemaker (1980) (see Table 5.1).

ORDER EFFECTS

How people answer questions can also be influenced by the ordering of questions or response alternatives. Usually these effects are fairly small, but in some cases they can be substantial. For instance, if two questions concern the same topic and there is a need on the part of respondents to appear consistent, then answers to the second question can be pulled in the direction of answers to the first.

In their book *Questions and Answers in Attitude Surveys*, Howard Schuman and Stanley Presser (1981) illustrated this effect with results from a survey on freedom of the press. Schuman and Presser asked a random sample of American adults the following two questions:

1. Do you think a Communist country like Russia should let American newspaper reporters come in and send back to America the news as they see it?
2. Do you think the United States should let Communist newspaper reporters from other countries come in and send back to their papers the news as they see it?

Roughly half the respondents were asked these questions in the order above, and the remainder were asked the questions in reverse order.

Schuman and Presser found that when respondents were first asked about American reporters, 82 percent said that American reporters should be allowed to report freely from Communist countries. Consistent with this answer, nearly 75 percent of the respondents also granted that Communist reporters should be allowed to report freely within the United States. On the other hand, when respondents were first asked about Communist reporters, only 55 percent approved of giving Communist reporters free license in the United States. In this case, presumably to remain consistent and avoid showing a double standard, only 64 percent of the respondents said that American reporters should be allowed into Communist countries (closer to 55 percent than 82 percent). Thus, a different ordering of the very same questions produced a marked change in the answers.

Answers can also be influenced by the order in which response alternatives are presented. Response-order effects are usually slight, and they rarely occur when questions involve very brief dichotomous choices (such as "agree" or "disagree") or fairly large sets of alternatives. One of the most common response-order effects is a recency effect, in which the same answer is chosen more frequently when it appears as the last alternative in a series.

Schuman and Presser (1981) found a moderately strong recency effect in two variations of a question on divorce. They asked approximately half the respondents in a national opinion poll the following question: "Should divorce in this country be **easier to obtain, more difficult to obtain**, or **stay as it is now?**"

In response to this question, 23 percent of the respondents said that divorce should be made easier, 36 percent said that it should be made more difficult, and 41 percent said it should stay as is (see Figure 5.1).

The remaining respondents were asked the same question, except that the order of the last two response alternatives was inverted: "Should divorce in this country be **easier to obtain, stay as it is now**, or be **more difficult to obtain?**"

In this case, 26 percent of the respondents said that divorce should be made easier, 29 percent favored the status quo, and 46 percent said that it should be made more difficult. In both variations of the question, the most popular response was the last alternative mentioned.

PSEUDO-OPINIONS

Although context and order can significantly influence the way people answer questions, responses are "plastic" only to a certain point (survey researchers refer to the malleability of responses as *plasticity*). When people are familiar with an issue, variations in context and order typi-

*Should divorce in this country
be easier to obtain, more difficult
to obtain, or stay as it is now?*

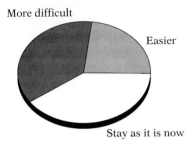

More difficult

Easier

Stay as it is now

*Should divorce in this country
be easier to obtain, stay as it is now,
or be more difficult to obtain?*

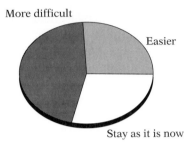

More difficult

Easier

Stay as it is now

FIGURE 5.1

In both versions of this question on divorce, respondents favored the last response alternative. *(Based on data from a national survey conducted by Howard Schuman and Stanley Presser, 1981.)*

cally produce marginal changes of less than 30 percent ("marginals" are the percentage of respondents giving each answer). When respondents know fairly little about an issue, however, they are more easily influenced by these variations. And when respondents know virtually nothing about an issue, a certain percentage will show the ultimate form of plasticity; depending upon how the question is asked, some portion will offer an opinion on a topic about which they have no real opinion. Such opinions are called, appropriately enough, "pseudo-opinions."*

One of the earliest studies to explore the prevalence of pseudo-opinions was published in 1946 by Eugene Hartley. In a survey of several hundred college students, Hartley found that more than 80 percent were willing to rate Danireans, Pireneans, Wallonians, and 32 other nationalities in terms of "social distance" (a widely used index of how close

---

*As Tom Smith (1984) has pointed out, opinions and pseudo-opinions (or attitudes and "nonattitudes," as they are sometimes called) are actually endpoints on a continuum, rather than qualitatively distinct terms. Still, it is useful to distinguish between the two (just as hot and cold are distinguished even though they are part of a continuum).

One further note on terminology: Throughout the book, "opinions" and "judgments" are used more or less interchangeably, and "attitudes" are used to signify *evaluative* judgments (judgments ordered along dimensions such as good-bad, like-dislike, or approve-disapprove). For example, although people can form a *judgment* or an *opinion* about how many beans are in a jar, they do not usually form an *attitude* about the number of beans. As most psychologists use the term, "attitude" refers only to evaluative judgments. In practice, however, it is often difficult to distinguish among attitudes, opinions, and judgments.

people feel to each other). The catch was that there is no such thing as a Danirean, Pirenean, or Wallonian—Hartley simply invented these nationalities in order to see how many students would pretend to have an opinion about them.

The next year, *Tide* magazine publicized a similar poll that asked respondents about a piece of fictitious legislation called the Metallic Metals Act:

> Which of the following statements most closely coincides with your opinion of the Metallic Metals Act?
>
> (a) It would be a good move on the part of the U.S.
> (b) It would be a good thing but should be left to individual states.
> (c) It is all right for foreign countries but should not be required here.
> (d) It is of no value at all.

Even though there was no such thing as a Metallic Metals Act, 70 percent of the respondents gave an opinion. Forty-one percent favored leaving the Metallic Metals Act to individual states, 15 percent thought it would be a good U.S. move, 11 percent felt it should not be required, and 3 percent said the act had no value at all (Gill, 1947, March 14).

The same article also discussed the results of a survey in which respondents were asked: "Are you in favor of or opposed to incest?" (in the 1940s, the word "incest" was not as well known as it is today). Of the respondents who expressed an opinion, two-thirds said they were opposed to incest and one-third said they favored it!

PSEUDO-OPINIONS IN POLITICAL AFFAIRS

After reviewing research on pseudo-opinions—including several experiments of their own—Schuman and Presser (1981) concluded that the problem, while significant, was not as serious as earlier studies had suggested. In their own survey work, only a third or a fourth of the respondents offered pseudo-opinions in response to questions about obscure legislation. Other researchers have found similar results (Bishop, Oldendick, Tuchfarber, & Bennett, 1980).

Although pseudo-opinions offered by 25 to 35 percent of all respondents may not appear serious, it is important to remember that in many democracies (including the United States), 30 percent of the public can elect a president. Political controversies are often decided by margins of only a few percent, and as a result, pseudo-opinions can decisively influence political affairs. Moreover, if respondents who know very little about an issue are added to those who have never heard of it, the percentage of pseudo-opinions frequently constitutes an absolute majority.

Pseudo-opinions are particularly common in judgments concerning foreign and military policy, where strong social pressures to express an

opinion often collide with low levels of political involvement or awareness. For instance, consider these examples of American "political illiteracy," taken from Plous (1989, March):

- A 1988 Gallup poll of American adults found that almost half did
  not know that the country with a government policy of apartheid
  was South Africa, and three-fourths could not name four countries
  that officially acknowledged having nuclear weapons.
- A 1985 survey of college students found that 45 percent could not
  name the two cities on which nuclear weapons have been dropped.
- According to a 1979 government survey reported in the *New York
  Times*, 40 percent of high school seniors mistakenly thought that
  Israel was an Arab nation.
- A 1983 *Washington Post* article, entitled "El Salvador Is Not In
  Louisiana," reported that three-fourths of the respondents in a
  national poll did not know the location of El Salvador (the title of
  the article was taken from an answer provided by one of the
  respondents).
- Other polls have shown that 68 percent of those surveyed were
  unaware that the United States has no means of defending itself
  from incoming ballistic missiles, and 81 percent falsely believed
  that U.S. policy was to use nuclear weapons against the Soviet
  Union only if the U.S.S.R. attacked first with nuclear weapons.

This level of political illiteracy tremendously complicates the interpretation of public opinion toward foreign and military policies. For
example, what does support for Israel mean if Israel is mistaken for an
Arab country? What does support for the Strategic Defense Initiative
mean when thousands of people believe that the United States can
already defend itself against ballistic missiles? For such political judgments to be comprehensible, true opinions must first be separated from
pseudo-opinions.

FILTERING OUT PSEUDO-OPINIONS

Historically, most public opinion surveys have used "unfiltered" questions. No effort has been made to exclude respondents who lack an
opinion, and response options have not explicitly included categories
such as "no opinion" or "don't know." Increasingly, though, survey
researchers have realized the usefulness of "filters." Filters are designed
to weed out respondents who have no opinion on a given topic.
    There are several ways in which filtering is usually accomplished. In
some polls, respondents are first asked whether they have heard or read
anything about a particular issue. If they reply affirmatively, they are
asked for their opinion; if not, they are asked about different issues.

Other polls begin by asking respondents whether they have thought much about an issue, or even more directly, whether they have formed an opinion on the topic. Yet another filtering technique is to explicitly mention "no opinion" or "don't know" as response alternatives.

Filters are generally effective in screening out pseudo-opinions. In some cases, though, they run the risk of biasing survey results. For example, "don't know" responses tend to be negatively correlated with educational level or interest in certain issues. If relatively uneducated or uninterested respondents are filtered out, survey results may not be representative of the population as a whole.

To assess the effects of filtering, Schuman and Presser (1981) conducted a number of experimental polls comparing filtered and unfiltered questions. Based on their findings, they concluded that most filters (1) shift at least one-fifth of the respondents from expressing an opinion to answering "don't know"; (2) do not significantly affect the relative proportion of respondents who give a particular answer (for example, the proportion who say "yes" versus "no"); and (3) do not strongly affect the correlation between answers to one question and answers to another.

For instance, the following pair of questions, which appeared in an American national survey in 1974, yielded results typical of those found by Schuman and Presser:

Unfiltered Version: "The Arab nations are trying to work for a real peace with Israel. Do you agree or disagree?"

Agree [17 percent]
Disagree [60 percent]
Don't Know (volunteered) [23 percent]

Filtered Version: "The Arab nations are trying to work for a real peace with Israel. Do you have an opinion on that? (If yes) Do you agree or disagree?"

Agree [10 percent]
Disagree [45 percent]
No opinion [45 percent]

Even though the filtered version drew 22 percent more "no opinion/don't know" responses than the unfiltered version, the ratio of disagreement to agreement remained fairly similar in both versions (about four respondents disagreeing for every one agreeing).

Of course, this similarity does not mean that the effect of filtering is unimportant. Suppose, for example, that a devious pollster wants to show that an absolute majority of the public disagrees with the statement: "The Arab nations are trying to work for a real peace with Israel." In that case, the pollster might ask the question without filtering it first.

On the other hand, if a pollster wants to show the lowest absolute level of agreement, then the filtered version would be a better choice. This kind of manipulation has been responsible for more than a few sensational headlines.

INCONSISTENCY: THE HOBGOBLIN OF ATTITUDES

Plasticity in choices and opinions is closely related to attitudinal inconsistency. Whereas *plasticity* usually refers to a discrepancy in how people answer two versions of the same question, *inconsistency* refers to a discrepancy between two related attitudes (attitude-attitude inconsistency) or between an attitude and a corresponding behavior (attitude-behavior inconsistency). One of the most striking demonstrations of attitude-attitude inconsistency was published in 1960 by James Prothro and Charles Grigg.

Prothro and Grigg were interested in whether Americans would support specific applications of popular democratic principles. At the time of the study, these principles were accepted by the vast majority of Americans. For example, the principles included:

1. Public officials should be chosen by majority vote.
2. Every citizen should have an equal chance to influence government policy.
3. The minority should be free to criticize majority decisions.

After Prothro and Grigg outlined these general principles, they derived 10 specific statements that either illustrated or contradicted the principles, such as:

> If an admitted Communist wanted to make a speech in this city favoring Communism, he should be allowed to speak.

or:

> In a city referendum, only people who are well informed about the problem being voted on should be allowed to vote.

Then Prothro and Grigg asked a random sample of registered voters in Ann Arbor, Michigan, and Tallahassee, Florida, whether they agreed or disagreed with each of the 10 derived statements.

What they found was surprising. Respondents failed to reach a 90 percent consensus on any of the 10 statements, and more often than not, their judgments about specific applications of democracy were inconsistent with widely accepted democratic principles. For example, 51 percent of the respondents endorsed the antidemocratic idea that only well-informed people should be permitted to vote, 79 percent said that only taxpayers should vote, and only 44 percent felt that a bona fide member of the Communist Party should be allowed to publicly advocate Communism. Commenting on the irony of these results, Prothro and Grigg (1960, p. 293) concluded: "Assuming that the United States is a democracy, we cannot say without qualification that consensus on fundamental principles is a necessary condition for the existence of democracy."

Although this study provides an extreme example of attitude-attitude inconsistency, subsequent research has confirmed the findings of Prothro and Grigg. Attitudes about abstract propositions are often unrelated to attitudes about specific applications of the same propositions. When it comes to specific applications, there are invariably complicating factors: situational constraints, other principles that present conflicts, and so forth. As the next section shows, research on attitude-behavior inconsistency suggests that abstract attitudes also bear little relation to specific actions.

ON THE ROAD AGAIN

In 1930, Richard LaPiere, a Stanford University sociologist, began traveling the United States with a young Chinese couple. For two years, LaPiere and the couple swept across the country, visiting a total of 184 eating establishments and 67 hotels, auto camps, and tourist homes. Despite the intense anti-Chinese prejudice that prevailed in those days, LaPiere observed racial discrimination only once in 251 encounters. In fact, LaPiere judged that his companions were received with "more than ordinary consideration" on 72 occasions. Based on this experience, LaPiere concluded that one would never suspect the American people of being prejudiced against the Chinese.

Yet prejudice was very apparent at the level of abstract opinion. Six months after visiting each establishment, LaPiere sent the proprietors a survey that asked, among other things: "Will you accept members of the Chinese race as guests in your establishment?" With persistence, LaPiere was able to obtain responses from 81 restaurants and cafes, and 47 hotels, auto camps, and tourist homes. Of the 128 respondents, 118 indicated that they would *not* accept Chinese guests (nine said that it would depend upon the circumstances, and one woman from an auto camp replied affirmatively, stating that she had hosted a Chinese gentleman and his wife during the previous summer—LaPiere's friends!). LaPiere also obtained identical results from a sample of 128 establishments that were located in similar regions of the country but had not been visited by the Chinese couple: 118 negative responses, 9 conditional responses, and 1 affirmative response (see LaPiere, 1934, for further details). These findings suggest that people can hold abstract opinions which have little or nothing to do with their actual behavior.

Three years after LaPiere published his study, Stephen Corey (1937) published an experiment that arrived at similar conclusions. Corey was interested in the relation between attitudes toward cheating and behavioral measures of cheating. He measured attitudes toward cheating by asking 67 college students to fill out several attitude scales concerning their opinions about cheating. These scales appeared to be anonymous, but in fact, Corey used a secret system of markings to identify individual respondents. In this way, he was able to elicit candid opinions that could later be related to actual measures of cheating.

The way Corey measured cheating was to administer five weekly true-false examinations to the students, secretly score each exam, return the unmarked exams to the students, and ask students to score their exams and report the grades. The total discrepancy between the scores students reported and their actual scores constituted the measure of cheating (the average cheating amounted to roughly two questions per 40- to 45-item exam).

What Corey found is that the correlation between attitudes and behavior was almost exactly zero. The attitudes students had about cheating apparently bore no significant relation to their own tendency to cheat. What *did* correlate significantly with cheating was test performance; the number of exam points that students missed correlated .46 with cheating. According to Corey (1937, p. 278): "Whether or not a student cheated depended in much greater part upon how well he had prepared for the examination than upon any opinions he had stated about honesty in examinations."

A PARABLE FOR OUR TIMES

In 1973, John Darley and Daniel Batson published a contender for the all-time most vivid demonstration of attitude-behavior inconsistency. Darley and Batson were interested in the factors that determine whether people will help someone in trouble. Their subjects were seminary students en route from one building to another to give either a speech about jobs at which seminary students would be effective, or a speech on the parable of the Good Samaritan (a biblical injunction to help those in need). An experimental assistant told the students that these speeches should be three to five minutes in length and would be recorded by another assistant. Then, as students made their way to the appropriate building, they were confronted with someone who appeared to need help. Darley and Batson wanted to see if helping was related to (a) whether the student was about to give a speech on the virtue of giving help and (b) how much of a hurry the student was in to get where he was going.

In the *high-hurry* condition of the experiment, the experimental assistant looked at his watch and suddenly said to the student: "Oh, you're late. They were expecting you a few minutes ago. We'd better get moving. The assistant should be waiting for you so you'd better hurry. It shouldn't take but just a minute." In the *intermediate-hurry* condition, the experimental assistant said: "The assistant is ready for you, so please go right over." And in the *low-hurry* condition, the experimental assistant announced: "It'll be a few minutes before they're ready for you, but you might as well head on over. If you have to wait over there, it shouldn't be long."

In order to get from one building to the other, each student had to pass through an alley, and in that alley Darley and Batson had placed a shabbily dressed man who sat slumped in a doorway, head down, eyes closed, motionless. As the seminary student went by, the man coughed twice and groaned without lifting his head. If the student stopped to ask if something was wrong, or if the student offered to help, the man acted startled and said somewhat groggily:

> Oh, thank you [cough]. . . . No, it's all right. [Pause] I've got this respiratory condition [cough]. . . . The doctor's given me these pills to take, and I just took one. . . . If I just sit and rest for a few minutes I'll be O.K. . . . Thanks very much for stopping though.

If the student insisted on taking the man into the building, the man accepted whatever help was offered and thanked the student for taking the trouble to be of assistance. Then, once the student left, the man rated the student on the following five-point scale:

0 = Failed to notice the man as possibly in need at all
1 = Perceived the man as possibly in need but did not offer aid
2 = Did not stop but helped indirectly (e.g., by telling someone about the man)
3 = Stopped and asked if the man needed help
4 = After stopping, insisted on taking the man inside the building

Darley and Batson (1973) found that students in a hurry were much less likely to offer help than were students not in a hurry, but that giving a speech on the parable of the Good Samaritan did not significantly influence whether students offered help. In fact, in several cases a seminary student en route to give a talk on the parable of the Good Samaritan literally stepped over the man in the alley so as not to be late! These results dramatically illustrate that abstract opinions—in this case, about the importance of helping people in need—can be at extreme variance with actual behavior.

INCONSISTENCY REVISITED

Are attitudes and behaviors usually this discrepant? In 1969, a psychologist named Allan Wicker published a research review that suggested the answer is yes, and in doing so, he dealt a major blow to attitude research. As the basis for his review, Wicker located 46 studies in which attitudes and corresponding behaviors were measured on separate occasions. The participants in these studies ranged from college students to insurance agents to industrial employees to maternity ward patients, and they numbered in the thousands. Likewise, the attitude topics ranged from public housing to football to civil rights activities and beyond.

After reviewing all 46 studies, Wicker (1969, p. 65) concluded that "it is considerably more likely that attitudes will be unrelated or only slightly related to overt behaviors than that attitudes will be closely related to actions." According to his findings, the correlation between attitudes and behavior often approached zero, and only in rare cases did it exceed .30. Indeed, two years after his initial review, Wicker (1971) went even further and suggested that it might be desirable to abandon the very idea of attitudes.

As you can imagine, these conclusions did not sit well with attitude researchers, and before long, a "revisionist" school was born. Adherents to the revisionist school argued that attitudes *are* consistent with behavior, provided certain conditions are met. These conditions include the following: (1) All measures of attitudes and behaviors must be carefully chosen to be as valid and reliable as possible; (2) whenever feasible, multiple items should be used to assess attitudes and behaviors; (3) to avoid intervening variables, attitudes and behaviors should be measured closely together in time; and (4) attitudes should match behaviors in terms of the action performed, the target of the action, the context in which the action occurs, and the time at which the action takes place.

In a 1977 literature review, Icek Ajzen and Martin Fishbein demonstrated the importance of several of these conditions. Ajzen and Fishbein classified attitude-behavior relations reported in more than 100 studies according to whether the attitudes and behaviors had high, partial, or low correspondence in terms of the target and action specified. In almost every instance in which the attitudes and behaviors were low in correspondence, Ajzen and Fishbein found no significant correlation between the two. On the other hand, attitudes and behaviors were always correlated at least .40 when they were measured appropriately and corresponded well in their targets and actions. In other words, if an attitude concerned a particular action directed at a particular target, then the attitude predicted that behavior fairly well. If the target of an attitude did not match the target of a behavior, however, attitude-behavior consistency was unlikely. Ajzen and Fishbein argued that LaPiere (1934) had observed low attitude-behavior consistency because the target of attitudes in his study (i.e., Chinese people *in general*) was far more general than the target of behaviors (i.e., a *particular* Chinese couple).

CONCLUSION

There is a wonderful Russian proverb that characterizes many of the findings discussed in this chapter. The proverb, as paraphrased by famous Russian émigré Alexander Rivilis, runs roughly like this: "Going through life is not so simple as crossing a field." When applied to judgment and decision research, the proverb might be rephrased: "Measuring an attitude, opinion, or preference is not so simple as asking a question."

Attitudes, opinions, and choices are often surprisingly plastic. In many cases, the wording of a question significantly influences the answers people give. Consequently, it is worth paying close attention to the structure and context of questions. Chapter 6 illustrates this point with a discussion of several ways in which subtle changes in wording can affect judgment and decision making.

THE EFFECTS OF QUESTION WORDING AND FRAMING

When asked whether their country's nuclear weapons made them feel "safe," 40 percent of the respondents in a 1986 British Gallup poll said yes, and 50 percent said no (the remaining 10 percent had no definite opinion). But when another pollster used the word "safer" rather than "safe," these percentages reversed: 50 percent of the respondents said that nuclear weapons made them feel safer, and 36 percent said that nuclear weapons made them feel less safe (Lelyveld, 1986, October 5).

These results illustrate the importance of subtle changes in wording. Sometimes changes of only a word or two—either in the response alternatives or the question itself—can profoundly affect how people answer a question (Borrelli, Lockerbie, & Niemi, 1987). Consider, for example, the mysterious case of the Missing Middle Category. . . .

A TRICKY ASSIGNMENT

The year is 1969. You, a Machiavellian pollster par excellence, *have infiltrated the Gallup polling organization. Secretly, your mission is to conduct a survey showing that the American public wants a speedy troop withdrawal from the Vietnam War. How will you attain your objective?*

In June of that year, Gallup told respondents that President Richard Nixon had "ordered the withdrawal of 25,000 troops from Vietnam in the next three months." Respondents were then asked whether "troops should be withdrawn at a faster or a slower rate" ("same as now" was not explicitly included in the response alternatives, but if respondents spontaneously declared that the present rate was about right, interviewers accepted this answer). Nearly half of the respondents (42 percent) said "faster," 16 percent said "slower," and 29 percent volunteered "same as now" (Converse & Schuman, 1970, June).

You release these results to the press, and the next day newspapers across the country run the headline: AMERICANS FAVOR SPEEDIER TROOP WITHDRAWAL. *Sitting back in your chair, you toast the successful completion of your mission. Or so you think.*

Soon after the Gallup poll, Harris conducted a similar survey using the following question: "In general, do you feel the pace at which the President is withdrawing troops is too fast, too slow, or about right?" In response to this question, approximately half of the respondents (49 percent) felt that the troop withdrawal was proceeding at about the right rate. Only 29 percent said they preferred a speedier withdrawal, and 6 percent said the withdrawal was too fast (Converse & Schuman, 1970, June).

Picking up a newspaper, you now read the following headline: AMERICANS FAVOR STATUS QUO; EARLIER POLL IN ERROR.

"Earlier poll in ERROR?" you say to yourself. Surely the poll conducted by Gallup is not in error. But if not, then which poll is correct?

Instead of asking which poll is correct—cases can be made for both—a more useful question is to ask what the results from each one mean. Gallup used a "forced choice" question that did not include an explicit middle category. As a consequence, people with very slight leanings came out for either faster or slower troop withdrawals. Questions without middle categories are often useful for assessing general inclinations, but to be entirely accurate, the Gallup headline should have read: WHEN FORCED TO CHOOSE BETWEEN FASTER AND SLOWER TROOP WITHDRAWALS, AMERICANS FAVOR A SPEEDIER WITHDRAWAL. Results from the Gallup poll do *not* indicate the percentage of Americans who were actually dissatisfied with the rate of troop withdrawals.

In contrast, the Harris survey explicitly offered respondents a middle category. The effect of adding a middle category is much the same as adding a "no opinion/don't know" filter; usually, 10 to 40 percent of the respondents shift their answers to this category, but the marginal proportions stay roughly the same (in this case, the proportion saying "too fast" or "too slow"). The *disadvantage* of including a middle category is that it is a "safe" answer, and in some instances, may therefore act as a magnet for pseudo-opinions.

OPEN PRIORITIES

Just as the inclusion of a middle category encourages people to choose that category, the inclusion of other response alternatives often increases the number of respondents who choose those alternatives. This pattern was clearly documented in a study published by Howard Schuman and Jacqueline Scott (1987).

Schuman and Scott asked respondents in a national survey to name "the most important problem facing this country today." As the first column of Table 6.1 shows, when respondents were asked this question in an "open" format (in which they answered in their own words), only 2 percent spontaneously named the energy shortage, the quality of public

TABLE 6.1

A QUESTION OF PRIORITIES

| | PERCENTAGE CHOOSING EACH ANSWER | |
Problems	Open Question	Closed Question
Quality of public schools	1	32
Pollution	1	14
Legalized abortion	0	8
Energy shortage	0	6
All other responses	98	40

Note: These data come from a survey by Howard Schuman and Jacqueline Scott (1987) in which 178 respondents were asked the open question "What do you think is the most important problem facing this country today?" and 171 respondents were asked the closed question "Which of the following do you think is the most important problem facing this country today—the energy shortage, the quality of public schools, legalized abortion, or pollution—or, if you prefer, you may name a different problem as most important."

schools, legalized abortion, or pollution (see Item #27 of the Reader Survey for your own answer). When Schuman and Scott included these infrequent answers in a "closed" version of the question, however, the story was very different (in a closed format, respondents select an answer from a list of offered alternatives). As you can see from the second column in Table 6.1, the majority of respondents chose an uncommon answer as the most important problem facing the country. Simply by mentioning these uncommon response alternatives, Schuman and Scott generated a thirtyfold increase in their popularity.

Although closed questions can distort the results of a survey when uncommon response alternatives would not otherwise come to mind, there are also cases in which open questions can yield misleading answers. For example, when people are asked to name the most important world event that has taken place in recent history, less than 2 percent spontaneously mention the invention of the computer. When the invention of the computer is explicitly included as a response alternative, however, approximately 30 percent of the respondents select this answer (Schuman & Scott, 1987). In this case, the closed question may come closer to measuring actual opinion than the open question.

Even answers to the most mundane questions can be affected by the number and type of response alternatives. For instance, one study found that reported television usage varied as a function of the response categories that were provided in the question (Schwarz, Hippler, Deutsch, & Strack, 1985). In this experiment, respondents used one of two scales to indicate how much television they watched per day. Both scales were divided into six half-hour increments, but the first scale began with "up to a half hour" and ended with "more than two and a half hours," whereas the second scale began with "up to two and a half hours" and

TABLE 6.2

WHERE LIES THE TRUTH?

Question	Mean Answer
Do you get headaches frequently, and if so, how often?	2.2/week
Do you get headaches occasionally, and if so, how often?	0.7/week
In terms of the total number of [headache] products, how many other products have you tried? 1? 5? 10?	5.2 products
In terms of the total number of [headache] products, how many other products have you tried? 1? 2? 3?	3.3 products
How long was the movie?	130 minutes
How short was the movie?	100 minutes
How tall was the basketball player?	79 inches
How short was the basketball player?	69 inches

Note: The top pair of questions are taken from a study by Elizabeth Loftus (1975), and the bottom pair of questions are taken from a study by Richard Harris (1973). All differences are statistically significant.

ended with "more than four and a half hours." Of the respondents who were given the first scale, 84 percent reported watching television two and a half hours or less per day. In contrast, of the respondents who used the second scale, only 63 percent gave this answer.

According to Norbert Schwarz and his colleagues (1985, pp. 388–389): "Response scales are not simply 'measurement devices' that respondents use to report their behaviors. Rather . . . respondents may use the range of behaviors described in the response alternatives as a frame of reference in estimating and evaluating their own behavior." Structured response alternatives—like questions—are never perfectly neutral, and they often convey an implicit range of acceptable answers (see Table 6.2 for some other questions that implicitly suggest appropriate responses). As the next section shows, response biases may also arise because certain answers are more socially desirable than others.

SOCIAL DESIRABILITY

In 1982, Richard Wirthlin, who used to be in charge of opinion polling for President Reagan, found that 58 percent of the respondents in a national survey agreed with this statement: "A freeze in nuclear weapons should be opposed because it would do nothing to reduce the danger of the thousands of nuclear warheads already in place and would leave the Soviet Union in a position of nuclear superiority." But then, several minutes later in the very same polling interview, 56 percent agreed with the statement: "A freeze in nuclear weapons should be favored because it would begin a much-needed process to stop everyone in the world from building nuclear weapons now and reduce the possibility of nuclear war in the future." In fact, 27 percent of the respondents actually endorsed *both* statements, in what Wirthlin called "the most singular inconsistency on any question we've ever asked" (Clymer, 1982, May 6).

Why the inconsistency? In the absence of a firm opinion concerning a nuclear freeze, respondents may have tried to give the most "socially desirable" answer. The first question equated support for a nuclear freeze with Russian nuclear superiority, and the second question associated it with world peace. Very few Americans are in favor of Russian nuclear superiority or opposed to world peace.

When people do not have deep convictions about an issue, they often respond to "catch phrases" that point them in a socially desirable direction. For example, *U.S. News & World Report* published the results of a poll in which 58 percent of the respondents favored aid to Nicaraguan rebels "to prevent Communist influence from spreading," but only 24 percent favored assistance to "the people trying to overthrow the government of Nicaragua" (Budiansky, 1988, July 11). To most Americans, "preventing Communism" is a commendable goal and "overthrowing governments" is not.

Schuman and Presser (1981) found similar results from a pair of opinion polls conducted in 1978. In the first poll, respondents were asked: "If a situation like Vietnam were to develop in another part of the world, do you think the United States **should** or **should not** send troops?" In response to this question, only 17 percent of those surveyed felt that the United States should send troops. When the threat of Communism was explicitly mentioned, however, support for sending troops doubled; 37 percent of the respondents supported sending troops when asked: "If a situation like Vietnam were to develop in another part of the world, do you think the United States **should** or **should not** send troops to stop a Communist takeover?"

Back in 1940, Hadley Cantril found essentially the same pattern of results in two polls on the U.S. involvement in World War II. Only 13 percent of Cantril's respondents agreed that "the U.S. should do more than it is now doing to help England and France," but this figure climbed to 22 percent when a second set of respondents were asked: "Do you think the U.S. should do more than it is now doing to help England and France in their fight against Hitler?" At the time, helping in the "fight against Hitler" was seen as more socially desirable than simply helping England and France.

TO ALLOW OR FORBID?

In another early pair of experimental polls, Rugg (1941) asked respondents one of two questions:

Do you think that the United States should allow public speeches against democracy?
Do you think that the United States should forbid public speeches against democracy?

Even though these questions seem as though they are asking the same thing, Rugg found that they led to very different responses. When people were asked whether the United States should *allow* public speeches against democracy, 62 percent said no. On the other hand, when people were asked whether the United States should *forbid* speeches against democracy, only 46 percent of all respondents said yes (the logical equivalent of *not allowing* such speeches). Of those respondents who expressed an opinion, about 20 percent more said they would "not allow" antidemocratic speeches than would "forbid" them!

Schuman and Presser (1981) repeated Rugg's experiment three times in the 1970s, and on each occasion they found results similar to those observed by Rugg (1941). Thus, in a total of four survey administrations spanning more than 30 years, the "forbid" version of the question led to substantially more support for free speech than did the "allow" version (presumably because of the loss in freedom associated with "forbidding" something). The only significant difference between Schuman and Presser's results and Rugg's results was that Americans in the 1970s were relatively more tolerant of free speech. In both forms of the question, roughly 30 percent more people supported free speech in the 1970s than in the 1940s.

The allow-forbid distinction has also been observed with respect to a number of other topics. For example, Hans-J. Hippler and Norbert Schwarz (1986) found differences between "not allowing" and "forbidding" peep shows, X-rated films, and the use of salt to melt snow on the highways. Other polls have found that only 29 percent of those surveyed were in favor of a constitutional amendment "prohibiting abortions," but 50 percent were in favor of a constitutional amendment "protecting the life of the unborn" (Budiansky, 1988, July 11).

FRAMING

As the foregoing results suggest, people respond differently to losses (e.g., prohibitions) than to gains (e.g., allowances). The importance of this difference was not widely appreciated, however, until psychologists Amos Tversky and Daniel Kahneman popularized the notion of "framing." According to Tversky and Kahneman (1981, p. 453), a decision frame is "the decision maker's conception of the acts, outcomes, and contingencies associated with a particular choice." Tversky and Kahneman (1981) proposed that decision frames are partly controlled by the formulation of the problem, and partly controlled by the norms, habits, and characteristics of the decision maker. What Tversky and Kahneman focused on in their research, though, was the effect of formulating problems in different ways.

To see how powerful these effects can be, consider the following pair of monetary bets (taken from an experiment by Tversky and Kahneman). In Decision 1, you must choose between Alternative A and Alternative B:

Alternative A: A sure gain of $240
Alternative B: A 25 percent chance to gain $1000, and a 75 percent chance to gain nothing

What would you choose? (See Item #25 of the Reader Survey for your answer.) After noting your preference, consider Decision 2:

Alternative C: A sure loss of $750
Alternative D: A 75 percent chance to lose $1000, and a 25 percent chance to lose nothing

What would you choose this time? (See Item #26 of the Reader Survey.)

Tversky and Kahneman (1981) found that Alternative A was preferred in Decision 1. Eighty-four percent of their subjects chose Alternative A over Alternative B. As mentioned in Chapter 5, people tend to be risk averse when gains are at stake (they prefer "a bird in the hand" to "two in the bush").

In Decision 2, however, people usually prefer to gamble. Eighty-seven percent of Tversky and Kahneman's subjects chose Alternative D. When losses are at stake, people tend to be risk seeking. Indeed, this pattern of risk seeking and risk aversion was so common that 73 percent of Tversky and Kahneman's respondents chose Alternatives A and D, and only 3 percent chose Alternatives B and C.

The interesting thing about this problem is that choosing B and C turns out to be better than choosing A and D. You can see this by simply adding the chosen alternatives together (see Figure 6.1). By choosing A and D, a sure gain of $240 is added to a 75 percent chance of losing $1000 and a 25 percent chance of losing nothing. This becomes a 75 percent chance of losing $760 and a 25 percent chance of gaining $240. By choosing B and C, a sure loss of $750 is subtracted from a 25 percent chance of gaining $1000 and a 75 percent chance of gaining nothing.

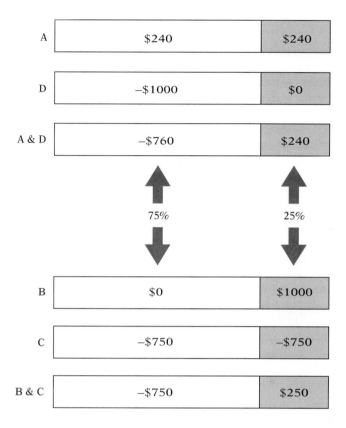

FIGURE 6.1
Even though Alternatives B and C yield a better outcome than A and D, Amos Tversky and Daniel Kahneman (1981) found that people choose A and D far more often than B and C.

This leaves a 25 percent chance of gaining $250 and a 75 percent chance of losing $750.

In other words, the combined choices are:

> **A and D:** A 75 percent chance of losing $760 and a 25 percent chance of gaining $240
>
> **B and C:** A 75 percent chance of losing $750 and a 25 percent chance of gaining $250

If you choose A and D, you stand to lose more or gain less than if you choose B and C. Regardless of whether you lose or gain, choosing B and C is better than choosing A and D.

A BITTER PILL TO SWALLOW

The effects of framing are particularly important in medical decision making. The earliest and most famous example of a framing problem related to medicine is Tversky and Kahneman's (1981) "Asian disease" question:

> Imagine that the U.S. is preparing for the outbreak of an unusual Asian disease, which is expected to kill 600 people. Two alternative programs to combat the disease have been proposed. Assume that the exact scientific estimate of the consequences of the programs are as follows:
>
> - If Program A is adopted, 200 people will be saved.
> - If Program B is adopted, there is 1/3 probability that 600 people will be saved, and 2/3 probability that no people will be saved.

Which of the two programs would you favor?

Tversky and Kahneman found that 72 percent of the people given this frame were risk averse; they preferred to save 200 lives for sure rather than gamble on saving a larger number of lives.

By changing the frame, however, Tversky and Kahneman were able to elicit a very different pattern of preferences. They gave a second set of respondents the same problem, except that the consequences were now described as follows:

> - If Program C is adopted 400 people will die.
> - If Program D is adopted there is 1/3 probability that nobody will die, and 2/3 probability that 600 people will die.

Even though Programs C and D in this frame are numerically equivalent to Programs A and B in the former frame, 78 percent of the respondents now became risk seeking; they preferred to gamble rather than accept a sure loss of 400 lives.

Similar results have been found in other studies of medical decision making (cf. Wilson, Kaplan, & Schneiderman, 1987). For example, an experiment published in the *New England Journal of Medicine* found that framing influenced physicians' decisions about how to treat lung cancer (McNeil, Pauker, Sox, & Tversky, 1982). The participants in this study were 424 radiologists, 491 graduate students who had completed coursework in statistics and decision theory, and 238 ambulatory patients with different chronic problems. All 1153 participants were presented with summary information on two forms of treatment for lung cancer (surgery and radiation therapy). Once they finished reading this summary information, they were asked which of the two treatments they would prefer.

In approximately half the cases, the summary information was framed in terms of the cumulative probability of survival after a particular amount of time (e.g., a 68 percent chance of living for more than one year). In the other cases, the summary information was cast in terms of mortality (e.g., a 32 percent chance of dying by the end of one year). Because the danger of dying during or immediately after surgery is the major disadvantage of treating lung cancer surgically, the experimenters hypothesized that surgery would be selected more frequently when the summary information was framed in terms of the probability of *living* than when it was framed in terms of the probability of *dying*.

And in fact, this is exactly what they found. Surgery was preferred to radiation therapy 75 percent of the time in the survival frame, but only 58 percent of the time in the mortality frame. This pattern was found among physicians and graduate students as well as patients. Thus, even in the case of life-and-death decisions made by highly trained special-ists, framing can significantly influence the choices that are made.

DEDUCTIVE LOGIC

In a thought-provoking essay on "economic reasoning," Harvard economist Thomas Schelling (1981) presented an interesting case in which "reframing" a choice can lead to surprising conclusions. Schelling began his discussion by noting that the U.S. income tax laws at that time allowed families to deduct $1000 for each child (i.e., to sub-tract $1000 per child in the process of converting gross income to tax-able income). The amount of this deduction was fixed; it did not depend on the total income a family earned.

Schelling raised the question, though, whether it might not be better to allow wealthy families to take larger tax deductions for each child. After all, wealthy families spend more on their children than do poor families, and the amount of money it costs for wealthy families to have children is much higher than the amount it costs poor families.

Most people would object to such a policy. "There is no reason," goes the argument, "to extend further privileges to the rich—and certainly not at public expense."

But consider (says Schelling) what would happen if the tax laws were reformulated. Suppose that instead of *deducting* the cost of children from a tax schedule based on childless families, a "childless premium" were *added* to a tax schedule that assumed the typical family had two or three children. In other words, suppose a childless family were charged "extra" taxes (instead of giving families with children a tax break). Should a poor family without children pay just as high a premium as a wealthy family without children?

In this case, it is tempting to argue that rich families should pay more than poor families. Because rich families spend more on their children than do poor families, it stands to reason that a rich family without chil-dren can afford to pay higher premiums than a poor family without children. The problem is, however, that this argument directly contra-dicts the earlier argument against allowing wealthy people to take larger deductions for their children. In the words of Schelling (1981, p. 55): "Since the same income tax can be formulated either as a base schedule for the childless couple with an adjustment for children, or as a base schedule for the family with children plus an adjustment for childlessness, it should not make any difference which way we do it."

But of course it *does* make a difference, and as long as there are deductions for children, people will argue—with good reason—that these deductions should be fixed in size.

PSYCHOLOGICAL ACCOUNTING

Not only do decision makers frame *choices*—they frame the *outcomes* of their choices. Tversky and Kahneman (1981) dubbed this process "psychological accounting." Psychological accounting has to do with whether an outcome is framed in terms of the direct consequences of an act (what Tversky and Kahneman called a "minimal account"), or whether an outcome is evaluated with respect to a previous balance (a more "inclusive" account).

The following pair of problems (taken from an experiment by Tversky & Kahneman, 1981) illustrates psychological accounting:

> **Problem 1.** Imagine that you have decided to see a play where admission is $10 per ticket. As you enter the theater you discover that you have lost a $10 bill. Would you still pay $10 for a ticket for the play?

Of the 183 people who Tversky and Kahneman asked, 88 percent said they would still buy a ticket to see the play. Most respondents did not link the loss of $10 with the purchase of a ticket; instead, they charged the loss to a separate account.

Now consider the second problem:

> **Problem 2.** Imagine that you have decided to see a play and paid the admission price of $10 per ticket. As you enter the theater you discover that you have lost the ticket. The seat was not marked and the ticket cannot be recovered. Would you pay $10 for another ticket?

Of the 200 people who Tversky and Kahneman asked, only 46 percent said they would purchase another ticket. Even though the loss of a ticket is financially equivalent to the loss of $10, most respondents apparently added the cost of a second ticket to the cost of the original ticket—and viewed $20 as excessive.

Here is another example of psychological accounting from Tversky and Kahneman:

> Imagine that you are about to purchase a jacket for $125, and a calculator for $15. The calculator salesman informs you that the calculator you wish to buy is on sale for $10 at the other branch of the store, located 20 minutes drive away. Would you make the trip to the other store?

In response to this question, 68 percent of Tversky and Kahneman's subjects said they would be willing to make the 20-minute drive to save $5.

But what if the calculator cost $125 and the jacket cost $15? Tversky and Kahneman presented this problem to 88 people:

> Imagine that you are about to purchase a jacket for $15, and a calculator for $125. The calculator salesman informs you that the calculator you wish to buy is on sale for $120 at the other branch of the store, located 20 minutes' drive away. Would you make the trip to the other store?

Now only 29 percent of Tversky and Kahneman's subjects said they would make the drive. When the calculator was valued at $125, more than two-thirds of the respondents said they would not drive 20 minutes to save $5, even though this price reduction is no different than the savings mentioned in the earlier problem.

Why? According to Tversky and Kahneman (1981), respondents frame the first problem in terms of a minimal account in which the 20-minute drive is weighed directly against $5 in savings. In the second problem, though, respondents include the entire purchase price in the account, and as a consequence, $5 seems rather negligible. More formally, George Quattrone and Amos Tversky (1988) have proposed that people make choices according to a "ratio-difference principle" in which the impact of any fixed positive difference between two amounts increases with their ratio. Thus, the difference between a price of $20 and $15 yields a ratio of 1.33, which is larger and more influential than the rather negligible ratio of 1.04 between $125 and $120. Richard Thaler (1985) has found similar framing effects in his research on the role of psychological accounting in consumer choices.

These findings, and the findings mentioned earlier in this chapter, do not mean that a clever salesperson or pollster can elicit *any* response from the public. Rather, they indicate only that question wording and framing often make a substantial difference, and that it pays to be aware of their effects. Although these observations may seem self-evident, they have been—as the next three chapters show—a long time in coming.

CONCLUSION

When people learn the results of a public opinion poll, they rarely think about whether the questions were filtered, whether a middle category was included among the response alternatives, whether the problem was framed in terms of gains or losses, and so forth. The natural tendency most people have is to assume that the survey respondents simply answered in keeping with their beliefs. A great deal of research suggests, however, that framing and question wording can significantly affect how people respond.

Before relying on results from survey research and other studies of judgment and decision making, it is important to consider how people's answers would have changed as a function of factors such as:

- ✔ The order in which the questions were presented
- ✔ The context in which the questions appeared
- ✔ Whether the question format was open or closed
- ✔ Whether the questions were filtered
- ✔ Whether the questions contained catch phrases
- ✔ The range of suggested response alternatives
- ✔ The order in which response alternatives were presented
- ✔ Whether middle categories were provided
- ✔ Whether problems were framed in terms of gains or losses

If you suspect that changes in these factors would have led to changes in how people answered, you should qualify your interpretation of the results until variations in wording can be tested. As Paul Slovic, Dale Griffin, and Amos Tversky (1990, p. 25) have argued: "If [the results from multiple procedures] are consistent, we may have some basis for trusting the judgment; if they are not, further analysis is required." Because judgments are so easily influenced by question wording and framing, the safest course of action is to elicit them in a variety of ways and compare the results.

SECTION III

MODELS OF DECISION MAKING

Despite the context-dependent nature of judgment and decision making, early models of decision making assumed that people had a fixed set of attitudes and preferences that did not change as a function of how they were elicited. Decision makers were treated as "rational actors" who sought to maximize their utility, or self-benefit, and who obeyed various principles of rational behavior. The chapters in this section review these models, their shortcomings, and alternative theories of decision making.

CHAPTER 7

EXPECTED UTILITY THEORY

In 1713, a Swiss professor named Nicolas Bernoulli posed an intriguing question. In rough translation, Bernoulli was interested in how much money people would pay to play a game with the following two rules: (1) An unbiased coin is tossed until it lands on Tails, and (2) the player is paid $2.00 if Tails comes up on the opening toss, $4.00 if Tails first appears on the second toss, $8.00 if Tails appears on the third toss, $16.00 if Tails appears on the fourth toss, and so forth. How much would you pay to play this game? (The Reader Survey included a version of this question as Item #30, so you might check to see how you answered.) Most people are willing to pay no more than a few dollars to play the game. → Paradox: should be infinite (ev).

Since Bernoulli first posed this problem, it has been dubbed the "St. Petersburg Paradox." It is a paradox because the expected value of the game (the average payoff you would expect if the game were played an endless number of times) is infinite, yet very few people are willing to pay huge sums of money to play. To verify that the average payoff is infinite, we can calculate the expected value of Bernoulli's game by multiplying the payoff for each possible outcome against the chances of that outcome occurring.[*] The chances of Tails on the first toss (which would result in a payoff of $2.00) are 1/2, the chances of one Heads followed by Tails (a payoff of $4.00) are 1/4, the chances of two Heads followed by Tails (a payoff of $8.00) are 1/8, and in general, the expected value (EV) (where K = number of tosses) is:

$$\text{EV(game)} = (\tfrac{1}{2})(\$2.00) + (\tfrac{1}{4})(\$4.00) + (\tfrac{1}{8})(\$8.00) + \cdots + (\tfrac{1}{2})^{K}(\$2.00)^{K}$$
$$= \quad \$1.00 \quad + \quad \$1.00 \quad + \quad \$1.00 \quad + \cdots + \quad \$1.00$$
$$= \textbf{an infinite amount of money}$$

---

[*]This section of the book is more mathematical and more theoretical than other sections. Consequently, some readers may find this material more challenging than the topics covered in previous chapters. If you are unfamiliar with notions such as "expected value," don't give up the ship—most of the main points should be understandable without any training in mathematics, and very little mathematics is used in later chapters.

The question is, then, why people are unwilling to pay more than a few dollars to play a game with an infinite expected return.

Twenty-five years after Nicolas Bernoulli posed the problem, his younger cousin, mathematician Daniel Bernoulli, arrived at a solution that contained the first seeds of contemporary decision theory. Daniel Bernoulli (1738/1954) reasoned that the value, or "utility," of money declines with the amount won (or already possessed). For example, according to the younger Bernoulli (1738/1954, p. 24): "A gain of one thousand ducats is more significant to a pauper than to a rich man though both gain the same amount." Specifically, Bernoulli argued that the value of money could be represented as follows:

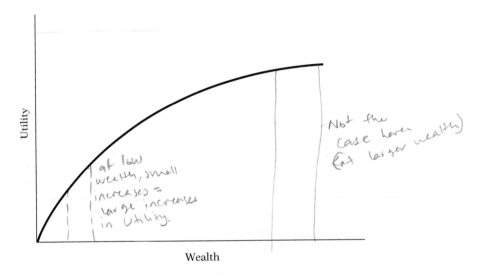

By assuming that the value of additional money declined with wealth, Bernoulli was able to show that the expected utility of the St. Petersburg game was not infinite after all.

EXPECTED UTILITY THEORY

Although scholars have debated whether Daniel Bernoulli actually solved the St. Petersburg Paradox (e.g., Lopes, 1981; Weirich, 1984), his observation of declining marginal utility set the stage for later theories of choice behavior. The most famous example of such a theory, now referred to as "expected utility theory," was published by John von Neumann and Oskar Morgenstern (1947). Von Neumann and Morgenstern proposed expected utility theory as a "normative" theory of behavior. That is, classical utility theory was not intended to describe how people *actually* behave, but how people *would* behave if they followed certain requirements of rational decision making.

One of the main purposes of such a theory was to provide an explicit set of assumptions, or axioms, that underlie rational decision making. Once von Neumann and Morgenstern specified these axioms, decision researchers were able to compare the mathematical predictions of expected utility theory with the behavior of real decision makers. When researchers documented violations of an axiom, they often revised the theory and made new predictions. In this way, research on decision making cycled back and forth between theory and observation.

What are the axioms of rational decision making? Most formulations of expected utility theory are based at least in part on some subset of the following six principles:

[handwritten: → Comparability ⌐ AXIOMS — Assumptions which underlie rational decision making]

- **Ordering of alternatives.** First of all, rational decision makers should be able to compare any two alternatives. They should either prefer one alternative to the other, or they should be indifferent to them. *[handwritten: ⟨what about refusing to choose?⟩]*

- **Dominance.** Rational actors should never adopt strategies that are "dominated" by other strategies (for our purposes, adopting a strategy is equivalent to making a decision). A strategy is *weakly dominant* if, when you compare it to another strategy, it yields a better outcome in at least one respect and is as good or better than the other strategy in all other respects (where "better" means that it leads to an outcome with greater utility). A strategy is *strongly dominant* if, when you compare it to another strategy, it yields an outcome that is superior in every respect. For example, Car A strongly dominates Car B if it is superior in mileage, cost, and looks, and it is weakly dominant if it gets better mileage than Car B but is equivalent in cost and looks. According to expected utility theory, perfectly rational decision makers should never choose a dominated strategy, even if the strategy is only weakly dominated.

- **Cancellation.** If two risky alternatives include identical and equally probable outcomes among their possible consequences, then the utility of these outcomes should be ignored in choosing between the two options. In other words, a choice between two alternatives should depend only on those outcomes that differ, not on outcomes that are the same for both alternatives. Common factors should cancel out. *[handwritten: A ≥ B if and only if (ApO) ≥ (BpC)]*

[handwritten in left margin: Independence]

- **Transitivity.** If a rational decision maker prefers Outcome A to Outcome B, and Outcome B to Outcome C, then that person should prefer Outcome A to Outcome C. *[handwritten: If A ≥ B ≥ C ∴ A ≥ C]*

- **Continuity.** For any set of outcomes, a decision maker should always prefer a gamble between the best and worst outcome to a sure intermediate outcome if the odds of the best outcome are good enough. This means, for example, that a rational decision maker should prefer a gamble between $100 and complete finan-

(If $A \geqslant B$ & at least some chance of A over B then take chance of A than sure avoidance of $\cancel{B} A$ & get B ?! ?!)

cial ruin to a sure gain of $10, provided the odds of financial ruin are one in 1,000,000,000,000,000,000,000,000,000,000,000. . . .

- *Invariance.* The Invariance Principle stipulates that a decision maker should not be affected by the way alternatives are presented. For example, a rational decision maker should have no preference between a compound gamble (e.g., a two-stage lottery with a 50 percent chance of success on each stage and a $100 payoff if both stages yield successful outcomes) and the simple gamble to which it can be reduced (i.e., a one-stage lottery with a 25 percent chance of winning $100).

Von Neumann and Morgenstern (1947) proved mathematically that when decision makers violate principles such as these, expected utility is not maximized. To take an example, suppose that in violation of the Transitivity Principle, you have intransitive preferences for Outcomes A, B, and C. You prefer Outcome A to Outcome B, Outcome B to Outcome C, and Outcome C to Outcome A. This means that I should be able to give you Outcome C and offer—say, for a penny—to take back Outcome C and give you Outcome B. Because you prefer Outcome B to Outcome C, you would undoubtedly accept my offer and pay the penny.

Now you have Outcome B. In the same way, I should be able to offer—for another penny—to take back Outcome B and give you Outcome A (which you prefer to Outcome B). This would leave you with Outcome A. But now, because your preferences are intransitive, I can offer—say, for a third penny—to take back Outcome A and give you Outcome C (which you prefer to Outcome A). The result is that you are back where you started from, minus three pennies (or $3, or $3000, or whatever). In other words, I can continue to use this intransitivity in preferences as a "money pump" until your supply of money runs out. In later chapters, we will discuss cases in which the Transitivity Principle and other principles of rational behavior are violated.

EXTENSIONS

After von Neumann and Morgenstern (1947) proposed their theory of expected utility, dozens of other theorists developed extensions and variations. One of the most notable variations is "subjective expected utility theory," initially developed by Leonard Savage (1954). The main difference between Savage's theory and the theory of von Neumann and Morgenstern is that Savage allowed for subjective, or personal, probabilities of outcomes. Before 1954, the probabilities in expected utility theory had been treated as objective probabilities in the classical sense (i.e., based on relative frequency). Savage generalized the theory to include people's subjective probabilities that an outcome would occur.

This generalization is particularly important in cases when an objective probability cannot be determined in advance or when the outcome will only occur once. For example, within the framework of subjective expected utility theory, it makes sense to consider the probability of an unrepeatable event such as worldwide nuclear war, even though there is no way to determine the probability of nuclear war based on relative frequency. In contrast, it is hard to know what "the likelihood of nuclear war" actually means within the context of classical utility theory.

Other theorists have improved on classical utility theory in additional ways. For example, Duncan Luce (1959) and others have developed what they call "stochastic" models of choice—models that treat preferences as though they have a random component. Until stochastic models were developed, utility theorists had a difficult time explaining why it is rational to prefer soup one day and salad the next. The way Luce solved this problem is to treat preferences for soup and salad as probabilistic, rather than fixed choices that occur 100 percent of the time.

Further extensions or alternatives to expected utility theory have been offered by Peter Fishburn (1984), Udar Karmarkar (1978), John Payne (1973), and Clyde Coombs (1975), among many others. Thus, even though expected utility theory is often discussed as though it were one unified theory, there is no one accepted utility theory. Expected utility theory is actually a *family* of theories (although "expected utility theory" is often used as a shorthand reference to the theory developed by von Neumann and Morgenstern).

CONCLUSION

In a comprehensive review of expected utility theory and its variants, Paul Schoemaker (1982, p. 529) wrote that: "It is no exaggeration to consider expected utility theory the major paradigm in decision making since the Second World War." Certainly it has generated more research and discussion than any other theory of decision making. As Chapter 8 shows, however, there are several thorny problems and paradoxes that undermine the assumptions of classical expected utility theory. These problems have led many decision researchers to forsake expected utility theory in search of more useful alternatives.

CHAPTER **8**

PARADOXES IN RATIONALITY

As sensible as the principles of expected utility theory sound, there are many cases in which decision makers violate them. For example, the framing effects discussed in Chapter 6 show that the Invariance Principle is often violated (for further violations of invariance, as well as violations of dominance, see Tversky & Kahneman, 1986). In this chapter, we will focus mainly on violations of the Cancellation Principle and the Transitivity Principle.

THE ALLAIS PARADOX ↗ *Independance Axiom*

According to the Cancellation Principle, a choice between two alternatives should depend only on how those two alternatives differ—not on any factor that is the same for both alternatives. Any factor that is the same for both alternatives should not affect the choice a rational person makes. For instance, if you are choosing between two cars, and they both get the same mileage, then the mileage factor should not influence which car you choose.

On the face of it, this principle seems very plausible; if two cars get the same mileage, why should your choice between them be affected by whether the mileage is high or low? Rational decision makers should only decide between alternatives on the basis of how the alternatives differ. In 1953, however, a French economist named Maurice Allais published a paper that seriously challenged the Cancellation Principle. In this paper, Allais (1953) outlined what is now known as the Allais Paradox—a paradox that shows how the Cancellation Principle is sometimes violated. Let's take a look at how the paradox works.

Suppose I offer you a choice between two alternatives, A and B. If you choose A, you will receive $1,000,000 for sure. On the other hand, if you choose B, you stand a 10 percent chance of getting $2,500,000, an 89 percent chance of getting $1,000,000, and a 1 percent chance of getting nothing at all. In other words, your choice is the following:

> **Alternative A:** $1,000,000 for sure
> **Alternative B:** A 10 percent chance of getting $2,500,000, an 89 percent chance of getting $1,000,000, and a 1 percent chance of getting $0

What would you choose? (See Item #28a for your answer in the Reader Survey.) Most people choose the sure outcome in Alternative A even though Alternative B has an expected value greater than $1,000,000. You can verify that the expected value (EV) of Alternative B is actually $140,000 greater than the sure outcome in Alternative A by multiplying the probability of each possible outcome in Alternative B against the payoff if that outcome were to occur:

$$EV(B) = (.10)(\$2,500,000) + (.89)(\$1,000,000) + (.01)(\$0) = \$1,140,000$$

Still, most people are content to receive a guaranteed payment of $1,000,000.

Now suppose I offer you another choice. This time, Alternative A is an 11 percent chance of receiving $1,000,000 and an 89 percent chance of getting nothing, whereas Alternative B is a 10 percent chance of receiving $2,500,000 and a 90 percent chance of getting nothing. In other words, you have the following choice:

> **Alternative A:** An 11 percent chance of getting $1,000,000, and an 89 percent chance of getting $0
> **Alternative B:** A 10 percent chance of getting $2,500,000, and a 90 percent chance of getting $0

What would you choose in this case? (See Item #28b of the Reader Survey for your answer.) Most people choose Alternative B. They usually reason that there is not much difference between a 10 percent chance of winning and an 11 percent chance of winning, but there is a large difference between $1,000,000 and $2,500,000. Also, Alternative B has the greatest expected value. The expected value of Alternative B is 10 percent of $2,500,000, or $250,000, which is more than twice the expected value of Alternative A (11 percent of $1,000,000, or $110,000). The problem, or paradox, is that anyone choosing Alternative A in the first situation should also choose Alternative A in the second—otherwise, the Cancellation Principle is violated.

To see how the Cancellation Principle is violated, suppose the payoffs

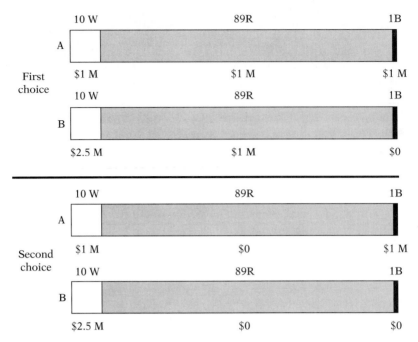

FIGURE 8.1

Illustration of the Allais Paradox. *(Based on Pool, 1988, and a freehand sketch by Elke Weber.)*

for each alternative are determined by drawing a ball randomly from a jar of 100 colored balls: 89 red, 10 white, and 1 blue. In the first choice, Alternative A yields $1,000,000 for a red, white, or blue ball (in other words, $1,000,000 no matter what), and Alternative B yields $1,000,000 for a red ball, $2,500,000 for a white ball, and nothing for a blue ball (see Figure 8.1). By the same logic, Alternative A in the second choice situation yields nothing for a red ball, $1,000,000 for a white ball, and $1,000,000 for a blue ball, whereas Alternative B yields nothing for a red ball, $2,500,000 for a white ball, and nothing for a blue ball.

Viewed in this way, you can see that the two choice situations offer identical alternatives, with the sole exception being that in the first problem, you get $1,000,000 for a red ball regardless of which alternative you choose, and in the second problem, you get $0 for a red ball regardless of which alternative you choose. In both problems, white and blue balls in Alternative A are worth $1,000,000, and white and blue balls in Alternative B are worth $2,500,000 and $0, respectively. Alternative A in the first problem is identical to Alternative A in the second problem except for the addition of an 89 percent chance of winning $1,000,000, and Alternative B in the first problem is identical to Alternative B in the second problem except for the addition of an 89 percent chance of winning $1,000,000.

Thus, the addition of equivalent consequences—a red ball worth $1,000,000 in the first problem or a red ball worth nothing in the second—leads many people to make different choices in the two situations. This difference violates the Cancellation Principle, which states that a choice between two alternatives should depend only on how those two alternatives differ, not on any factor that is common to both alternatives.

ELLSBERG'S PARADOX

Independance Axiom

Another famous violation of the Cancellation Principle was documented by Daniel Ellsberg (1961). Ellsberg's Paradox (as it is now called) goes like this: Suppose an urn contains 90 balls. Thirty of these balls are red, and the remaining 60 balls are either black or yellow, in unknown proportions. One ball is to be drawn from the urn, and the color of that ball will determine your payoff according to the scheme listed in Figure 8.2a.

What color would you bet on—red or black? Most people choose red in order to avoid the uncertain mix of black and yellow balls. But suppose you are faced with the payoff scheme contained in Figure 8.2b. What would you bet on then? In the second situation, most people prefer to bet on a black or yellow ball rather than a red or yellow ball, again in order to avoid the uncertainty associated with the ratio of black and yellow balls. In other words, many people choose Alternative 1 in the first problem and Alternative 2 in the second.

According to the Cancellation Principle, though, people should

FIGURE 8.2a

This is the payoff scheme for the first part of Ellsberg's Paradox.

Betting Alternatives	30 BALLS	60 BALLS	
	Red	Black	Yellow
Alternative 1: A red ball	$100	$0	$0
Alternative 2: A black ball	$0	$100	$0

cancelled out
Most pick Red.

FIGURE 8.2b

This is the payoff scheme for the second part of Ellsberg's Paradox. The only change is that a yellow ball is now worth $100 rather than $0.

Betting Alternatives	30 BALLS	60 BALLS	
	Red	Black	Yellow
Alternative 1: A red or yellow ball	$100	$0	$100
Alternative 2: A black or yellow ball	$0	$100	$100

cancelled out
Most pick Black or Yellow

choose the same alternative in both problems. As you can see from Figure 8.2, the two payoff schemes are equivalent in every respect except that a yellow ball is worth no money in the first scheme and $100 in the second. Because a yellow ball is always worth the same amount in Alternative 1 and Alternative 2 ($0 in the first scheme and $100 in the second), the value of a yellow ball should not influence which choice is made within each scheme (just as equal mileage should not influence a choice between two cars). Contrary to expected utility theory, however, people often choose differently in the two problems.

INTRANSITIVITY

Another principle of rational decision making is the Transitivity Principle, which states that a decision maker who prefers Outcome A to Outcome B, and who prefers Outcome B to Outcome C, should prefer Outcome A to Outcome C. Chapter 7 discussed how a decision maker with intransitive preferences can be used as a "money pump." Another example of intransitivity is given in Figure 8.3.

Suppose you have to choose between three job applicants (listed as Applicants A, B, and C in Figure 8.3), and you have information about each applicant's intelligence and work experience. Suppose further that your decision rule is the following: If the difference in IQ between any two applicants is greater than 10 points, choose the more intelligent applicant. If the difference between applicants is equal to or less than 10 points, choose the applicant with more experience.

This sounds like a reasonable enough rule, but let's look at what happens if you follow it. If we compare Applicant A with Applicant B, we should choose B because A and B do not differ by more than 10 points in IQ, and B is more experienced than A. Similarly, if we compare Applicant B with Applicant C, we should choose C because B and C do not differ by more than 10 points in IQ, and C is more experienced than B. Yet if we compare Applicants C and A, we should choose A because the

FIGURE 8.3

The following decision rule leads to intransitive preferences for Applicants A, B, and C: If the difference in intelligence between any two applicants is greater than 10 points, choose the more intelligent applicant. If the difference between applicants is equal to or less than 10 points, choose the applicant with more experience.

		DIMENSIONS	
		Intelligence (IQ)	Experience, Years
	A	120	1
APPLICANTS	B	110	2
	C	100	3

IQ of A is more than 10 points higher than the IQ of C. Thus, Applicant B is preferred to Applicant A, Applicant C is preferred to Applicant B, and Applicant A is preferred to Applicant C. This intransitivity arises because the decision rule is based on two different dimensions—intelligence and experience—that increase in small steps and are inversely related.

Do people actually violate the Transitivity Principle? In 1969, Amos Tversky published a study in which one third of the experimental participants behaved intransitively. Tversky began the study by presenting 18 Harvard undergraduates with the five gambles listed in Figure 8.4. As you can see, the expected value of each gamble increased with the odds of winning and decreased with the payoff amount. The students were randomly presented with a pair of gambles and asked to choose which one they preferred. After they chose three times between all 10 possible pairings (A and B, A and C, and so on), Tversky selected eight subjects who showed some tendency toward intransitivity, and he asked them to return to his laboratory once a week for an intensive five-week study.

What he found was that six of the students showed highly reliable intransitivities. When two alternatives had a very similar probability of winning (e.g., Gambles A and B), subjects chose the one with the higher payoff. In contrast, when the difference in probabilities was extreme (e.g., Gambles A and E), subjects chose the alternative with the higher probability of winning. Thus, Gamble A was preferred to Gamble B, Gamble B to Gamble C, Gamble C to Gamble D, and Gamble D to Gamble E, but Gamble E was preferred to Gamble A. Tversky (1969) also found intransitivities using problems similar to the job applicant example above.

Intransitivity is more than an experimental curiosity; it can have important implications for decision makers. For example, consider the "committee problem," as it is known among decision analysts. In a typical version of the committee problem, there are five members of a faculty search committee: Ann, Bob, Cindy, Dan, and Ellen. Their task

FIGURE 8.4

These gambles were used in an experiment on intransitivity by Amos Tversky (1969). The expected value (EV) for each gamble is calculated by multiplying the payoff amount by the probability of winning.

Gamble	Probability of a Win	Payoff, $	EV, $
A	7/24	5.00	1.46
B	8/24	4.75	1.58
C	9/24	4.50	1.69
D	10/24	4.25	1.77
E	11/24	4.00	1.83

	COMMITTEE MEMBERS				
Candidates	Ann	Bob	Cindy	Dan	Ellen
Joe Schmoe	1	1	2	3	3
Jane Doe	2	3	3	1	1
Al Einstein	3	2	1	2	2

FIGURE 8.5

These are ranked preferences in a typical version of the committee problem. Lower numbers indicate greater preferences (for example, Ann prefers Joe Schmoe to Jane Doe, and she prefers Jane Doe over Al Einstein).

is to hire a new professor, and their top three preferences are given in Figure 8.5.

Suppose you are chair of the faculty committee, you know everyone's preferences, and you want to control the balloting so that Al Einstein is chosen. What should you do?

The answer is that you should avoid any direct votes between Einstein and Jane Doe, because three of the five committee members prefer Doe to Einstein (Ann, Dan, and Ellen). Instead, you should ask committee members to vote on whether to hire Schmoe or Doe, and after Schmoe wins, you should ask for a second vote between Schmoe and Einstein. On the other hand, if you prefer to hire Doe, you should first call for a vote between Schmoe and Einstein, and after Einstein has won, ask for a vote between Einstein and Doe. Because the committee's preferences are intransitive with a majority rule based on pairwise comparisons, the person setting the agenda has complete control over the outcome.

PREFERENCE REVERSALS

As if intransitivity were not bad enough, in some cases preferences actually "reverse" depending on how they are elicited. One of the first studies documenting preference reversals was published by Sarah Lichtenstein and Paul Slovic (1971). Lichtenstein and Slovic reasoned that choosing between a pair of gambles might involve different psychological processes than bidding for each one separately (i.e., setting a dollar value on their worth). Specifically, they hypothesized that choices would be determined primarily by a gamble's probabilities, whereas bids would be affected predominantly by the amount to be won or lost.

They tested this hypothesis in three experiments. In each study, they first presented experimental subjects with several pairs of bets. Each pair of bets had very similar expected values, but one bet always had a high probability of winning, and the other always had a high payoff for

Pair	High Probability	EV	High Payoff	EV
1	.99 Win $4.00	$3.95	.33 Win $16.00	$3.94
	.01 Lose $1.00		.67 Lose $2.00	
2	.95 Win $2.50	$2.34	.40 Win $8.50	$2.50
	.05 Lose $.75		.60 Lose $1.50	
3	.95 Win $3.00	$2.75	.50 Win $6.50	$2.75
	.05 Lose $2.00		.50 Lose $1.00	
4	.90 Win $2.00	$1.60	.50 Win $5.25	$1.88
	.10 Lose $2.00		.50 Lose $1.50	
5	.80 Win $2.00	$1.40	.20 Win $9.00	$1.40
	.20 Lose $1.00		.80 Lose $.50	
6	.80 Win $4.00	$3.10	.10 Win $40.00	$3.10
	.20 Lose $.50		.90 Lose $1.00	

FIGURE 8.6

These gambles were used by Sarah Lichtenstein and Paul Slovic in an experiment on preference reversals. EV = expected value. (Based on Lichtenstein and Slovic, 1971.)

a win (see Figure 8.6). After subjects indicated which bet they preferred within each pair, they made a bid for each gamble considered separately. Bids were elicited by telling subjects that they owned a ticket to play the gamble and asking them to name the minimum dollar amount for which they would be willing to sell the ticket.

In the first experiment, college students indicated which bets they preferred and how much they would be willing to sell their tickets for. As a measure of preference reversal, Lichtenstein and Slovic calculated the percentage of times that the selling price for the *high-payoff* gamble exceeded the selling price for the *high-probability* gamble, given that the high-probability gamble had been chosen when the two gambles were paired. Lichtenstein and Slovic found that 73 percent of the subjects always showed this reversal in preference. The second experiment basically replicated the first one with a different bidding procedure, and the third experiment found that even when lengthy and careful instructions were administered to each subject individually, and the gambles were actually played, people showed reliable preference reversals.

Of course, the preference reversals Lichtenstein and Slovic (1971) found were carefully produced in a laboratory experiment, and there is still the question of whether these reversals occur outside the laboratory. To answer this question, Lichtenstein and Slovic (1973) replicated their experiment in a casino in Las Vegas. Armed with a computer and a roulette wheel, they were able to collect data on 44 gamblers (including seven professional dealers).

Their results were impressive. Of the cases in which people preferred the high-probability gamble to the high-payoff gamble, 81 percent set a larger dollar value on the high-payoff gamble. This proportion of reversals is even higher than the proportion found in the first experiment. It seems, then, that preference reversals are not limited to the laboratory; they also exist for experienced decision makers who have financial incentives to perform well.

Since the time of these early experiments, several studies have replicated and extended the basic findings of Lichtenstein and Slovic (Grether & Plott, 1979; Schkade & Johnson, 1989; Slovic, Griffin, & Tversky, 1990; Slovic & Lichtenstein, 1983; Tversky, Slovic, & Kahneman, 1990). Preference reversals are robust, and they do not diminish with financial incentives (Tversky, Slovic, & Kahneman, 1990). When people are asked to *choose* between two bets, they pay particular attention to the probability of winning, but when they are asked to *set a price* for how valuable the bet is, they look at how large the potential payoffs are.

ARE VIOLATIONS OF EXPECTED UTILITY THEORY TRULY IRRATIONAL?

There is little doubt that people violate the principles of expected utility theory, but we might ask whether these violations show that people are truly irrational. Do such findings mean that the way people make decisions is unreasonable?

The answer is almost certainly *no* because we have no information about the cost of people's errors compared with the cost of following normatively rational principles such as cancellation and transitivity (this point will be discussed further in the Afterword). As Lichtenstein and Slovic (1971, p. 55) have written: "The approximations subjects follow in order to simplify the difficult task of bidding might prove to be rather efficient, in the sense that they reduce cognitive effort and lead to outcomes not too different from the results of optimal strategies. In using such approximations, the decision maker assumes that the world, unlike the present experiments, is *not* designed to take advantage of his approximation methods." A decision strategy that cannot be defended as logical may nonetheless be rational if, over the long run, it provides a quick and easy approximation to normative strategies that maximize utility.

CONCLUSION

The studies in this chapter have been presented as though they examine specific principles of rationality in isolation, but as Duncan Luce (1990) has observed, it is sometimes difficult to pinpoint which principle an experiment is testing. For example, preference reversals are frequently interpreted as evidence against the Transitivity Principle, but recent research suggests that preference reversals may be better characterized as violations of the Invariance Principle (Bostic, Herrnstein, & Luce, 1990; Tversky, Sattath, & Slovic, 1988; Tversky, Slovic, & Kahneman, 1990). Regardless of how this debate is settled, however, it is clear that expected utility theory does not adequately describe how people make decisions.

In the aftermath of von Neumann and Morgenstern's (1947) seminal work, many decision theorists tried to use expected utility theory as a descriptive model of decision making. Yet these efforts frequently met with failure, and as the pillars of cancellation, transitivity, invariance, and dominance fell, a number of formerly loyal utility theorists turned to other models of decision making. Several of these alternative models are discussed in Chapter 9.

CHAPTER 9

DESCRIPTIVE MODELS OF DECISION MAKING

In 1977, Jay Russo published a field study on the effect of unit pricing schemes in supermarkets (unit prices are breakdowns of the cost per ounce, per gram, or per whatever unit the product comes in). In this study, Russo discovered several interesting things about the way people shop. First, when shelf tags include unit price information, shoppers save an average of 1 percent in their cost per unit. The way they save this money is almost always by buying larger sizes of the product, rather than buying cheaper brands (1 percent may not seem like much money, but keep in mind that *billions* of dollars are spent in supermarkets). Second, Russo found that when the supermarket displayed a list comparing the unit prices of different brands, shoppers saved an average of 3 percent per unit. The main way shoppers saved money in this case was by switching to store brands and other less expensive products.

The latter finding is somewhat surprising, because a comparison of unit prices does not add any new information; it merely lists the unit prices already displayed beside each brand. According to the Invariance Principle of expected utility theory, decisions should not be influenced by the way in which choices are presented. Nonetheless, Russo (1977) found that the presentation of a unit price list had a significant effect upon consumers. When unit prices for different brands appeared together on a single sheet, shoppers tended to buy less expensive brands. By listing unit price information on the same piece of paper, the supermarket was able to influence consumer choices.

SATISFICING

Expected utility theory makes a number of simplifying assumptions in order to yield mathematically tractable problems and analytically elegant solutions. Typically, decision makers are assumed to have complete information about the probabilities and consequences attached to each alternative course of action. Expected utility theory also assumes that decision makers understand this information, and that they are able to implicitly or explicitly calculate the advantages and disadvantages of each alternative. Finally, the theory postulates that decision makers compare these calculations and choose the course of action that maximizes expected utility.

Clearly, decision makers do not operate this way. Information about alternatives is often missing or inherently uncertain, and perception is highly selective. Memory is fraught with biases. The consequences attached to various alternatives are frequently misunderstood, and as Russo showed, unaided decision makers do not necessarily compare all available alternatives. Thus, although expected utility is useful as a *normative* model of decision making (a model about how rational actors would behave if certain assumptions were met), it is not very useful as a *descriptive* model (a model of how people actually make decisions). To describe how people actually arrive at their decisions, it is necessary to turn to other theoretical models.

One of the earliest alternatives to expected utility theory was proposed by Nobel Laureate Herbert Simon (1956). Simon proposed that people "satisfice" rather than optimize when they make decisions. To satisfice is to choose a path that satisfies your most important needs, even though the choice may not be ideal or optimal. For example, in renting an apartment, people tend to search for an alternative that satisfies certain needs (price, location, space, safety, and so on). They do not conduct an exhaustive search of all available apartments and choose the apartment that has the highest overall utility. As Simon (1956, p. 129) wrote: "However adaptive the behavior of organisms in learning and choice situations, this adaptiveness falls far short of the ideal of 'maximizing' in economic theory. Evidently, organisms adapt well enough to 'satisfice'; they do not, in general, 'optimize.'"

PROSPECT THEORY

Many alternatives to expected utility theory have been proposed since the time of Simon's paper, but the most widely accepted is "prospect theory." Prospect theory was developed by Daniel Kahneman and Amos Tversky (1979), and it differs from expected utility theory in a number of important respects.

First, it replaces the notion of "utility" with "value." Whereas utility is usually defined only in terms of net wealth, value is defined in terms of gains and losses (deviations from a reference point). Moreover, the value function for losses is different than the value function for gains. As you can see in Figure 9.1, the value function for losses (the curve lying below the horizontal axis) is convex and relatively steep. In contrast, the value function for gains (above the horizontal axis) is concave and not quite so steep. These differences lead to several noteworthy results.

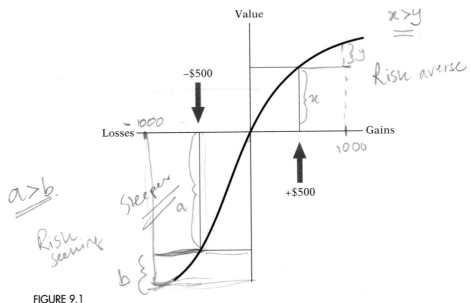

FIGURE 9.1

A hypothetical value function in prospect theory. *(Figure adapted from Kahneman and Tversky, 1979.)*

Because the value function for losses is steeper than that for gains, losses "loom larger" than gains. For instance, a loss of $500 is felt more strongly than a gain of $500 (see Figure 9.1). As George Quattrone and Amos Tversky (1988) have pointed out, this asymmetry, or "loss aversion," is consistent with the advantage that incumbent politicians have over challengers (i.e., voters weigh the potential loss from an unfavorable change in leadership more heavily than the potential gain from a favorable change in leadership). Quattrone and Tversky (1988, p. 726) also note that loss aversion may complicate bargaining and negotiation, because "each party may view its own concessions as losses that loom larger than the gains achieved by the concessions of the adversary. . . . In negotiating over missiles, for example, each superpower may sense a greater loss in security from the dismantling of its own missiles than it senses a gain in security from a comparable reduction made by the other side."

Another result of loss aversion is the so-called "endowment effect," in which the value of a good increases when it becomes part of a person's endowment (Thaler, 1980). For example, when people are asked to name a selling price for something they own (e.g., a chocolate bar, pen, or coffee mug), they often require much more money than they would pay to own the very same item (Kahneman, Knetsch, & Thaler, 1990; Knetsch & Sinden, 1984). According to Richard Thaler and his colleagues, the reason for this effect is that losses (of the item in question)

are felt more strongly than equivalent gains. This asymmetry is routinely exploited by companies that offer products on a trial basis. Trial own-
ership often increases the value of a product and makes it more difficult
to return.

Unlike expected utility theory, prospect theory predicts that preferences will depend on how a problem is framed. If the reference point is
defined such that an outcome is viewed as a gain, then the resulting
value function will be concave and decision makers will tend to be risk
averse. On the other hand, if the reference point is defined such that an
outcome is viewed as a loss, then the value function will be convex and
decision makers will be risk seeking. As an illustration, consider the following pair of problems (adapted from an experiment by Kahneman
and Tversky, 1979):   *Gain - Goncave - averse*
                        Loss - Convex - seeking

Problem 1. In addition to whatever you own, you have been given
$1000. You are now asked to choose between Alternative A and
Alternative B.

> **Alternative A:**   A 50 percent chance of gaining $1000
> **Alternative B:**   A sure gain of $500

Of the 70 respondents who were given a version of this problem by
Kahneman and Tversky, 84 percent chose the sure gain. As the upper
half of Figure 9.1 shows, this answer makes a good deal of sense,
because the value function rises more from $0 to $500 than from $500
to $1000. If you do not value the second $500 as much as the first $500,
then you should not accept an even wager for the second $500.

Now look at the second problem, a variant of which was given to 68
respondents:

Problem 2. In addition to whatever you own, you have been given
$2000. You are now asked to choose between Alternative C and
Alternative D.

> **Alternative C:**   A 50 percent chance of losing $1000
> **Alternative D:**   A sure loss of $500

In this case, nearly 70 percent of those surveyed chose the risky alternative. As the bottom half of Figure 9.1 shows, risk seeking makes sense
when losses are at stake because more value is lost from $0 to $500 than
from $500 to $1000 (so losing $500 for sure is worse than a 50 percent

chance of losing $1000). Thus, even though the two problems are numerically equivalent, they lead to very different choices. As a consequence of having an "S-shaped" value function, people are generally risk averse when it comes to gains and risk seeking when it comes to losses. And because value is always defined with respect to a reference point, prospect theory—unlike expected utility theory—predicts that preferences will be affected when the reference point shifts (as with the framing problems in Chapter 6).

Prospect theory also differs from expected utility theory in the way it handles the probabilities attached to particular outcomes. Classical utility theory assumes that decision makers value a 50 percent chance of winning as exactly that: a 50 percent chance of winning. In contrast, prospect theory treats preferences as a function of "decision weights," and it assumes that these weights do not always correspond to probabilities. Specifically, prospect theory postulates that decision weights tend to overweight small probabilities and underweight moderate and high probabilities. As you can see in Figure 9.2, a typical weighting function lies above the diagonal for low probabilities and below it for moderate and high probabilities.

Kahneman and Tversky (1979) illustrated people's tendency to overweight small probabilities with a pair of problems similar to the following:

Problem 1. Choose between Alternative A and Alternative B.

FIGURE 9.2
Hypothetical decision weights according to prospect theory. *(Figure adapted from Kahneman and Tversky, 1979.)*

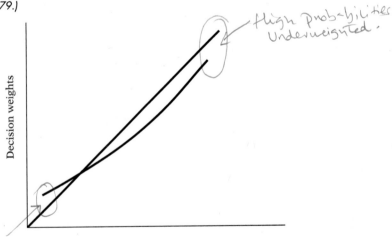

[handwritten margin notes: "When learnt ↗ from description!"; "High probabilities Underweighted."; "Small Probabilities Overweighted"]

> **Alternative A:** A 1 in 1000 chance of winning $5000 ✓
> **Alternative B:** A sure gain of $5

Of 72 respondents who were presented with a variant of this problem, nearly three in four chose the risky alternative. Thousands of people make much the same choice each day when they purchase lottery tickets. But consider the second problem:

Problem 2. Choose between Alternative C and Alternative D.

> **Alternative C:** A 1 in 1000 chance of losing $5000   *overweigh chances*
> **Alternative D:** A sure loss of $5 ✓   *of large loss*

Of the 72 respondents who were given a version of this problem, more than four out of five preferred the sure loss. Kahneman and Tversky explained this preference in terms of a tendency to overweight the chances of a large loss—a tendency that greatly benefits the insurance industry.

THE CERTAINTY EFFECT

Still another difference between prospect theory and expected utility theory is that prospect theory predicts a "certainty effect" in which "a reduction of the probability of an outcome by a constant factor has more impact when the outcome was initially certain than when it was merely probable" (Tversky & Kahneman, 1981, p. 455). The certainty effect was exploited by Maurice Allais (1953) in his famous counterexample to expected utility theory, and a very concrete example of how it works has been provided by economist Richard Zeckhauser. Zeckhauser observed that most people would pay more to remove the only bullet from a gun in Russian roulette than they would to remove one of four bullets. Even though the probability of being shot is reduced by the same amount with each bullet removed, people regard the difference between 0 and 1 bullet as more important than the difference between 3 and 4 bullets. This effect is predicted by prospect theory, but not by expected utility theory. ⟹ *Making a probability certain is more valued.*

To see why prospect theory predicts a certainty effect, consider the results from a survey Kahneman and Tversky (1979) conducted on "probabilistic insurance." In this survey, Kahneman and Tversky asked college students to suppose they were evaluating some insurance against theft or damage to property, and to suppose further that, after weighing the insurance premiums against the benefits of insurance, they had no clear preference whether to insure or not. Then the students were asked whether they would be interested in purchasing a new type of policy called "probabilistic insurance," in which the premium would be cut in half but there would be only a 50 percent chance that their losses would be covered in the event of an accident (with a full refund of the premium if the loss was not covered). In other words, under probabilistic insurance, they would pay only 50 percent of the premium and would be covered against theft or damage only 50 percent of the time. This problem may seem contrived, but as Kahneman and Tversky pointed out, there are many forms of protective action in which the probability of an undesirable event is reduced without being eliminated (installing a burglar alarm, replacing old tires, quitting smoking, and so on).

When faced with this problem, 80 percent of the students indicated that they would not buy probabilistic insurance (see Item #23 of the Reader Survey for your own answer to the problem). Kahneman and Tversky argued that reducing the probability of a loss from whatever it is (say p) to half that amount ($p/2$) is less valuable than reducing the probability from half ($p/2$) to zero. People would much rather *eliminate* risk than *reduce* it, even if the probability of a catastrophe is diminished by an equal amount in both cases. This finding is predicted by prospect theory, because in prospect theory the decision weights "overweight" small probabilities and thereby inflate the importance of improbable events. In contrast, expected utility theory predicts that probabilistic insurance should actually be *more* attractive than regular insurance (the proof for this statement is somewhat complicated and can be found on page 270 of Kahneman & Tversky, 1979).

PSEUDOCERTAINTY

In addition to the certainty effect, Tversky and Kahneman (1981) have discussed a "pseudocertainty effect." The pseudocertainty effect is similar to the certainty effect, except that in this case the certainty is apparent rather than real. Paul Slovic, Baruch Fischhoff, and Sarah Lichtenstein (1982a) published a clever demonstration of the pseudocertainty effect.

Slovic and his colleagues presented 211 respondents with one of two descriptions concerning a vaccination program. In the *probabilistic protection* condition, respondents were asked whether they would volunteer to receive a vaccine that protected half the recipients from a disease that was expected to afflict 20 percent of the population. In other words, the vaccine would reduce the risk of disease from 20 percent to 10 percent. Only 40 percent of the respondents indicated that they would be interested in receiving such a vaccine.

In the *pseudocertainty* condition, respondents were told that there were two mutually exclusive and equally probable strains of the disease, each of which was expected to afflict 10 percent of the population. Respondents were told that the vaccine would give complete protection against one of the strains and no protection against the other. Thus, here again the overall risk of disease would be reduced from 20 percent to 10 percent. Of the respondents in this condition, however, 57 percent indicated that they would get vaccinated. According to Slovic, Fischhoff, and Lichtenstein (1982), the vaccine was more popular in the pseudo-certainty condition because it appeared to eliminate risk rather than simply reduce it.

Marketing professionals often use analogous techniques to enhance the perceived value of price reductions. For example, instead of advertising a 25 percent price reduction, a dry cleaner may offer to clean one shirt free with each order of three. The idea is that a free service will be more appealing than a discounted service, even if the free service does not represent a greater overall price reduction.

REGRET THEORY

As prospect theory makes clear, decision makers evaluate their alternatives relative to a reference point. The status quo is probably the most common reference point, but in some cases, people compare the quality of their decisions to what might have happened if they had made a different choice. The comparison of imaginary outcomes is sometimes referred to as "counterfactual reasoning," because it relies on hypothetical events (Dunning & Parpal, 1989).

Counterfactual reasoning forms the basis of regret theory, an economic theory of choice independently proposed by David Bell (1982; see also 1985) and Graham Loomes and Robert Sugden (1982, 1983, 1987). In the words of Loomes and Sugden (1982, p. 820): "Regret theory rests on two fundamental assumptions: first, that many people experience the sensations we call regret and rejoicing; and second, that in making decisions under uncertainty, they try to anticipate and take account of those sensations." For example, if people are faced with a choice between $1000 for sure and $2000 if an unbiased coin lands on Heads, they may choose the sure bet to avoid any regret they would feel if the coin landed on Tails.

This is the same risk aversion predicted by prospect theory, but regret theory predicts this choice by adding a new variable, regret, to the normal utility function. With the addition of this variable, regret theory is able to account for many of the same paradoxes as prospect theory, including the Allais Paradox, Ellsberg's Paradox, preference reversals, the avoidance of probabilistic insurance, and so on. Indeed, Loomes and Sugden (1982) explicitly offered regret theory as an alternative to prospect theory. The anticipation of regret need not be viewed as inconsistent with prospect theory, however, and in decisions involving a risk of death (e.g., open heart surgery), it makes no sense to speak of regret following a negative outcome.

MULTI-ATTRIBUTE CHOICE

In many choice situations, the outcomes cannot be scaled along a single metric such as money or risk of disease. When trade-offs must be made (such as the trade-off between cost and quality), there is not an objectively optimal solution in the same sense as when only one criterion is involved. Instead of objective optimality, there is only consistency with one's goals and values (Einhorn & Hogarth, 1981). As a result, much of the research on "multi-attribute choice" concerns *how*, rather than *how well*, people make decisions.

People use a number of different decision strategies to make multi-attribute choices, and these strategies vary quite a bit depending on problem type. When decision makers are faced with simple choices between two alternatives, they often use what are known as "compensatory" strategies (Payne, 1982). A compensatory strategy trades off low values on one dimension against high values on another. For instance, a car buyer might trade off poor gas mileage against stylish looks, or a candidate for an untenured faculty position at Harvard might forsake long-term job security in return for academic prestige.

There are several possible ways to make such trade-offs (cf. Hogarth, 1987). One strategy is to use a "linear model." In a linear model, each dimension is weighted according to its importance, and the weighted values are summed to form an overall index of value. For example, in choosing among graduate school applicants, an admissions committee might form a weighted index based on grade point average, test scores, and letters of recommendation. Even though people do not normally use linear equations to arrive at their decisions, linear decision rules often yield choices that agree closely with the choices people make (and can therefore be used to model human decision making, or at times, even replace it).

Another compensatory strategy is known as the "additive difference model." This model is similar to the linear model, except that in the linear model, each alternative is evaluated on all the dimensions and then compared with other alternatives, whereas in the additive difference model, each dimension is first evaluated across alternatives, and only the *differences* among alternatives are weighted and summed together. Focusing on differences has at least two advantages—it greatly simplifies the choice between two alternatives, and as a model of decision making, it seems closer to how people actually make decisions. For example, a car buyer would be much more likely to focus on the difference between two cars than to examine every dimension of each car and sum the weighted values (as in the case of a linear model).

Still another compensatory strategy is the "ideal point model." The ideal point model is algebraically similar to the linear model, but it is very different in principle. According to this model, decision makers have a representation of what an ideal alternative would be (for example, an ideal job or an ideal car). Then the actual alternatives are evaluated in terms of how far they are from the ideal on each dimension.

NONCOMPENSATORY STRATEGIES

When people are confronted with complex choices among a number of alternatives, they typically use "noncompensatory" strategies. In contrast to compensatory strategies, these strategies do not allow trade-offs. Four well-known examples of noncompensatory strategies are the conjunctive rule, the disjunctive rule, the lexicographic strategy, and elimination-by-aspects (Hogarth, 1987).

Decision makers using the conjunctive rule eliminate any alternatives that fall outside certain predefined boundaries. For example, applicants to graduate school might be excluded from consideration if their Graduate Record Examination (GRE) score falls below 1000, their college grade point average is less than 3.0, or their letter of application contains three or more spelling mistakes. The conjunctive rule is an example of satisficing, rather than optimizing.

On the other hand, a decision maker using the disjunctive rule might be willing to allow quite a few misspellings if the applicant's GRE score or grade point average is high enough. According to the disjunctive rule, each alternative is evaluated in terms of its best attribute, regardless of how poor other aspects of the alternative may be. To take an extreme example, a graduate admissions committee using the disjunctive rule might admit an applicant whose cover letter was typed by a chimpanzee, provided the applicant had attained high enough GRE scores.

The third noncompensatory choice strategy is lexicographic. A decision maker using this strategy begins by identifying the most important dimension for comparison and choosing the most desirable alternative or alternatives on this dimension. If more than one alternative remains, the alternatives are compared on the next most important dimension, then the next, and so on until only one alternative is left.

The fourth noncompensatory choice strategy, proposed by Tversky in 1972, is known as elimination-by-aspects (EBA) and is essentially a probabilistic variation of the lexicographic strategy. According to EBA, each dimension—or aspect—of comparison is selected with a probability proportional to its importance. The alternatives are first compared with respect to a selected aspect, inferior alternatives are then eliminated, another aspect of comparison is selected, additional alternatives are eliminated, and so forth until only one alternative remains. Tversky (1972, p. 285) illustrated EBA this way: "In contemplating the purchase of a new car, for example, the first aspect selected may be automatic transmission: this will eliminate all cars that do not have this feature. Given the remaining alternatives, another aspect, say a $3000 price limit, is selected and all cars whose price exceeds this limit are excluded. The process continues until all cars but one are eliminated."

THE MORE IMPORTANT DIMENSION

Although a number of theoretical and mathematical papers have been written on multi-attribute choice strategies, relatively few experiments have been conducted on this topic. One notable exception, however, is a series of experiments published by Slovic (1975).

Slovic was interested in how people choose between two equally valued alternatives. His hypothesis was that, given a choice between two equally valued alternatives, people tend to choose the alternative that is superior on the more important dimension. Slovic called this the "more important dimension hypothesis."

To test this hypothesis, Slovic first had subjects equate two alternatives in value (e.g., two baseball players in value to their teams). For example, they were asked questions similar to the following:

> Player 1 has hit 26 home runs and has a batting average of .273. Player 2 has hit 20 home runs. What would Player 2's batting average have to be in order to make the two players of *equal* ability and value to their teams?

After subjects equated the two alternatives (and some time had elapsed), Slovic asked them to rate the relative importance of the dimensions and to choose between the alternatives. The results strongly supported the more important dimension hypothesis. By an overwhelming margin, subjects tended to choose the alternatives that were superior on the more important dimension.

These results show that when faced with equally valued alternatives, people do not choose randomly. Nor are they paralyzed by indecision, as in the case of Dante's tortured soul who starved to death when confronted with two equally appealing foods. Instead, people usually select the alternative that is superior on the most important dimension under consideration.

CONCLUSION

Just as the St. Petersburg Paradox led to the development of expected utility theory, problems such as the Allais Paradox and Ellsberg's Paradox resulted in the development of alternatives to expected utility theory. The most widely accepted of these alternatives is prospect theory. Although many decision analysts still use expected utility theory as a normative model, prospect theory provides a more accurate description of how people actually make decisions. It can also be applied rather easily to a range of common situations.

For example, the loss aversion predicted by prospect theory means that credit card companies will profit by promoting cash discounts rather than credit card surcharges (Thaler, 1980). Surcharges are perceived as out-of-pocket losses, whereas cash discounts are viewed as gains; thus, even though the fee structure is equivalent in both cases, prospect theory predicts that surcharges will be felt more strongly than the absence of a cash discount. Similar strategies are adopted by stores that use "suggested retail prices" to shift the consumer's reference point and make sale prices seem like "savings" (Thaler, 1985).

Loss aversion has also been used to encourage women to perform self-examinations for breast cancer. Beth Meyerowitz and Shelly Chaiken (1987) presented college-aged women with one of three pamphlets: (1) a pamphlet that framed the benefits of breast self-examination (BSE) in terms of *gains* in protection against cancer, (2) a pamphlet that warned against a *loss* in protection, or (3) a pamphlet that contained neither frame. For instance, the gain-frame pamphlet said: "By doing BSE now, you can learn what your normal, healthy breasts feel like so you will be better prepared to notice any small, abnormal changes that might occur as you get older." In contrast, the loss-frame pamphlet pointed out that: "By not doing BSE now, you will not learn what your normal, healthy breasts feel like so you will be ill prepared to notice any small, abnormal changes that might occur as you get older." The no-frame pamphlet simply omitted these statements.

Meyerowitz and Chaiken found that, four months later, 57 percent of the women who were given a loss-frame pamphlet reported an increase in BSE, compared with only 38 percent of those given a gain-frame pamphlet and 39 percent given a no-frame pamphlet. According to Meyerowitz and Chaiken, women who received a loss-frame pamphlet were more likely to perform BSE because the prospect of a loss in health protection was perceived as more important than an equal gain in protection—even though the two are logically equivalent. These results show how loss aversion can be used to improve the health and welfare of society.

Prospect theory represents a great improvement over classical expected utility theory. Indeed, many violations of expected utility theory are explicitly predicted by prospect theory. Section IV reviews a number of additional ways in which decision makers deviate from normative principles of rationality. As its chapters show, decision makers are prone to a range of biases in judgment and choice behavior, but in many cases, these biases are systematic and can be controlled or predicted in advance.

SECTION IV

HEURISTICS AND BIASES

When people are faced with a complicated judgment or decision, they often simplify the task by relying on heuristics, or general rules of thumb. In many cases, these shortcuts yield very close approximations to the "optimal" answers suggested by normative theories. In certain situations, though, heuristics lead to predictable biases and inconsistencies. This section of the book focuses on several of the best-known heuristics and biases.

CHAPTER 10

THE REPRESENTATIVENESS HEURISTIC

How do people come to their decisions? How do they choose among different options? And how do they form judgments of the value or likelihood of particular events or outcomes? This section of the book focuses on two related issues: the *processes* by which decision makers reach their conclusions, and the *biases* that can result as a consequence of these processes.

Amos Tversky and Daniel Kahneman (1974) have proposed that decision makers use "heuristics," or general rules of thumb, to arrive at their judgments. The advantage of heuristics is that they reduce the time and effort required to make reasonably good judgments and decisions. For example, it is easier to estimate how likely an outcome is by using a heuristic than by tallying every past occurrence of the outcome and dividing by the total number of times the outcome could have occurred. In most cases, rough approximations are sufficient (just as people often satisfice rather than optimize).

Normally, heuristics yield fairly good estimates. The disadvantage of using heuristics, however, is that there are certain instances in which they lead to systematic biases (i.e., deviations from normatively derived answers). The heuristic discussed in this chapter is known as "representativeness," and it leads to very predictable biases in certain situations. As mentioned earlier, the reason for focusing on biases rather than successes is that biases usually reveal more of the underlying processes than do successes. In fact, virtually all current theories of decision making are based on the results of research concerning biases in judgment.

THE A, B, C's OF REPRESENTATIVENESS

According to Tversky and Kahneman (1974, p. 1124), people often judge probabilities "by the degree to which A is representative of B, that is, by the degree to which A resembles B." Tversky and Kahneman called this rule of thumb the "representativeness heuristic."

What are "A" and "B"? It depends on the judgment you are making. If you are estimating the probability that A came from B, then A might be an instance or a sample, and B might be a category or a parent population. For example, A might be a person, B might be a group, and the judgment in question might be the probability that A is a member of B. On the other hand, if you are trying to estimate the probability that A was produced by B, then A might be an event or an effect, and B might be a process or cause. For instance, B might be the process of flipping an unbiased coin, A might be the event of getting six Heads in a row, and the judgment might concern the chances of observing such an event with an unbiased coin. Because this definition of representativeness is abstract and a little hard to understand, let's consider some concrete examples of how the representativeness heuristic works and how it can lead to biases in certain situations.

Item #1 of the Reader Survey provides one example. This problem, taken from a study by Tversky and Kahneman (1982), reads as follows:

> Linda is 31 years old, single, outspoken, and very bright. She majored in philosophy. As a student, she was deeply concerned with issues of discrimination and social justice, and also participated in antinuclear demonstrations. Please check off the most likely alternative:
>
> ❏ Linda is a bank teller.
> ❏ Linda is a bank teller and is active in the feminist movement.

Most people feel that Linda is more likely to be a feminist bank teller than a bank teller. When Tversky and Kahneman (1982) put this question to 86 people, nearly 9 of every 10 respondents answered this way. If you think about it, though, this response violates a fundamental rule of probability. The conjunction, or co-occurrence, of two events (e.g., "bank teller" and "feminist") cannot be more likely than the probability of either event alone (e.g., "bank teller"). For this reason, Tversky and Kahneman (1983) called this phenomenon the "conjunction fallacy" (see also Leddo, Abelson, & Gross, 1984; Morier & Borgida, 1984).

You can verify the conjunction rule by looking at Figure 10.1. The circle on the left represents the universe of all bank tellers, the circle on the right represents the universe of all feminists, and the shaded area represents all bank tellers who are feminists. Because some bank tellers are *not* feminists, the chances of being a bank teller (whether feminist or not) will always be greater than the chances of being a bank teller who is feminist.

Just to make sure that people were not interpreting "bank teller" to mean "bank teller who is not active in the feminist movement," Tversky and Kahneman (1982) ran additional experiments in which different groups of subjects were presented with a set of alternatives that included one of the alternatives from Item #1 but not the other (so that the two alternatives were never directly compared). Even in these experi-

Feminist bank tellers

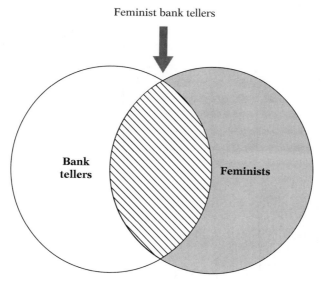

FIGURE 10.1

The overlapping worlds of bank tellers and feminists.

ments, subjects assigned a higher probability to Linda being a feminist bank teller than to Linda being a bank teller.

Tversky and Kahneman (1982) also found similar results with problems about "Bill" (who was thought more likely to be an accountant and jazz player than simply a jazz player), a Wimbledon tennis player (who was thought more likely to lose the first set but win the match than simply to lose the first set), and a former president of the United States (who was thought more likely to provide federal support for unwed mothers and to cut federal support to local governments than simply to provide federal support for unwed mothers).

From results such as these, Tversky and Kahneman (1982, p. 98) concluded: "As the amount of detail in a scenario increases, its probability can only decrease steadily, but its representativeness and hence its apparent likelihood may increase. The reliance on representativeness, we believe, is a primary reason for the unwarranted appeal of detailed scenarios and the illusory sense of insight that such constructions often provide. . . . For example, the hypothesis 'the defendant left the scene of the crime' may appear less plausible than the hypothesis 'the defendant left the scene of the crime for fear of being accused of murder,' although the latter account is less probable than the former."

This conclusion is further supported by the way that most people respond to Item #11 of the Reader Survey. This question asked which of the following two scenarios was more likely:

> **Scenario 1:** An all-out nuclear war between the United States and Russia
>
> **Scenario 2:** A situation in which neither country intends to attack the other side with nuclear weapons, but an all-out nuclear war between the United States and Russia is triggered by the actions of a third country such as Iraq, Libya, Israel, or Pakistan

As with the bank teller problem, most people feel that the more specific event (an all-out war triggered by a third country) is more probable than the more general event (an all-out war). Indeed, the Pentagon has spent decades developing war plans and procuring weapons to handle highly detailed but extremely improbable scenarios. According to Tversky and Kahneman, specific scenarios appear more likely than general ones because they are more representative of how we imagine particular events.

THE LAW OF SMALL NUMBERS

Another consequence of the representativeness heuristic is that people tend to believe in what Tversky and Kahneman (1971) call "the law of small numbers." The law of small numbers is a tongue-in-cheek reference to a law in statistics known as the law of large numbers (a law stating that the larger a sample you draw from a population, the closer its average will be to the population average). A belief in the law of *small* numbers is a belief that random samples of a population will resemble each other and the population more closely than statistical sampling theory would predict.

For example, when people are asked to write down a random sequence of coin tosses without actually flipping a coin, they often try to make the string look random at every point (Kahneman and Tversky, 1972, call this "local representativeness"). As a consequence, they tend to exclude long runs and include more alternations between Heads and Tails than you would normally find in a chance sequence. In a chance sequence, there are many points at which the series does not look random at all. To verify this fact, you can approximate a chance sequence by tossing a coin 100 times and recording the pattern of Heads and Tails.

An illustration of the law of small numbers is given in Item #15 of the Reader Survey. This problem comes from a study by Tversky and Kahneman (1971), and it runs as follows:

> The mean IQ of the population of eighth graders in a city is *known* to be 100. You have selected a random sample of 50 children for a study of educational achievements. The first child tested has an IQ of 150. What do you expect the mean IQ to be for the whole sample?

Most people answer that the mean IQ should still be 100, but in fact, the correct answer is that the average IQ should be 101. The correct answer is 101 because the first child has an IQ of 150 and the 49 remaining children have an expected IQ of 100 each. This makes a total of 5050 IQ points (150 + 4900) which, when divided by 50 children, comes out to an average expected IQ of 101.

If you answered 100 rather than 101, you probably assumed that there would be low IQ scores to "balance out" the high score of 150. Such a view implicitly assumes, however, that chance is self-correcting. Chance does *not* correct or cancel out high scores with correspondingly low scores; it merely "dilutes" high scores with additional scores that are closer to the average (in this case 100). Tversky and Kahneman (1971) have argued that the tendency to view chance as self-correcting is an example of a bias resulting from the representativeness heuristic, because samples are expected to be highly representative of their parent population.

In the same vein, Tversky and Kahneman (1971) proposed that the representativeness heuristic leads people to commit the "gambler's fallacy"—the belief that a successful outcome is due after a run of bad luck (or, more generally, the belief that a series of independent trials with the same outcome will soon be followed by an opposite outcome). Item #31 of the Reader Survey examined your tendency to commit the gambler's fallacy. You were asked:

> Suppose that an unbiased coin is flipped three times, and each time the coin lands on Heads. If you had to bet $100 on the next toss, what side would you choose?

Because the coin is unbiased, the normatively correct answer is that you should have no preference between Heads and Tails. Some people erroneously believe, however, that Tails is more probable after a run of three Heads. Tversky and Kahneman explain this answer in terms of the mistaken belief that chance sequences must be locally representative (i.e., that every part of the sequence must appear random).

THE HOT HAND

One of the most entertaining demonstrations of the law of small numbers was published by Thomas Gilovich, Robert Vallone, and Amos Tversky (1985). Instead of looking at coin tosses, these researchers examined people's perceptions of a "hot hand" in basketball. A player with a hot hand (also known as a "streak shooter" or an athlete "on a roll") is a player who has a better chance of making a basket after one or more successful shots than after having missed a shot.

What Gilovich, Vallone, and Tversky discovered is that Philadelphia 76er basketball fans—and several players and coaches as well—perceived streak shooting when statistical analyses showed that none existed. That is, people thought that the chances of making a basket increased after a player had made several successful shots, when in truth the chances of making the next basket were not significantly different from the player's overall probability of making a basket. Gilovich and his associates found the same results with free-throw records from the Boston Celtics and with laboratory experiments (or, more precisely, *gymnasium* experiments) on men and women from Cornell's varsity basketball teams.

For a short time, these findings created a national uproar in the sports community. How could Gilovich, Vallone, and Tversky say that streak shooting was simply an illusion? Anyone who has played or watched basketball *knows* that players are sometimes hot or cold! Basketball teams even alter their strategies in order to defend against streak shooters. The idea that basketball shots made by the same player are statistically unrelated seems very hard to swallow.

In order to find out why people strongly perceive streak shooting when successes and failures are statistically independent of one another, Gilovich, Vallone, and Tversky (1985) conducted an experiment in which subjects viewed six different series of X's and O's (which you might think of as "hits" or "misses" in a basketball game). Each series contained 11 X's and 10 O's, and the probability of alternating between the two letters was set at .40, .50, .60, .70, .80, or .90. For example, the string "XOXOXOOOXXOXOXOOXXXOX" represented an alternation probability of .70 (because it alternated between X and O on 14 of 20 possible alternations).

Gilovich, Vallone, and Tversky found that subjects selected the .70 and .80 sequences as the best examples of a chance series, rather than correctly selecting the .50 sequence. The sequence with a .50 probability of alternation was classified as a chance series by only 32 percent of the subjects. Indeed, 62 percent of the subjects classified the .50 sequence as "streak shooting."

To see how you would have performed on this task, take a look at your answer to Item #38 of the Reader Survey. The first string (XOXXXOOOOXOXXOOOXXXOX) alternates on half of all possible occasions (similar to what might be expected from a chance series). In contrast, the second sequence (XOXOXOOOXXOXOXOOXXXOX) represents an alternation probability of .70—far higher than the .50 expected by chance alone. If you thought that the first sequence contained runs that were too long to have been generated randomly, you were expecting too many alternations between X and O in the series (just as people do when they see "streak shooting" in chance sequences). Chapter 14 discusses the perception of randomness in greater detail.

NEGLECTING BASE RATES

In some instances, a reliance on representativeness leads people to ignore "base rate" information (a base rate is the relative frequency with which an event occurs). Kahneman and Tversky have demonstrated this tendency in a series of experiments. In one study, for example, Kahneman and Tversky (1973, p. 241) told subjects that:

> A panel of psychologists have [sic] interviewed and administered personality tests to 30 engineers and 70 lawyers, all successful in their respective fields. On the basis of this information, thumbnail descriptions of the 30 engineers and 70 lawyers have been written. You will find on your forms five descriptions, chosen at random from the 100 available descriptions. For each description, please indicate your probability that the person described is an engineer, on a scale from 0 to 100.

For example, here is a thumbnail description that Kahneman and Tversky intended to be fairly representative of an engineer:

> Jack is a 45-year-old man. He is married and has four children. He is generally conservative, careful, and ambitious. He shows no interest in political and social issues and spends most of his free time on his many hobbies which include home carpentry, sailing, and mathematical puzzles.

Using the same five thumbnail descriptions, Kahneman and Tversky also gave a second group of subjects identical instructions with the proportion of engineers and lawyers reversed (that is, 70 engineers and 30 lawyers), but because the results are comparable, we will focus exclusively on the condition with 30 engineers.

Once subjects rated the probability that each of the five people might be an engineer, they were asked to estimate the probability that someone randomly selected from the pool of 100 descriptions (a person about whom they were given no information) would be an engineer. Not surprisingly, on average subjects rated the chances that a randomly chosen person would be an engineer as roughly 30 percent. In other words, they used the base rate given in the problem.

On the other hand, when subjects were provided with descriptive information—even information that had nothing to do with being an engineer or lawyer—they tended to ignore base rates. For example, Kahneman and Tversky (1973) deliberately constructed the following portrait to be equally descriptive of an engineer or a lawyer:

> Dick is a 30-year-old man. He is married with no children. A man of high ability and high motivation, he promises to be quite successful in his field. He is well liked by his colleagues.

Such a description is entirely uninformative with respect to Dick's profession; consequently, the probability of being an engineer in this case should be equal to the base rate of 30 percent. Kahneman and Tversky (1973) found, however, that subjects given this description gave a median probability estimate of 50 percent. Apparently, subjects ignored the base rate information and simply judged the description as equally representative of an engineer or a lawyer.

A good deal of research has investigated the conditions under which people tend to use or neglect base rate information (Bar-Hillel, 1980, 1990; Fischhoff & Bar-Hillel, 1984; Osberg & Shrauger, 1986). For example, Icek Ajzen (1977) found that people often use base rate information when it is consistent with their intuitive theories of cause and effect. In one experiment, Ajzen asked subjects to predict a student's grade point average based on either causal factors (such as the number of hours per week the student studied) or noncausal information (such as the student's weekly income). Ajzen found that people used base rates more often when the information was causal than when it was not— even when they were told that the noncausal factors predicted grade point average just as well as the causal factors.

NONREGRESSIVE PREDICTION

People also tend to neglect the diagnosticity of the information on which they base their predictions, and as a result, they make "nonregressive" predictions. For example, Item #35 of the Reader Survey (based on a problem from Kahneman and Tversky, 1973) posed the following question:

> Suppose that scores on a high school academic achievement test are moderately related to college grade point averages (GPAs). Given the percentiles below [shown in Figure 10.2], what GPA would you predict for a student who scored 725 on the test?

How did you respond? Most people predict a GPA between 3.5 and 3.7 (a GPA highly "representative" of a 725 test score). This answer makes sense if the achievement test is perfectly diagnostic of a student's GPA. If there is an exact correspondence between test scores and GPAs, then a score of 725 would translate into a GPA of about 3.6. According to the problem, though, scores on the achievement test are *not* perfect predictors of GPA. The problem states that scores on the test are only "moderately related to college grade point average." Because test scores are only moderately predictive of GPA, the best GPA prediction lies between 3.6 and the average GPA of 2.5—thereby allowing for "regression to the mean."

FIGURE 10.2

The relationship between performance on an achievement test and grade point average. *(Taken from Item #35 of the Reader Survey.)*

Student Percentile	Achievement test	GPA
Top 10%	> 750	> 3.7
Top 20%	> 700	> 3.5
Top 30%	> 650	> 3.2
Top 40%	> 600	> 2.9
Top 50%	> 500	> 2.5

Regression to the mean is a statistical phenomenon in which high or low scores tend to be followed by more average scores, just as very tall parents tend to have children who are closer to average height. Because a test score of 725 is quite high, a student who is tested a second time would probably receive a score that is somewhat closer to the average of 500 (and, by the same logic, would have a correspondingly lower GPA). You can think of it this way: A GPA of 2.5 is the best guess if you have no information about the student, and a GPA of 3.6 is the best guess if high school achievement test scores correlate perfectly with college GPAs. Because test scores are only *moderately* predictive of GPAs, the best choice is somewhere between 2.5 and 3.6 (i.e., somewhat higher than the average, but not nearly as high as 3.6).

Most psychologists think of test scores as being made up of two independent components: the "true score" and "error." The true score is the score that a student would receive if the test were a perfect measure of ability, and the error component is the result of all the factors that have nothing to do with ability but nonetheless influence a particular test score (amount of sleep the previous night, blood sugar level, mood, lighting conditions, and so on). In most cases these factors tend to cancel each other out, but occasionally they combine so as to dramatically increase or decrease a test score. Because this fluctuation is independent of the true score, however, future test scores are likely to "regress" toward the true score.

The tendency to overlook regression can lead to critical errors in judgment. For example, Kahneman and Tversky (1973) discuss a case in which instructors in a flight school concluded that praising pilots for well-executed flight maneuvers caused a decline in subsequent performance. Does this decline mean that teachers should stop reinforcing successes? Not at all! On the basis of regression alone, outstanding performances will be followed by performances that are closer to the average. Likewise, poor performances that are punished will improve regardless of whether punishment is genuinely effective.

In their book on human inference, Richard Nisbett and Lee Ross (1980, pp. 163, 165) describe some additional consequences of misinterpreting regression:

> Such mislabeling of simple regression phenomena (whereby extremely good or bad performances will, on the average, be followed by less extreme performances whenever there is an element of chance in such performances) is common in everyday experience. One disconcerting implication of such mislabeling is that measures designed to stem a "crisis" (a sudden increase in crime, disease, or bankruptcies, or a sudden decrease in sales, rainfall, or Olympic gold medal winners) will, on the average, seem to have greater impact than there actually has been. . . . Superstitions about what one must change to end a "bad streak" of outcomes, or must *not* change for fear of ending a "good streak," will arise from the observation of simple regression phenomena.

George Gmelch (1978, August), a professional baseball player who later became a social science researcher, chronicled several examples of such superstition in an article entitled "Baseball Magic." According to Gmelch, the New York Giants refused to clean their uniforms during a 16-game winning streak for fear of "washing away" their good fortune. Similarly, Leo Durocher wore the same black shoes, grey slacks, blue coat, and knotted tie for three and a half weeks while the Brooklyn Dodgers clinched a pennant victory in 1941.

Regression toward the mean can also explain why highly successful athletes and teams tend to experience a drop in performance immediately after appearing on the cover of *Sports Illustrated* magazine. Athletes typically appear on the cover following an unusually good performance, and from regression alone, a decline in performance would be expected. The *"Sports Illustrated* Jinx," as it is known, is not a jinx at all—most likely, it is nothing more than regression to the mean.

CLINICAL VERSUS ACTUARIAL PREDICTION

The tendency people have to neglect information on base rates and diagnosticity contributes to a very surprising and embarrassing state of affairs. As documented in nearly 100 studies in the social sciences (Dawes, Faust, & Meehl, 1989), the accuracy of "actuarial" predictions (predictions based solely on empirical relations between a given set of variables and an outcome) is equal to or better than the accuracy of "clinical" predictions (predictions based on the judgment of human beings). In other words, contrary to common sense, predictions are usually more accurate when they are *not* made by a human decision maker—even when the decision maker has full access to actuarial information.

For example, in one study on clinical prediction, the judgments of 21 psychiatric staff members were compared with the weight of patients' compensation claim files in predicting readmission for psychiatric care (Lasky, Hover, Smith, Bostian, Duffendack, & Nord, 1959). The weight of claim files was used as a crude measure of past hospitalizations. As it turned out, staff judgments were not significantly more accurate in predicting readmission than were folder weights (the correlations were .62 and .61, respectively).

Apparently, the expertise of staff members and the advantage of having additional information were more than offset by other factors. Because clinical judges generally rely on heuristics such as representativeness—and are therefore susceptible to a variety of biases—their predictions are rarely more accurate than predictions based exclusively on actuarial relations.

CONCLUSION

Research on the representativeness heuristic suggests several ways to improve judgment and decision making skills, including the following tips:

- ✔ *Don't Be Misled by Highly Detailed Scenarios.*   The very specificity that makes detailed scenarios seem representative also lessens their likelihood. In general, the more specific a scenario is, the lower its chances are of occurring—even when the scenario seems perfectly representative of the most probable outcome.
- ✔ *Whenever Possible, Pay Attention to Base Rates.*   Base rates are particularly important when an event is very rare or very common. For example, because the base rate is so low, many talented applicants never get admitted to graduate school (and it would be a mistake to interpret nonadmission as indicating that an applicant lacks academic ability). Conversely, because the base rate is so high, many unskilled drivers are awarded a driver's license. When base rates are extreme, representativeness is often a fallible indicator of probability.
- ✔ *Remember That Chance Is Not Self-Correcting.*   A run of bad luck is just that: a run of bad luck. It does not mean that an equivalent run of good luck is bound to occur, and it does not mean that things are doomed to stay the same. If a chance process (like tossing an unbiased coin) has a certain probability of producing a certain outcome, past events will have no effect on future outcomes.
- ✔ *Don't Misinterpret Regression Toward the Mean.*   Even though a run of bad luck is not necessarily balanced by a run of good luck (or vice versa), extreme performances tend to be followed by more

average performances. Regression toward the mean is typical whenever an outcome depends in part upon chance factors. Every once in awhile these factors combine to produce an unusual performance, but on subsequent occasions, performance usually returns to normal.

By keeping these suggestions in mind, it is possible to avoid many of the biases that result from a reliance on the representativeness heuristic. Chapter 11 focuses on another well-known heuristic, "availability," and the biases that often result from it.

CHAPTER 11

THE AVAILABILITY HEURISTIC

According to Amos Tversky and Daniel Kahneman (1974, p. 1127), the availability heuristic is a rule of thumb in which decision makers "assess the frequency of a class or the probability of an event by the ease with which instances or occurrences can be brought to mind." Usually this heuristic works quite well; all things being equal, common events are easier to remember or imagine than are uncommon events. By relying on availability to estimate frequency and probability, decision makers are able to simplify what might otherwise be very difficult judgments.

As with any heuristic, however, there are cases in which the general rule of thumb breaks down and leads to systematic biases. Some events are more available than others *not* because they tend to occur frequently or with high probability, but because they are inherently easier to think about, because they have taken place recently, because they are highly emotional, and so forth. This chapter examines three general questions: (1) What are instances in which the availability heuristic leads to biased judgments? (2) Do decision makers perceive an event as more likely after they have imagined it happening? (3) How is vivid information different from other information?

AVAILABILITY GOES AWRY

Which is a more likely cause of death in the United States—being killed by falling airplane parts or by a shark? Most people rate shark attacks as more probable than death from falling airplane parts (see Item #7 of the Reader Survey for your answer). Shark attacks certainly receive more publicity than do deaths from falling airplane parts, and they are far easier to imagine (thanks in part to movies such as *Jaws*). Yet the chances of dying from falling airplane parts are 30 times greater than the chances of being killed by a shark (Death Odds, 1990, September 24). In this case, availability is a misleading indicator of frequency.

Item #8 of the Reader Survey contains additional comparisons that many people find surprising (taken from Combs & Slovic, 1979). For instance, contrary to the relatively scarce media coverage they receive, diabetes and stomach cancer kill roughly *twice* as many Americans annually as homicide or car accidents, and lightning claims more lives than tornadoes do. According to Tversky and Kahneman, these kinds of statistics are counterintuitive because most people estimate the frequency of an event by how easy it is to bring instances of the event to mind. Because car accidents, tornadoes, and murders are all headline grabbers, they are more "available" than higher frequency causes of death such as stomach cancer, lightning, and diabetes.

Availability can also lead to biased judgments when examples of one event are inherently more difficult to generate than examples of another. For instance, Tversky and Kahneman (1973) asked people the following question: In a typical sample of text in the English language, is it more likely that a word starts with the letter K or that K is its third letter (not counting words with less than three letters)? Of the 152 people who were asked questions such as this, 105 generally thought that words with the letter in the first position were more probable. In truth, however, there are approximately twice as many words with K in the third position as there are words that begin with it. Because it is easier to generate words that start with K than have K as the third letter, most people overestimate the relative frequency of these words.

Still another way that availability can lead to biases is when one type of outcome is easier to visualize than another. Item #37 of the Reader Survey illustrates this kind of bias:

Consider the two structures, A and B, which are displayed below.

Structure A: Structure B:

X X X X X X X X   X X
X X X X X X X X   X X
X X X X X X X X   X X
                                        X X
                                        X X
                                        X X
                                        X X
                                        X X
                                        X X

A *path* is a line that connects an X in the top row of a structure to an X in the bottom row by passing through one (and only one) X in each row. In other words, a path connects three X's in Structure A (one in each of the three rows) and nine X's in Structure B (one in each of the nine rows).

(a) In which of the two structures are there more paths?
(b) Approximately how many paths are in Structure A? Structure B?

Most people find it easier to visualize paths running through Structure A than Structure B, and as a consequence, they guess that Structure A contains more paths than Structure B. Of the respondents who Tversky and Kahneman (1973) presented with a version of this problem, 85 percent thought there were more paths in Structure A than Structure B. The median estimates they gave were 40 paths in Structure A and 18 paths in Structure B.

In reality, both structures contain the same number of paths. In Structure A, there are eight elements to choose from in the top row, eight in the middle row, and eight in the third row. This yields $8 \times 8 \times 8$ (or 512) possible combinations. In Structure B, there are $2 \times 2 \times 2 \times 2 \times 2 \times 2 \times 2 \times 2 \times 2$ potential combinations, which also comes out to a total of 512 paths. Thus, both structures have an equal number of paths, even though the paths in Structure A are easier to see than those in Structure B (the paths in Structure A are more distinctive than the paths in Structure B because, on the average, two paths in Structure A share only about one-eighth of their elements, whereas two paths in Structure B overlap in half of their elements).

AN IMAGINATIVE STUDY

In 1978, John Carroll published a study that linked the availability heuristic with the act of imagining an event. Carroll reasoned that if easily imagined events are judged to be probable, then perhaps the very act of imagining an event will increase its availability and make it appear more likely. He tested this hypothesis in two experiments.

In the first experiment, conducted one day before the American presidential election in 1976, subjects were asked to imagine watching televised coverage of the presidential election results either the night of the election or the following morning. Roughly half the experimental subjects were told to imagine that:

> Ford wins the election as Carter fails to hold some key states and Ford wins much of the Midwest and West. He wins 316 electoral votes to Carter's 222, and a listing of states and electoral votes under columns for Carter and Ford shows Ford with 32 states and Carter with 18 states and the District of Columbia.

The remaining experimental subjects were instructed to imagine that:

> Carter wins the election as his strength in the South and East builds an insurmountable lead that Ford's near sweep of the West cannot overtake. He wins 342 electoral votes to Ford's 196, with 28 states and the District of Columbia to 22 states for Ford.

These scenarios were constructed using the most up-to-date polls at the time of the study, and subjects were asked not only to imagine that the scenario they were given was true, but to imagine the winner's victory speech and the loser's concession of defeat. Thus, the overall image was intended to be as plausible and as vivid as possible. Then, after subjects had imagined a particular outcome, Carroll asked them to predict how they thought the election would actually turn out.

The results showed that subjects who imagined Carter winning believed that Carter would win, and subjects who imagined Ford winning believed that Ford would win. According to Carroll, imagining a given outcome made that outcome more available and increased subsequent probability estimates that it would occur.

In the second experiment, Carroll (1978) asked University of Pittsburgh students to imagine either that their football team did well during the 1977 season or that it did poorly (Pittsburgh won the national championship in 1976, but the coach and several top players did not stay on in 1977). Although the results of the second experiment were not uniformly positive, there was again some indication that imagining an outcome made it seem more likely. For example, of the 35 subjects who imagined Pittsburgh having a good season, 63 percent predicted a major bowl bid in the 1977 season, but of the 38 subjects who imagined Pittsburgh having a poor season, only 40 percent did so. On the whole, then, Carroll was able to conclude that imagining an outcome made it appear more likely, and, since the time of his study, several other researchers have replicated and extended this finding (Anderson, 1983; Gregory, Cialdini, & Carpenter, 1982).

THE LIMITS OF IMAGINATION

What if an outcome is difficult to imagine? If a decision maker tries unsuccessfully to imagine an outcome, does the perceived likelihood of that outcome increase or decrease? In 1985, Jim Sherman, Robert Cialdini, Donna Schwartzman, and Kim Reynolds published a study that examined this question.

Sherman and his associates asked subjects to read about one of two diseases that were reported to be growing in prevalence on campus. Both diseases were referred to as "Hyposcenia-B," but they were described differently depending upon the experimental condition. In the "easy-to-imagine" conditions, subjects read about a disease with concrete symptoms such as muscle aches, low energy level, and frequent severe headaches. In the "difficult-to-imagine" conditions, subjects read about a disease with abstract symptoms such as a vague sense of disorientation, a malfunctioning nervous system, and an inflamed liver.

Subjects in the control groups simply read the description they were given of Hyposcenia-B—whether easy or difficult to imagine—and judged how likely they were to contract the disease in the future. Subjects in the experimental groups, on the other hand, were asked to read about the disease "with an eye toward imagining a three-week period during which they contracted and experienced the symptoms of the disease." Experimental subjects were also asked to write detailed descriptions of how they thought they would feel during these three weeks.

Sherman and his colleagues found that control subjects were not significantly influenced by how easy the symptoms were to imagine, but experimental subjects were strongly affected. Experimental subjects in the easy-to-imagine condition thought they were relatively *more* likely to contract the disease, but those in the difficult-to-imagine condition actually rated themselves as *less* likely to contract the disease than did control subjects who never imagined the disease. Sherman et al. (1985) concluded that imagining an outcome does not guarantee that it will appear more likely; if an outcome is difficult to envision, the attempt to imagine it may actually reduce the perceived likelihood that it will occur.

DENIAL

Another case in which imagining an event may not increase its apparent likelihood is when the outcome is extremely negative. Some events are so upsetting that the very act of contemplating them leads to denial that they might occur (Rothbart, 1970).

For many people, the most extreme example of such an event is nuclear war. In 1989, I published a study in which approximately 2000 people were asked to estimate the chances of a nuclear war within the next ten years. Although Chapter 13 will examine this study in detail, there are two findings relevant to availability. First, asking people to vividly imagine what a nuclear war would be like (i.e., increasing "outcome availability") had no significant effect on how likely they judged nuclear war to be. Second, asking them to consider the likelihood of various paths to nuclear war (i.e., increasing "path availability") had an equally insignificant effect on probability estimates. The latter finding is especially surprising in light of several studies that have documented the importance of path availability (Hoch, 1984; Levi & Pryor, 1987; Ross, Lepper, Strack, & Steinmetz, 1977; Sherman, Zehner, Johnson, & Hirt, 1983).

What may have happened is that the event subjects were asked to imagine—which included the incineration of close friends and family members—was so aversive as to elicit a feeling of denial that nuclear war could ever occur. If so, then this denial may have canceled out the effect of increased availability, leaving probability estimates unchanged. Thus, if the prospect of an event is so horrifying that it leads to denial, then imagining its occurrence may not make it seem more likely.

VIVIDNESS

A close cousin of availability is vividness. Vividness usually refers to how concrete or imaginable something is, although occasionally it can have other meanings. Sometimes vividness refers to how emotionally interesting or exciting something is, or how close something is in space or time. A number of studies have shown that decision makers are affected more strongly by vivid information than by pallid, abstract, or statistical information (Nisbett & Ross, 1980).

For example, Eugene Borgida and Richard Nisbett (1977) published a study that contrasted the effectiveness of a statistical summary of college course evaluations and a more vivid form of presenting such evaluations. The subjects in their experiment, mostly prospective psychology majors at the University of Michigan, were assigned to one of three experimental conditions: (1) a *base rate* condition, in which they read through a statistical summary of 5-point course evaluations from "practically all the students who had enrolled in the course during the previous semester"; (2) a *face-to-face* condition, in which subjects heard between one and four student panelists evaluate the 10 courses (these panelists prefaced their remarks with 5-point ratings that were, on average, equal to the ratings given in the base rate condition); and (3) a *no evaluation* control condition, in which they neither heard nor read any evaluations of the courses. Then, after either reading the statistical summary or listening to the panel presentation (or, in the case of the control group, receiving no evaluation at all), students were asked to indicate which of 27 college courses they were likely to take in the future.

Because the base rate condition included a nearly exhaustive summary of student evaluations, the most "logical" result would have been for base rate subjects to follow course recommendations more often than face-to-face subjects. As shown in Table 11.1, however, Borgida and Nisbett found just the opposite. Subjects were more persuaded by a few other students talking in a panel presentation than by a comprehensive statistical summary of course evaluations. In fact, subjects in the base rate condition did not plan to take significantly more of the recommended courses or fewer of the nonrecommended courses than subjects in the control group. Only subjects in the face-to-face condition differed from subjects in the control group. Students in the face-to-face condition indicated that they would take an average of 1.4 more recommended courses and 0.9 fewer nonrecommended courses than students in the control condition.

These results show that a handful of individual testimonials can outweigh comprehensive statistical summaries. As many new car buyers are aware, vivid stories about one person's lemon can quickly erode the confidence that might otherwise come from reading an endorsement in *Consumer Reports* (Nisbett, Borgida, Crandall, & Reed, 1976). Similarly, particularly vivid crimes or terrorist actions can overshadow crime statistics and other summary reports. Because vivid information is more "available" and easier to recall than pallid information, it often has a disproportionate influence on judgments.

TABLE 11.1
THE POWER OF VIVID TESTIMONIALS

Condition	Recommended Courses	Nonrecommended Courses
Face-to-face	4.73	.50
No evaluation (control)	3.33	1.39
Base rate	4.11	.94

Note: This table is adapted from a study by Eugene Borgida and Richard Nisbett (1977). Students in the face-to-face condition planned to take significantly more recommended courses and fewer nonrecommended courses than did students in the control condition, but students in the base rate condition did not differ significantly from control subjects.

THE LEGAL SIGNIFICANCE OF GUACAMOLE

The power of vivid information is widely appreciated by advertising executives, politicians, and many other "professional persuaders." One area in which vividness can be absolutely pivotal is a court of law. Robert Reyes, Bill Thompson, and Gordon Bower (1980) illustrated this point in a study on the way that vivid information influences mock jury decisions. The experiment took place over two sessions.

In the first session, subjects read about a court case involving drunk driving. The defendant had run a stop sign while driving home from a Christmas party and had collided with a garbage truck. The defendant's blood alcohol level had not been tested at the time, and he was now being tried on the basis of circumstantial evidence. The defense was arguing that the defendant had not been legally drunk.

After reading a brief description of the defendant's character, subjects were presented with nine written arguments by the defense about why the defendant was innocent, and nine written arguments by the prosecution about why the defendant was guilty. Each of these 18 statements contained one piece of evidence, and each was presented in either a pallid style or a vivid style. For example, the pallid version of one of the prosecution's arguments went like this:

> On his way out the door, Sanders [the defendant] staggered against a serving table, knocking a bowl to the floor.

The vivid version of the same information went as follows:

> On his way out the door, Sanders staggered against a serving table, knocking a bowl of guacamole dip to the floor and splattering guacamole on the white shag carpet.

Similarly, a pallid argument for the defense went like this:

> The owner of the garbage truck admitted under cross-examination that his garbage truck is difficult to see at night because it is grey in color.

The vivid version stated the same information but added:

> The owner said his trucks are grey "Because it hides the dirt," and he said, "What do you want, I should paint them pink?"

Roughly half the subjects were given vivid arguments by the defense and pallid statements by the prosecution, and the remaining subjects received vivid arguments by the prosecution and pallid arguments by the defense.

After reading all 18 statements, subjects were asked to make three judgments: (1) How drunk do you think Sanders was at the time of the accident? (2) What is your personal opinion about Sanders' innocence or guilt? (3) If you were a member of a jury obligated to follow the rule of "guilty beyond a reasonable doubt," what would your verdict be? (These three judgments were later averaged to form one overall index of how guilty subjects thought Sanders was.) This ended the first session, and subjects were asked to return forty-eight hours later for the second part of the experiment.

When subjects arrived for the second session, they were asked to write brief descriptions of as many of the 18 arguments as they could remember. They were also asked to indicate their current opinion on the same three questions they had answered at the end of the first session. The instructions explained that subjects did not need to answer the same way they had during the first session, and that they should make their judgments as though they "were deciding the case now for the first time."

What Reyes, Thompson, and Bower found is that vividness had no significant effect on judgments of guilt during the first session, when subjects had just finished reading the 18 arguments, but that it had a substantial effect forty-eight hours later. Subjects in the vivid prosecution condition later judged the defendant to be significantly more guilty than did subjects in the pallid prosecution condition. Reyes, Thompson, and Bower (1980) explained this delayed effect in terms of vivid information being easier to remember than pallid information. Thus, as in the case of Borgida and Nisbett (1977), vivid information ultimately had more influence than pallid information, presumably because it was relatively more available, or easier to retrieve.

A DISCLAIMER

As convincing as these results are, it is worth noting that one prominent review of research on the "vividness effect" found relatively little support for the hypothesis that vivid information is more influential than pallid information. In an exhaustive review of laboratory studies on the vividness effect, Shelley Taylor and Suzanne Thompson (1982, p. 178) found that most research had turned up mixed results or no vividness effect whatsoever, and they therefore concluded that, at least with respect to laboratory research, the vividness effect was "weak if existent at all."

This conclusion should certainly temper any judgments concerning the superior impact of vivid information. At the same time, there are several reasons to suspect that the vividness effect exists in at least some situations. First, Taylor and Thompson noted a number of exceptions to their general conclusion. For example, they found that case histories were often more persuasive than statistical or abstract information, and that, under certain conditions, videotaped presentations were more persuasive than written or oral presentations. Second, as Taylor and Thompson were well aware, there are many ways to explain the *absence* of a research finding. The failure to find a vividness effect in a given experiment can be explained just as well by flaws in the experiment as by a true absence of the vividness effect, and in several studies vividness was confounded with other factors. Finally, and again pointed out by Taylor and Thompson themselves, there is reason to believe that laboratory settings work against the vividness effect by focusing attention on material that people might normally ignore. Hence, laboratory research may seriously underestimate the impact of vivid material in daily life.

In the last analysis, then, it seems likely that the vividness effect exists in at least some situations, but that its size and scope are limited. Also, in keeping with the availability heuristic, vivid examples of an event may increase probability and frequency estimates more than pallid examples.

CONCLUSION

In many cases, the availability heuristic provides reasonably accurate estimates of frequency and probability. In some situations, though, the availability heuristic can lead to critical biases in judgment. For example, public health depends on an awareness of mortality rates from dread diseases such as stomach cancer. If the incidence of these diseases is underestimated, people will be less likely to take preventive measures (Kristiansen, 1983). Similarly, if vivid but infrequent causes of death are overestimated, attention and funding may be diverted from more common dangers. Some writers have suggested, for example, that Americans overestimate the danger of terrorist attacks during travel abroad (Paulos, 1986, November 24).

One way to correct this problem is by explicitly comparing over- and underestimated dangers with threats that are misperceived in the opposite direction. For example, the American Cancer Society might launch a public information campaign that compares the mortality rate from stomach cancer with death rates from highly publicized dangers, such as homicide or car accidents. Billboards might declare: "THIS YEAR,

MORE PEOPLE WILL DIE FROM STOMACH CANCER THAN FROM CAR ACCIDENTS." Such a comparison would undoubtedly lead people to see stomach cancer as a more common cause of death than they had thought (although it may also have the unwanted effect of reducing frequency estimates of traffic fatalities). Travel agents use the same strategy when they promote tourism by pointing out that travelers stand a greater chance of dying in a traffic accident overseas than being killed in a terrorist plot.

When it comes to probability and frequency estimates, no heuristic is more central than the availability heuristic. Nonetheless, it is important to keep in mind that the availability heuristic is only one factor influencing probability and frequency judgments. Chapter 12 discusses several other factors that affect probability estimates, and it offers a number of suggestions on how to minimize common sources of bias.

CHAPTER 12

PROBABILITY AND RISK*

Probability and risk are everywhere: in the brakes of our cars, in the clouds above our heads, in the food we eat, and in the trust we place in others. Yet risk is often difficult to quantify, and even very basic problems in probability can be extremely challenging. Consider, for example, the infamous "game show problem" discussed by columnist Marilyn vos Savant (1990, September 9, p. 13):

> Suppose you're on a game show, and you're given the choice of three doors: Behind one door is a car; behind the others, goats. You pick a door, say No. 1, and the host, who knows what's behind the doors, opens another door, say No. 3, which has a goat. He then says to you, "Do you want to pick door No. 2?" Is it to your advantage to switch your choice?

Before reading further, take a guess at the answer. No

Many people respond that it makes no difference whether you switch doors. They reason that there are only two doors left after the host has opened one, and that the car is equally likely to be behind either of these doors. This is not, however, the correct answer.

The correct answer is that you should switch doors. As vos Savant explains:

> When you first choose door No. 1 from among the three, there's a 1/3 chance that the prize is behind that one and a 2/3 chance that it's behind one of the others. *But then the host steps in and gives you a clue.* If the prize is behind No. 2, the host shows you No. 3; and if the prize is behind No. 3, the host shows you No. 2. So when you switch, you win if the prize is behind No. 2 *or* No. 3. *YOU WIN EITHER WAY!* But if you *don't* switch, you win only if the prize is behind door No. 1.

(See Table 12.1 for an overview of outcomes.)

1/3

CONFUSION OF THE INVERSE

Here is another difficult problem: Suppose you are a physician who has just examined a woman for breast cancer. The woman has a lump in her breast, but based on many years of experience, you estimate the odds of

---

*Portions of this chapter are adapted from Plous (1991).

131

TABLE 12.1

OUTCOMES IN THE GAME SHOW PROBLEM

Car is in:	You choose:	Host opens:	You switch to:	Result:
Door 1	Door 1	Door 2 or 3	Door 2 or 3	You Lose
Door 1	Door 2	Door 3	Door 1	You Win
Door 1	Door 3	Door 2	Door 1	You Win
Door 2	Door 1	Door 3	Door 2	You Win
Door 2	Door 2	Door 1 or 3	Door 1 or 3	You Lose
Door 2	Door 3	Door 1	Door 2	You Win
Door 3	Door 1	Door 2	Door 3	You Win
Door 3	Door 2	Door 1	Door 3	You Win
Door 3	Door 3	Door 1 or 2	Door 1 or 2	You Lose

Note: This table shows that if you switch doors in the game show problem, you will win a car in six of nine possible outcomes (adapted from Selvin, 1975, February). Thus, switching is a better strategy than not switching.

a malignancy as 1 in 100. Just to be safe, though, you order a mammogram. A mammogram is an X-ray test that accurately classifies roughly 80 percent of malignant tumors and 90 percent of benign tumors.

The test report comes back, and much to your surprise, the consulting radiologist believes that the breast mass is malignant.

Question: Given your prior view that the chances of a malignancy were only 1 percent, and given test results that are 80 or 90 percent reliable, what would you say the overall chances of a malignancy are now? (Do not continue reading until you have formed an opinion.)

According to David Eddy (1982), 95 of 100 physicians who were asked this question estimated the probability of cancer given a positive test to be about 75 percent. In reality, though, the normatively correct answer is only 7 or 8 percent—a tenth of the typical answer found by Eddy. Apparently, physicians assumed that the chances of *cancer* given a *positive test result* were roughly equal to the chances of a *positive test result* given *cancer*. Decision researcher Robyn Dawes calls this mistake "confusion of the inverse."

To see why the correct answer should be only 7 to 8 percent, it is necessary to understand a fairly subtle rule of probability called "Bayes' theorem." According to Bayes' theorem, the correct way to estimate the odds of cancer given positive test results is as follows:

$$p(\text{cancer} \mid \text{positive}) = \frac{p(\text{positive} \mid \text{cancer})p(\text{cancer})}{p(\text{positive} \mid \text{cancer})p(\text{cancer}) + p(\text{positive} \mid \text{benign})p(\text{benign})}$$

The way to read "p(cancer)" is "the probability of cancer," and the way to read "p(cancer|positive)" is "the probability of cancer given that the test results are positive." The former quantity is a *simple* probability, and the latter is a *conditional* probability.

The probability on the left side of the equation is the quantity Eddy asked physicians to estimate, and the quantities on the right side of the equation were given in the problem as:

p(cancer) = .01 [the original estimate of a 1 percent chance of cancer]

p(benign) = .99 [the chances of not having cancer]

p(positive|cancer) = .80 [an 80 percent chance of a positive test result given cancer]

p(positive|benign) = .10 [a 10 percent chance of falsely identifying a benign tumor as malignant]

Once these values are known, it is a simple matter to plug them into the equation and calculate the conditional probability of cancer given a positive test result:

$$p(\text{cancer} \mid \text{positive}) = \frac{(.80)(.01)}{(.80)(.01) + (.10)(.99)} = \frac{.008}{.107} = .075 = 7.5 \text{ percent}$$

These results come as a surprise to many people, but what is equally surprising is the way that the physicians in Eddy's study reacted when they were informed of their mistake. In the words of Eddy (1982, p. 254):

> The erring physicians usually report that they assumed that the probability of cancer given that the patient has a positive X-ray . . . was approximately equal to the probability of a positive X-ray in a patient with cancer. . . . The latter probability is the one measured in clinical research programs and is very familiar, but it is the former probability that is needed for clinical decision making. It seems that many if not most physicians confuse the two.

Although confusion of the inverse is by no means limited to physicians, there are very few areas in which it is more important than medical diagnoses. In the event that life and death decisions must be made, there is little solace in answering the wrong question correctly.

What should you do in such a situation if using Bayes' theorem is impractical? The answer is to pay close attention to what statisticians call the "prior probability." The prior probability is the best probability estimate of an event before a new piece of information (e.g., a mammogram result) is known. In the breast cancer problem, the prior probability is the original estimate of a 1 percent chance of cancer. Because the prior probability is extremely low and the mammogram test is only 80 to 90 percent reliable, the postmammogram estimate should not be much higher than the prior probability. The same principle is true with virtually any outcome that is initially thought to be extremely improbable (or probable) and is "updated" with a somewhat unreliable piece of information. According to normative rules such as Bayes' theorem, the absolute difference between the revised probability and the prior probability should not be large.

IT'LL NEVER HAPPEN TO ME

Probability estimates are also influenced by the "valence" of an outcome (that is, the degree to which an outcome is viewed as positive or negative). Since the early 1950s, scores of studies have documented that, all things being equal, positive outcomes are viewed as more probable than negative outcomes (Blascovich, Ginsburg, & Howe, 1975; Crandall, Solomon, & Kellaway, 1955; Irwin, 1953; Irwin & Metzger, 1966; Irwin & Snodgrass, 1966; Marks, 1951; Pruitt & Hoge, 1965). This finding holds whether people are asked to rate the probability of an outcome occurring, guess which of two outcomes will occur, or bet on a given outcome occurring, and it persists even when there are financial incentives for accuracy (though the effect is somewhat diminished).

A straightforward demonstration of this bias was published by David Rosenhan and Samuel Messick in 1966. Rosenhan and Messick used a series of 150 cards with line drawings of either a smiling face or a frowning face (see Figure 12.1). In one experimental condition, 70 percent of the cards showed a smiling face and 30 percent showed a frowning face, and in another, 70 percent showed a frowning face and 30 percent showed a smiling face. The task for subjects was simply to guess on each of the 150 trials whether the card would show a smiling face or a frowning face when it was turned over.

Rosenhan and Messick found that when 70 percent of the cards had smiling faces, subjects were quite accurate. Over the course of the experiment, subjects predicted a smiling face on 68.2 percent of the trials. On the other hand, when 70 percent of the cards showed a frowning face, subjects predicted a frown on only 57.5 percent of the trials—significantly less than 70 percent. Thus, the valence of the dominant outcome influenced estimates of the probability of that outcome.

This is not a trivial finding limited to smiling faces. The same result is found when people are asked to predict the chances of positive or negative events in their lives. For example, Neil Weinstein (1980) documented this tendency in a study of Cook College students at Rutgers University. Weinstein asked students the following question: *Compared to other Cook students—same sex as you—what do you think are the chances that the following events will happen to you?* Students were given a list of 18 positive life events and 24 negative life events, and they

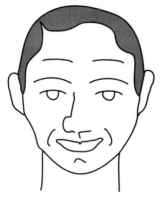

FIGURE 12.1

These are the stimuli used by David Rosenhan and Samuel Messick (1966) in their study of probability estimation.

were asked to indicate in percentages how likely they were (relative to other students) to experience the events.

Weinstein found that on the average, students rated themselves as 15 percent more likely than others to experience positive events and 20 percent less likely to experience negative events. To take some extreme examples, they rated themselves as 42 percent more likely to receive a good starting salary after graduation, 44 percent more likely to own their own home, 58 percent less likely to develop a drinking problem, and 38 percent less likely to have a heart attack before the age of 40. If you are a college student, you can compare these estimates with your own ratings in answer to Items #5a to #5d of the Reader Survey.

COMPOUND EVENTS

In probability theory, single events are known as "simple" events, and multiple events are known as "compound" events. For example, a one-stage lottery is a simple event, and a two-stage lottery (in which you must win the drawing in each stage to win the whole lottery) is a compound event. If the compound event is of the form A *and* B (e.g., winning *both* stages of a lottery), the event is called "conjunctive." If the compound event is of the form A *or* B (e.g., winning *either* stage of a lottery), the event is called "disjunctive." When it comes to estimating the probability of compound events, the difficulties people normally have in judging probabilities are complicated even further.

To begin with, people often overestimate the probability of conjunctive events. John Cohen, E. I. Chesnick, and D. Haran (1971) illustrated this tendency by asking subjects to estimate the probability of several multi-stage lotteries. When the lottery involved two stages, each with equally likely outcomes, subjects gave an average estimate of 45 percent—nearly twice the correct answer (if you think of this lottery as two tosses of an unbiased coin, it is clear that any particular outcome, such as Heads-Heads, has a 1/2 × 1/2, or 1/4, chance of occurring). Similarly, subjects overestimated the probability of a given outcome in a five-alternative, two-stage lottery as 30 percent, rather than 1 in 25 (1/5 × 1/5).

These are sizable overestimates, but they pale in comparison to the overestimates that Cohen, Chesnick, and Haran found when the lottery involved several stages and several alternatives. For instance, subjects set the odds of a given outcome in an eight-alternative, eight-stage lottery as 1 in 20. This estimate is almost one million times too high!

The tendency to overestimate the probability of conjunctive events is especially important when people are asked to estimate the probability that a complex system will function properly. For example, suppose you were able to build a ballistic missile defense that depended on the successful performance of 500 independent parts or subsystems (with current technology, an actual ballistic defense system would require many *thousands* of independent parts), and suppose that each part or subsystem were 99 percent reliable when used the very first time. What are the chances that such a system would work on its first attempt?

The answer, which surprises many people, is less than 1 percent.

Why does this figure seem so low? As Chapter 13 will explore in greater detail, decision makers tend to get "anchored," or stuck, on the probabilities of simple events that make up a compound event (in this case, each simple event has a probability of .99). Once decision makers have these probabilities fixed in mind, they fail to adjust sufficiently for the large number of simple events that must *all* occur in order for the conjunctive event to take place. Thus, the probability of conjunctive events is overestimated most when the event is comprised of many simple events. Furthermore, the same principle applies in the *underestimation* of disjunctive events. When disjunctive events are comprised of many low probability events, people tend to underestimate the probability that at least one of these events will occur. For example, people often underestimate the probability of at least one pregnancy occurring over several years of contraceptive use (Shaklee & Fischhoff, 1990).

Maya Bar-Hillel (1973) has documented the tendency decision makers have to overestimate the probability of conjunctive events and underestimate the probability of disjunctive events. Bar-Hillel asked subjects to choose between simple bets (such as drawing a colored marble randomly from an urn that contained 2 colored marbles and 18 white marbles) and compound bets (such as consecutively drawing 4 colored marbles from an urn with 10 colored marbles and 10 white marbles, replacing the marble after each drawing). Subjects were presented with four or five pairs of bets (made up of one simple bet and

FIGURE 12.2

Maya Bar-Hillel (1973) found that people prefer compound bets over equally probable simple bets when the compound events are conjunctive. For example, people prefer trying to draw a colored marble from the right-hand urn four times in a row rather than drawing a colored marble once from the urn on the left. In contrast, people prefer simple bets over equally probable compound bets when the compound events are disjunctive (see text).

one compound bet) and were told that one of their preferred bets would be randomly chosen and played for money after the experiment (so as to motivate subjects to do their very best).

Bar-Hillel found that, given bets with roughly the same expected value, people favored compound bets when the events were conjunctive and simple bets when the events were disjunctive. For instance, when presented with the pair of bets mentioned above, 12 of 15 subjects chose the conjunctive four-marble bet (which has a win probability of .06) over the simple one-marble bet (which has a win probability of .10). At the same time, when the compound bet was disjunctive (meaning that a bet was won if any of the drawn marbles were colored), 14 of 20 subjects chose a simple one-marble bet (with a .70 win probability) over a compound six-marble bet (in which the chances of drawing a colored marble were .20, and the overall chance of drawing a colored marble at least once in six tries was .74). These results suggest that people systematically overestimate the likelihood of conjunctive events and underestimate the likelihood of disjunctive events (see also Barclay & Beach, 1972; Wyer, 1976).

CONSERVATISM

To make matters worse, once people have formed a probability estimate, they are often quite slow to change the estimate when presented
with new information. This slowness to revise prior probability estimates is known as "conservatism" (Phillips & Edwards, 1966). Conservatism is the tendency to change previous probability estimates more
slowly than warranted by new data. Most often, slowness is defined relative to the amount of change prescribed by normative rules such as
Bayes' theorem (Hogarth, 1975).

   Consider, for example, Item #29 of the Reader Survey, which was
modeled after a problem proposed by Ward Edwards (1968):

> Imagine two urns filled with millions of poker chips. In the first urn, 70
> percent of the chips are red and 30 percent are blue. In the second urn,
> 70 percent are blue and 30 percent are red. Suppose one of the urns is
> chosen randomly and a dozen chips are drawn from it: eight red chips
> and four blue chips. What are the chances that the chips came from the
> urn with mostly red chips? (Give your answer as a percentage.)

   If you are like most people, you guessed that the chances are around
70 or 80 percent. In essence, you revised an initial probability of .50 (an
urn "chosen randomly") to .70 or .80 in light of having drawn more red
chips than blue chips. According to Bayes' theorem, however, the correct answer should be a whopping 97 percent (see Edwards, 1968, for
details). Most people revise their probability estimates far more conser-
vatively than warranted by the data. In fact, Edwards (1968, p. 18) has
argued that: "A convenient first approximation to the data would say
that it takes anywhere from two to five observations to do one observation's worth of work in inducing the subject to change his opinions."*

THE PERCEPTION OF RISK

Smoking causes more than one out of every six deaths in the United
States (Hilts, 1990, September 26). On the average, a male smoker
who deeply inhales cigarette smoke reduces his life expectancy by 8.6
years, and a female smoker who deeply inhales cigarette smoke loses
4.6 years (Cohen & Lee, 1979). By one estimate, smoking only 1.4
cigarettes increases the odds of death by the same amount as living
within 20 miles of a nuclear power plant for 150 years (Wilson, 1979,
February).

---

   *It should be noted, though, that in some instances people are "anticonservative" (that
is, they jump to conclusions on the basis of insufficient evidence). Future research might
fruitfully explore the conditions under which conservatism and anticonservatism are most
likely to occur.

These statistics illustrate some different ways that the very same risk can be described. Perceptions of risk are highly subjective, and the value people place on preventive behaviors depends in part upon the way a particular risk is presented and the type of risk it is (Stone & Yates, 1991). For example, Chauncey Starr has argued that people are willing to accept far greater "voluntary" risks (e.g., risks from smoking or skiing) than "involuntary" risks (e.g., risks from electric power generation). As Starr (1969, p. 1235) puts it: "We are loathe to let others do unto us what we happily do to ourselves." Although this generalization does not always hold (Fischhoff, Lichtenstein, Slovic, Derby, & Keeney, 1981), there are certainly many cases in which it is true.

Risk perception is an exceedingly important topic—a topic that will only become more critical as the world faces tough decisions about the global environment, international security, medical epidemics, and so forth. But what do people mean when they talk about risk? Is risk basically equivalent to the expected number of fatalities from a given action? What are the characteristics that make something appear risky?

As it happens, perceptions of risk are often complicated. To most people, risk means much more than the expected number of fatalities from a particular course of action.

Paul Slovic and his colleagues have uncovered three basic dimensions connected with public perceptions of risk. The first dimension, known as "dread risk," is characterized by a "perceived lack of control, dread, catastrophic potential, fatal consequences, and the inequitable distribution of risks and benefits" (Slovic, 1987, p. 283). This dimension corresponds closely to the general public's perception of risk, and the most extreme examples of this type of risk have to do with nuclear weapons and nuclear power. The second dimension, called "unknown risks," involves those aspects of risk "judged to be unobservable, unknown, new, and delayed in their manifestation of harm." Genetic and chemical technologies are extreme examples of this kind of risk. Finally, the last important dimension concerns the number of people who are exposed to a given risk. Although there are obviously a variety of other factors that influence the perception of risk—such as conservatism in probability estimation, the vividness or availability of a threat, and the recency of a catastrophe—a number of studies have replicated the three basic dimensions emphasized by Slovic and his colleagues.

One of the most interesting results these researchers have found is that lay people differ quite a bit from experts in how they perceive risk (Slovic, Fischhoff, & Lichtenstein, 1979, April). Lay people do a moderately good job of estimating the annual fatalities from various risks, but their overall perceptions of risk are more related to factors such as "catastrophic potential" and "threat to future generations" than to annual fatalities. Experts, on the other hand, do a very good job of estimating annual fatalities, and their perceptions of risk correlate highly with these fatality estimates.*

To take an example, the general public sees nuclear power as a terrible risk (based on factors such as the catastrophic potential and threat to future generations), whereas experts tend to see nuclear power as a relatively minor risk (based mainly on annual fatalities). In fact, when Slovic and his associates (1979, April) asked college students to rate 30 different activities and technologies in terms of risk, the students rated nuclear power as the single greatest risk. When a group of nationally respected risk assessors were presented with the same list, however, they rated nuclear power as twentieth—well behind riding a bicycle!

DO ACCIDENTS MAKE US SAFER?

On June 3, 1980, officers at the U.S. Strategic Air Command (SAC) were routinely watching for signs of a Russian missile attack. The shift had thus far passed uneventfully, and there were no signs of what was about to happen.

Suddenly, a computer display warned that the Russians had just launched a sortie of land- and submarine-based nuclear missiles. In several minutes, the missiles would reach the United States.

SAC responded immediately. Across the country, more than 100 nuclear-armed B-52 bombers were put on alert and prepared for take-off. Nuclear submarine commanders were also alerted, and missile officers in underground silos inserted their launch keys into position. The United States was ready for nuclear war.

Then, just three minutes after the warning had first appeared, it became clear that the alert was a false alarm. American forces were quickly taken off alert, and a number of investigations were initiated. Following a second false alert several days later, the Defense Department located the source of error. As it turned out, a computer chip worth $0.46 had malfunctioned. Instead of registering the number of incoming missiles as a string of zeros, the chip had intermittently inserted 2s in the digital readout.

The reaction people had following these false alerts was fascinating. By and large, opponents of nuclear deterrence reported feeling *less* safe, and supporters (who pointed out that the United States did not, after all, go to war) reported feeling *more* safe. For example, U.S. Representative Frank Horton warned that false alarms "are a serious threat to our national security [and] could trigger an overreaction by the Soviets that

---

*It is an open question as to which set of perceptions—lay or expert—is most adaptive in the long run. Cases can be made for each.

could lead to nuclear confrontation," whereas General James V. Hartinger, Commander in Chief of the North American Aerospace Defense Command at the time of the false missile alerts, concluded that "I really have more confidence in the system now because it was demonstrated that we could cope with such a fault" (U.S. Congress, 1981, May 19–20, pp. 131–133).

A similar reinforcement of preexisting views took place following the near meltdown at Three Mile Island (Mitchell, 1982; Rubin, 1981; Slovic, Fischhoff, & Lichtenstein, 1982a; Weinberg, 1981). As Allan Mazur (1981, pp. 220–221) concluded in his survey of 42 scientists who had publicly advocated or opposed nuclear power development before the accident at Three Mile Island: "None of the prominent scientists discussed here realigned themselves on the nuclear issue because of Three Mile Island. . . . Most respondents interpreted the accident to fit into their preconceptions about nuclear power. Thus, opponents tended to see it as a near catastrophe, symptomatic of the inability of private corporations and government regulators to manage reactors in a safe manner. Proponents emphasized that no one was killed; that the radiation release was relatively small, and therefore the safety system worked." Each side assimilated the evidence in keeping with its own biases; nuclear energy opponents tended to be upset by the very occurrence of a serious breakdown and tended to view the breakdown as proof that a future catastrophe would occur, whereas nuclear energy supporters tended to be reassured by the safeguards and tended to believe that future catastrophes would be averted.

Of course, even though these reactions to the breakdowns at SAC and Three Mile Island seem to reflect biases in judgment, they may also have been a function of selective media exposure or the role requirements imposed on public figures. To control for these factors, I conducted three studies in which respondents of differing political persuasions read *identical* descriptions of noncatastrophic technological breakdowns. For instance, in one experiment, two dozen Reserve Officers Training Corps (ROTC) cadets (the pronuclear subjects) and 21 peace activists (the antinuclear subjects) read identical accounts of four serious breakdowns concerning nuclear weapons. These breakdowns—all real but none well known—included:

- An American missile simulation test in which an error by the maintenance crew led to the initiation of an actual missile launch
- A Russian missile that accidentally began heading for Alaska
- A phony U.S. Coast Guard advisory that the president had been assassinated and the vice president had declared World War III
- A Russian naval alert falsely declaring a state of war with the United States and ordering ship commanders to prepare to engage American forces in combat

After subjects finished reading about these breakdowns, they were asked, among other things, two key questions. The first question was: "When a human or technological breakdown occurs, which factor is more significant *in assessing the likelihood of an inadvertent nuclear war in the future*—that the safeguards worked as planned, or that the breakdown happened in the first place?" Two-thirds of the pronuclear subjects felt that the most important factor was that the safeguards had worked as planned. In contrast, all but one antinuclear subject felt that the most important factor was that the breakdown had happened in the first place. As predicted, pronuclear subjects and antinuclear subjects emphasized different aspects of the same event.

The second question was designed to assess the consequences of this difference. The item read: "Several serious human and technological breakdowns have taken place without leading to nuclear war between the superpowers. Do such breakdowns give you greater confidence that an inadvertent nuclear war will not occur in the future, less confidence, or neither?" Here again, the results were unambiguous. Four out of five subjects expressed a change in confidence, but the direction of this change depended upon whether subjects were pronuclear or antinuclear. Eighty-four percent of the pronuclear subjects who reported a change said that noncatastrophic breakdowns gave them *greater* confidence that a war would not occur, while all of the reported changes among antinuclear subjects were in the direction of *less* confidence that a war would not occur (see Figure 12.3).

Similar results were found in the other two experiments (for details, see Plous, 1991). Supporters of a given technology tended to focus on the fact that the safeguards worked and tended to be reassured by non-catastrophic breakdowns, whereas opponents focused on the very fact that the breakdowns occurred and tended to be disturbed that something serious had gone wrong. Moreover, supporters and opponents used the breakdowns to arrive at different conclusions about the probability of a future catastrophe. After reading about a given breakdown, supporters reported seeing the chances of a future catastrophe as *lower* than before, whereas opponents reported seeing the chances as *greater* than before.

These results were found regardless of whether the breakdown was human or mechanical, American or Russian, energy-related or military-related, or previously known or unknown. Attitude polarization was also apparent irrespective of whether subjects were identified as extreme in advocacy. Thus, over a wide range of situations, perceptions of risk were strongly biased in the direction of preexisting views.

RECOMMENDATIONS

Decision makers can take several steps to reduce biases in probability and risk estimation, including the following simple measures:

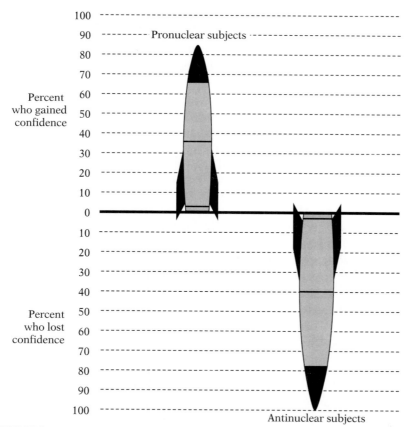

FIGURE 12.3

These percentages are based on answers to the following question: "Several serious human and technological breakdowns have taken place without leading to nuclear war between the superpowers. Do such breakdowns give you greater confidence that an inadvertent nuclear war will not occur in the future, less confidence, or neither?" *(Figure is adapted from Plous, 1991.)*

✔ *Maintain Accurate Records.*   By keeping track of how frequently particular events have occurred in the past, it is possible to minimize primacy and recency effects, availability biases, and other distortions that can arise from the serial presentation of information (e.g., Hintzman, 1969; Ward & Jenkins, 1965).

✔ *Beware of Wishful Thinking.*   In many cases, the probability of desirable events is overestimated and the probability of undesirable events is underestimated (although there are obviously exceptions to this rule, such as cases in which the availability of a feared outcome inflates probability estimates). One of the best ways to protect against wishful thinking is to ask uninvolved (but informed) third parties for independent assessments.

✔ ***Break Compound Events into Simple Events.*** If compound events are made up of statistically independent simple events (i.e., those whose outcomes are unrelated), a useful strategy is to estimate outcome probabilities for each simple event alone. Then, if the compound event is conjunctive, multiply these probabilities together. For example, to estimate the probability of a coin landing on Heads three times in a row (a compound event made up of three simple events), multiple .50 by .50 by .50 (for a final probability estimate of .125). Conversely, if the compound event is disjunctive, subtract each simple probability estimate from 1; multiply each of these numbers together, and subtract the resulting product from 1. For instance, to estimate the probability of a coin landing on Heads at least once in three tosses, calculate the chances of three Tails in a row (again .125) and subtract this number from 1 (for a final estimate of .875). This technique can be used whenever a compound event is comprised of statistically independent simple events (like coin tosses), but it should not be used when the outcomes of simple events are contingent upon one another.

CONCLUSION

As the last three chapters have shown, probability and risk estimates are susceptible to a range of biases. Some of these biases are the natural result of a reliance on heuristics such as representativeness and availability, others are a consequence of motivational factors, and still others arise from prior expectations or the way a problem is framed. Although many of these biases can be corrected, they underscore the fallibility of probability judgments. Chapter 13 discusses another source of bias, called "anchoring and adjustment," that influences probability estimates and many other types of judgment.

CHAPTER 13

ANCHORING AND ADJUSTMENT*

In front of you is a wheel of fortune. The perimeter is lined with an array of numbers, and after the wheel is given a spin, the needle lands on 65. You are confronted with a question: Is the percentage of African countries in the United Nations greater or less than 65? Not a matter you have thought much about, but nonetheless, you are fairly sure that the percentage is less than 65.

What, you are next asked, is the *exact* percentage of African countries in the United Nations? After some thought, you respond with an estimate of 45 percent. A researcher records your response, thanks you for your time, and off you go.

Now you are another person, a person who has not yet answered questions about the United Nations, a person for whom the wheel of fortune will land on 10 rather than 65. After the wheel has stopped moving, the researcher asks: Is the percentage of African countries in the United Nations greater or less than 10? More, you say—certainly it must be more.

What is the *exact* percentage of African countries in the United Nations?

After some thought, you respond with an estimate of 25 percent.

In fact, just such a procedure, yielding identical results, was conducted by Amos Tversky and Daniel Kahneman (1974). Subjects who were randomly assigned to an experimental condition in which the needle landed on 65 subsequently gave a median estimate of 45 percent, and subjects for whom the needle landed on 10 gave a median estimate of 25 percent. Tversky and Kahneman explained this phenomenon in terms of "anchoring and adjustment"—that is, the insufficient adjustment up or down from an original starting value, or "anchor."

Since the time of Tversky and Kahneman's (1974) study, anchoring has been documented in estimates as diverse as the percentage of working mothers with children under age 5, the proportion of Iranians who are Islamic, the percentage of chemistry professors who are women,

---

*Portions of this chapter are adapted from Plous (1989).

and the share of soap operas carried by NBC (Quattrone, Lawrence, Warren, Souza-Silva, Finkel, & Andrus, 1984). Anchoring has also been found with nonnumerical problems (Quattrone, 1982). For example, George Quattrone and his colleagues (1984) showed that randomly assigned anchors, in the form of positive or negative essays, can affect opinions about the SALT II arms control treaty. And Daniel Cervone and Philip Peake (1986) discovered that arbitrary anchors can influence people's estimates of how well they will perform at various problem-solving tasks—estimates which in turn affect their persistence in working on such tasks.

Surprisingly, the effects of anchoring do not disappear with monetary incentives for accuracy (Tversky & Kahneman, 1974; Wright & Anderson, 1989) or with outrageously extreme anchors (Quattrone et al., 1984). In one experiment, Quattrone and his associates (1984) solicited exact numerical estimates after first asking whether the number of Beatles records that had made the top 10 fell above or below 100,025 albums, whether the average price of a college textbook was more or less than $7128.53, or whether the average temperature in San Francisco was greater or less than 558°. Quattrone's research team found that absurdly high anchor values worked just as well as more plausible anchor values. From this result, they concluded that anchoring is a robust phenomenon in which the size of the effect grows with the discrepancy between the anchor and the "preanchor estimate" (the average estimate people offer before being exposed to an explicit anchor) until the effect reaches an asymptotic level. If true, these findings suggest that negotiators, advertisers, politicians, and other persuasion specialists will generally be most successful by staking out extreme initial positions.

THINKING ABOUT THE UNTHINKABLE

Unfortunately, most studies of anchoring have tended to focus on issues about which people have little familiarity or concern: the percentage of African nations in the United Nations, soap operas carried by NBC, female chemistry professors, and so forth. Relatively few studies have focused on whether estimates can be anchored when people care deeply about the topic, when they have previously thought about the issue, or when they know the area fairly well. Perhaps the most extreme example of such an issue is the likelihood of nuclear war. In contrast to other topics in the anchoring literature, the likelihood of nuclear war is an issue most people have already thought about and care about a great deal. The question is, then, whether a manipulation as simple as providing a high or low anchor value can affect beliefs about whether there will be a nuclear war. To answer this question, I distributed several variations of an anchoring survey to more than 2000 respondents between January 1985 and May 1987.

In the *low-anchor* condition the survey asked respondents whether the chances of a nuclear war between the United States and the Soviet Union were greater or less than 1 percent, and in the *high-anchor* condition it asked whether the chances of a war were greater or less than 90 percent (or in one version, 99 percent). Once respondents had answered this question, they were asked to give their best estimate, in percentage terms, of the *exact* chances of a nuclear war. In a third, *no-anchor* condition, respondents were never presented with the first question and were simply asked to give their best estimate of the chances of a nuclear war.

In all variations of the survey, anchoring exerted a strong influence on likelihood estimates of a nuclear war. Respondents who were initially asked whether the probability of nuclear war was greater or less than 1 percent subsequently gave lower estimates than people who were not provided with an explicit anchor, whereas respondents who were first asked whether the probability of war was greater or less than 90 (or 99) percent later gave estimates that were higher than those given by respondents who were not given an anchor. These differences were not significantly influenced by whether the estimates were cast in terms of a nuclear war occurring or not occurring, and they did not seem to be a function of how familiar respondents were with nuclear issues or how concerned they were about nuclear war.

At least two implications follow from these results. First, questions that include arbitrary numerical references may have unintended effects. For example, a national poll conducted in 1984 asked respondents: "Would you support a U.S. attempt to build a defensive system against nuclear missiles and bombers [if it were] able to shoot down 90 percent of all Soviet nuclear missiles and bombers?" (cited in Graham & Kramer, 1986). By mentioning a figure of 90 percent (a very high percentage by most standards), such a question may unwittingly anchor later estimates of the effectiveness of strategic defenses. Second, when advocates use worst-case or best-case examples to illustrate their positions, they may inadvertently anchor people's opinions to an opposing position. For instance, in 1986 a guest columnist for the *New York Times* argued: "A defense that can protect against 99 percent of the Soviet nuclear arsenal may be judged as not good enough, given the destructive potential of the weapons that could survive" (Gliksman, 1986, February 13). Contrary to his aim, this columnist provided readers with an anchor value that strategic defenses are 99 percent effective.

HOW REAL IS REAL ESTATE?

The effects of anchoring are in no way limited to ethereal estimates such as the likelihood of nuclear war or the effectiveness of strategic defenses. For example, budgetary appropriations from one year may anchor appropriations for the next, and initial positions in a negotiation may anchor later ones. There is also evidence that telling jurors to consider verdicts in an order that runs from harshest to most lenient—currently standard practice in murder trials—leads to harsher verdicts than telling them to consider lenient verdicts first (Greenberg, Williams, & O'Brien, 1986).

Anchoring can even influence real estate prices, as Gregory Northcraft and Margaret Neale (1987) have shown. In this study, dozens of real estate agents were given an opportunity to tour one of two houses for sale in Tucson, Arizona—one that had been appraised at $74,900, or another that had been appraised at $135,000. During these visits, the agents were given a 10-page packet that included all the information normally used to determine the value of a residential property (except the official appraisal): the standard Multiple Listing Service (MLS) summary sheet for the property, MLS listings for other properties currently being sold in the neighborhood, information about nearby properties that had been recently sold, and so forth. All agents who inspected a given property received the same packet of information, with one exception: For some agents, the price of the home was listed at 11 to 12 percent below the true appraised value; for others it was 4 percent below value; for others it was 4 percent above the appraised value; and for still others it was 11 to 12 percent above value. Northcraft and Neale wanted to see whether these differences in apparent listing prices would lead to differences in later evaluations of the property.

The agents were given twenty minutes to walk through and around the property, after which time they provided their best estimate of (1) the appraised value of the property, (2) an appropriate advertised selling price, (3) a reasonable price to pay for the house, and (4) the lowest offer they would accept for the house if they were the seller. Table 13.1 summarizes these four estimates for agents who evaluated the $135,000 property (the $74,900 property produced similar results). As you can see, the agents consistently saw the listing price as too high (regardless of what the listing price was), and all four estimates showed significant evidence of anchoring. Interestingly, however, when asked what their top three considerations were in making these judgments, only 1 agent in 10 mentioned the listing price.

These results are important for several reasons. First, they demonstrate the power of anchoring in a real-world setting. By changing only one piece of information (listing price) in a 10-page packet of materials, Northcraft and Neale were able to shift real estate appraisals by more than $10,000. Second, the results show that experts are not immune to the effects of anchoring. Most of the agents had sold real estate for several years, yet this expertise did not prevent their judgments from being anchored. Finally, very few agents identified the listing price as an important consideration in their deliberations. Although some agents may have been reluctant to admit relying on pricing information sup-

TABLE 13.1

THE EFFECTS OF ANCHORING ON REAL ESTATE PRICES

Apparent Listing Price, $	MEAN ESTIMATES GIVEN BY REAL ESTATE AGENTS			
	Appraised Value, $	Recommended Selling Price, $	Reasonable Purchase Price, $	Lowest Offer, $
119,900	114,204	117,745	111,454	111,136
129,900	126,772	127,836	123,209	122,254
139,900	125,041	128,530	124,653	121,884
149,900	128,754	130,981	127,318	123,818

Note: This table is adapted from a study by Gregory Northcraft and Margaret Neale (1987).

plied by someone else, it is likely that many of the agents were simply unaware of being anchored by the listing price.

FURTHER EXAMPLES OF ANCHORING

The Reader Survey contains several other examples of anchoring. In one problem, Item #12a, you were asked to estimate how thick a piece of paper would be if it were folded in on itself 100 times. Only rarely do people give estimates larger than a few yards or meters, yet the correct answer, given an initial sheet of paper 0.1 millimeter thick, is roughly 1.27×10^{23} kilometers—more than 800,000,000,000,000 times the distance between the earth and the sun! This answer surprises many people because they begin by imagining the first few folds (a very low anchor) and do not adjust their estimate upward sufficiently for the doubling effect of later folds. The correct answer can be found by multiplying the thickness of the paper (0.1 millimeter) by the total number of layers (2^{100}). This number works out to be 1.27×10^{29} millimeters, or 1.27×10^{23} kilometers.

Another example of anchoring can be found in Item #17 of the Reader Survey. This question asked how wide a cube-shaped tank would have to be in order to hold all the human blood in the world. Most people formulate their answer by first trying to imagine the size of the world's population. This initial image provides a very large anchor. Then, when people scale down this image to the size of a cube-shaped container of blood, they do not adjust away from the anchor sufficiently. The correct answer, as estimated by John Allen Paulos (1988), is a mere 870 feet. Paulos arrived at this figure by assuming a world population of 5 billion people and an average of 1 gallon of blood per person. Because a cubic foot holds about 7.5 gallons, the total amount of blood comes out to 670 million cubic feet. This is equivalent to a cube 870 feet on each side (870^3 = 670 million).

Still another illustration of anchoring, reported by Tversky and Kahneman (1974), involves the multiplication problem given in Item #22 of the Reader Survey. When Tversky and Kahneman put this question to a group of students, they obtained a median estimate of 2250. In contrast, when they asked a second group of students to estimate $1 \times 2 \times 3 \times 4 \times 5 \times 6 \times 7 \times 8$, the median estimate was only 512. Apparently, students who were given a descending sequence were anchored to the product of 8, 7, 6, and 5, and students who were given an ascending sequence were anchored to the smaller product of 1, 2, 3, and 4. In truth, however, *both* groups of students were strongly anchored downward. The correct answer is 40,320.

Finally, Item #13 of the Reader Survey posed the following problem:

> Including February 29, there are 366 possible birthdays in a year. Consequently, a group would need to contain 367 members in order to be absolutely sure that at least two people shared the same birthday. How many people are necessary in order to be 50 percent certain?

Most people give an answer somewhere around 183 (half the days in a year). The correct answer is that only 23 people are needed. That is, any random grouping of 23 people has better than even odds of containing at least two people with the same birthday.

To see why this answer is correct, consider first the probability that any two randomly selected people will *not* share the same birthday (for example, if Person 1 happens to be born on March 11, consider the probability that Person 2 was not born on March 11). This probability is 365/366, or 99.73 percent, because 365 of the 366 possible birthdays for Person 2 do not fall on the birthday of Person 1 (for simplicity, we are assuming here that birthdays are evenly distributed over each day of the year).

Now consider the chances that three people will not share a birthday. This figure is equal to the probability that two people will not share a birthday (365/366, as given above) multiplied by the probability that the third person will not share a birthday with either Person 1 or Person 2 (364/366). In other words, the probability that three people will not share a birthday is (365/366)(364/366), or 99.18 percent.

Using the same logic, the probability that any four people will not share a birthday is (365/366)(364/366)(363/366), or 98.37 percent. And the probability that 23 people will not share a birthday is:

$$\frac{365 \times 364 \times 363 \times \cdots \times 344}{(366)^{22}} \quad \text{or 49 percent}$$

Consequently, if there is a .49 probability that any 23 people will *not* share a birthday, there are better than even odds that they *will* share a birthday.

Although this problem is difficult for reasons apart from anchoring, there is no question that many people first react by adopting a high anchor value (such as 183) and later find it hard to adjust that anchor value downward as they think about the problem. This pattern is consistent with the research by Maya Bar-Hillel (1973) discussed in Chapter 12. People tend to underestimate the probability of a disjunctive event—in this case, the probability of at least one match in birthdays among 23 people.

The effects of anchoring are also apparent in a related question:

> How large would a group have to be in order to be 50 percent sure that at least one member has a *particular* birthday—say, the 4th of July?

Before you continue reading, take a guess at the answer.

The way to solve this problem is similar to the way the last one was solved. The probability that any one person will *not* be born on the 4th of July is 365/366. Likewise, because birthdays are independent of one another, the probability that any two people will not be born on the 4th of July is (365/366)(365/366), or $(365/366)^2$. And in general, the probability of any N people *not* being born on the 4th of July is $(365/366)^N$. As it turns out, this probability is just less than 50 percent when N is equal to 254. Thus, in a group of 254 people, there are better than even odds that at least one person *will* be born on the 4th of July. As in the previous birthday problem, many people initially suspect that the group would need to have roughly 183 members, and they find it difficult to adjust their estimate away from this early hunch.

After discussing these problems, Paulos (1988, p. 37) made the following observation: "The moral . . . is that some unlikely event is likely to occur, whereas it's much less likely that a particular one will. . . . The paradoxical conclusion is that it would be very unlikely for unlikely events not to occur." Only 23 people are needed to be 50 percent sure that two group members will share an *unspecified* birthday, but more than 10 times as many people are needed to be 50 percent sure that at least one person has a *particular* birthday. Coincidences are common, but *particular* coincidences are not. Chapter 14 examines several remarkable coincidences in detail.

CONCLUSION

The effects of anchoring are pervasive and extremely robust. More than a dozen studies point in the same direction: People adjust insufficiently from anchor values, regardless of whether the judgment concerns the chances of nuclear war, the value of a house, or any number of other topics.

It is difficult to protect against the effects of anchoring, partly because incentives for accuracy seldom work, and partly because the anchor values themselves often go unnoticed. The first step toward protection, then, is to be aware of any suggested values that seem unusually high or low. These are the anchor values most likely to produce biases in judgment.

In an ideal world, decision makers might discount or ignore these values, but in practice it is difficult to do so (Quattrone et al., 1984). Consequently, the most effective approach may be to generate an alternate anchor value that is equally extreme in the opposite direction. For example, before estimating the value of a house that seems grossly overpriced, a decision maker might imagine what the value would seem like if the selling price had been surprisingly low. Such a technique is similar to the development of multiple frames advocated in Chapter 6.

One further point bears repeating. Because extreme anchor values produce the largest anchoring effects, and because the effects of anchoring often go unnoticed, it is important to realize that a discussion of best- or worst-case scenarios can lead to unintended anchoring effects. For instance, after considering the profitability of a business venture under ideal conditions, it is difficult to arrive at a realistic projection. Similarly, after estimating the largest stockpile of weapons an adversary might have, it is hard to render an accurate military assessment. Again, it may be worth considering multiple anchors before attempting to make a final estimate.

CHAPTER 14

THE PERCEPTION OF RANDOMNESS

In his book on probability theory and the perception of luck, Warren Weaver (1982) tells the story of a rather unusual business trip taken by his next door neighbor, George D. Bryson. According to Weaver, Bryson traveled by train from St. Louis to New York. After boarding the train, Bryson asked a conductor whether it would be possible to stop over for a few days in Louisville, Kentucky—a city he had never seen before. The conductor replied affirmatively, and Bryson got off in Louisville. At the train station, Bryson inquired about hotel accommodations and was directed to the Brown Hotel, where he registered and was assigned Room 307. Then, on a whim, Bryson asked whether there was any mail waiting for him. The clerk calmly handed him a letter addressed to "Mr. George D. Bryson, Room 307." As it turned out, the previous resident of the room had been another George D. Bryson!

What are the chances of a coincidence like this? The natural reaction many people have is to say that the odds are less than one in a million. After all, it's not every day that successive occupants of a particular room at a particular hotel in a particular city share a name as uncommon as "George D. Bryson."

But thinking about the coincidence this way is misleading. The question is not whether this *particular* episode is likely to happen. The question is whether it is likely that successive occupants of *some* room in *some* hotel in *some* city at *some* point in time will share the same name. As with the birthday problem discussed in Chapter 13, the probability of an unspecified match is much greater than the probability of a particular match.

Indeed, coincidences based on duplicate names are more common than many people suspect (see Figure 14.1). Here are two further examples:

On October 5, 1990, the *San Francisco Examiner* reported that Intel Corporation, a leading computer chip manufacturer, was suing another chip maker for infringing on Intel's 386 microprocessor trademark (Sullivan, 1990, October 5). Intel had learned that the rival company was planning to release a chip called the "Am386." What is remarkable

Mixup in Cars Proves Startling Coincidence

MILWAUKEE, April 2 (AP) — The police estimated the odds as "a million to one."

Two men with the same surname, each owning a car of the same model and make and each having an identical key, wound up at a Sheboygan shopping center at the same time on April Fool's Day.

Richard Baker had taken his wife in their 1978 maroon Concord model of an American Motors Corporation automobile to shop at the Northgate Shopping Center in Sheboygan.

He came out before she did, put his groceries in the trunk and drove around the lot to pick her up.

The two were coming back from another errand when, "My wife said, 'Whose sunglasses are these,'" Mr. Baker said.

"I noticed I had a heck of a time getting the seat up and it was way back when I got in," he said. "My wife said: 'Something's wrong. Look at all this stuff in here. This isn't our car.'"

A check of the license plates confirmed it: The Bakers had the wrong car.

Meanwhile, Thomas J. Baker, no relation to Richard Baker, had reported his car stolen.

Thomas Baker and the police were waiting for Richard Baker and his wife when they drove back into the shopping center parking lot.

The police tried the keys on the cars and both keys operated and unlocked both cars.

Sgt. William Peloquin said estimated the odds of such an incident as "a million to one."

FIGURE 14.1
One in a million? *(Associated Press)*

about this story is *how* Intel discovered the infringement. As fate would have it, both companies employed someone named Mike Webb, and both Mike Webbs had checked into the same hotel in Sunnyvale, California, at the same time. Then, after both men had checked out, the hotel received a package addressed to one of the Mike Webbs. The package—which contained documents referring to an Am386 chip—was then misdelivered to the Mike Webb at Intel, who in turn forwarded it to Intel's attorney!

The second coincidence took place in the summer of 1990, when Frank William Bouma and his wife, Trudy, sent their fiftieth wedding anniversary picture to the *Grand Rapids Press* (a Michigan newspaper). At roughly the same time, the newspaper received a fifty-fifth anniversary announcement from another Frank William Bouma and his wife, Nella. Amazingly enough, both couples were celebrating their anniversary on July 9. Thinking the coincidence would make an interesting story, the *Grand Rapids Press* ran an article that detailed other similarities between the two Frank Boumas, such as the fact that both men had a daughter named Marcia (Malone, 1990, September 9). The story was then picked up by the Associated Press wire service and ultimately appeared in the *National Enquirer* (Carden, 1990, September 25).

AN UNLIKELY DEVELOPMENT

Can you think of a coincidence so unlikely that you would be forced to assume it was not simply a random occurrence? Consider a story told by Richard Blodgett (1983, November, p. 17):

> A German mother . . . photographed her infant son in 1914 and left the film at a store in Strasbourg to be developed. In those days, film plates were sold individually. World War I broke out and, unable to return to Strasbourg, the woman gave up the picture for lost. Two years later she bought a film plate in Frankfurt, nearly 200 miles away, to take a picture of her newborn daughter. When developed, the film turned out to be a double exposure, with the picture of her daughter superimposed over the earlier picture of her son. Through some incredible twist of fate, her original film had apparently never been developed, had been mislabeled as unused, and had eventually been resold to her.

This coincidence is quite famous because it is one of the stories that led Swiss psychiatrist Carl Jung to propose his theory of "synchronicity". According to Jung, coincidences occur much more frequently than one would expect by chance and are actually the work of an unknown force seeking to impose universal order.

In many ways, Jung's theory is similar to religious interpretations that characterize coincidences as acts of God. One coincidence that was widely interpreted this way appeared in *Life* magazine in 1950 (Edeal, 1950, March 27). On March 1 of that year, 15 members of the West Side Baptist Church choir in Beatrice, Nebraska, were due to practice at 7:15 PM, but for one reason or another, all 15 members were late that particular night. The minister's family was late because his wife ironed their daughter's dress at the last minute; a couple of choir members were late because their cars wouldn't start; the pianist had intended to get to church half an hour early but had fallen asleep after dinner; and so on. In all, there were at least 10 rather ordinary and seemingly unconnected reasons why people were late that night.

As things turned out, though, it was fortunate that everyone was late. According to the report in *Life*: "At 7:25, with a roar heard in almost every corner of Beatrice, the West Side Baptist Church blew up. The walls fell outward, the heavy wooden roof crashed straight down like the weight in a deadfall. . . . Firemen thought the explosion had been caused by natural gas [but] the Beatrice choir members . . . began . . . wondering at exactly what point it is that one can say, 'This is an act of God.'"

Of course, this "coincidence" may well have been an act of God, and Jung's theory of synchronicity may well be true. Such explanations are not subject to empirical confirmation or disconfirmation. Even the most improbable events are unlikely to turn skeptics into believers, because skeptics can always explain improbable events as a function of the astronomical number of opportunities for coincidences to arise (e.g., Alvarez, 1965). Likewise, most believers would probably be unmoved by the skeptic's explanation, because they base their beliefs on more than probabilities alone.

What *can* be empirically investigated, however, are the answers to two interrelated questions: (1) Do people tend to see meaningful patterns in random arrangements of stimuli? (2) Can people behave randomly?

An answer to the first question was given partially in Chapter 10, when the discussion focused on the illusion of streak shooting in basketball. The next section reviews other research on the perception of randomness.

LUCK AND SUPERSTITION

An estimated 40 percent of Americans believe that some numbers are especially lucky for some people ("*Harper's* Index," 1986, October). Does such a belief make sense?

As Robert Hooke (1983, p. 51) wrote in *How to Tell the Liars from the Statisticians*:

> A person claiming to be "lucky" is making perfectly good sense if by this it is meant that he or she has had good luck up until now. If the

claim extends to the future by implying a greater chance of winning a lottery than the rest of us have, then it becomes a superstitious claim, and this is the kind of luck that many are speaking of when they say they don't believe in luck.

One of the earliest experiments on the creation of superstitious beliefs was published by Harold Hake and Ray Hyman (1953). On each of 240 trials, Hake and Hyman presented subjects with one of two stimuli—either a horizontal row of lighted neon bulbs or a vertical column of lighted bulbs. Before each trial, subjects were asked to predict whether the stimulus would be horizontal or vertical. Hake and Hyman presented subjects with one of four different orderings of the stimuli, but the most interesting series was random—half of the trials were horizontal and half were vertical, in no detectable pattern (there is some question as to whether a series can ever be completely random, so the word *random* will simply be used here to indicate a series with no discernible pattern).

Hake and Hyman found that subjects who viewed a random series predicted a horizontal stimulus roughly half the time, regardless of whether they had predicted a horizontal stimulus on the previous trial. In this respect, their guesses resembled the random series they observed.

Subjects did not choose entirely at random, however; they were strongly influenced by whether their previous prediction had been correct. After correctly guessing horizontal on the previous trial, they guessed horizontal again 64 percent of the time, and after correctly guessing horizontal on the previous two trials, they repeated this guess 72 percent of the time. In other words, subjects superstitiously based their predictions on previous correct identifications, even though the series was random. As Hake and Hyman (1953, p. 73) concluded: "If our subjects are typical, [this means that people] will always perceive an ambiguous series of events as being more structured than it really is. This must follow whenever subjects allow their own past behavior to influence their predictions of the future occurrence of series of events which are, in fact, completely independent of the behavior of subjects."

A similar experiment was published by John Wright (1962). Wright presented subjects with a panel that had 16 regularly-spaced pushbuttons arranged in a circle around a seventeenth pushbutton. Subjects were told that by pressing the correct sequence of outside buttons, followed by the center button, they could sound a buzzer and score a point on a counter. If the sequence they chose was incorrect, pressing the center button would simply advance them to the next trial. In reality, there were no correct or incorrect sequences; the rewards were distributed randomly. In one condition of the experiment, subjects were randomly rewarded on 20 percent of the trials; in another, on 50 percent of the trials; and in another, on 80 percent of the trials. Wright found much the same result as Hake and Hyman—subjects tended to see patterns in the random feedback. They tended to develop superstitious behaviors, or preferences for certain patterns of buttons, and this tendency was most pronounced when the probability of reward was highest (80 percent).

RECOGNIZING RANDOMNESS

In the studies by Hake and Hyman (1953) and Wright (1962), subjects were presented with random feedback after each trial in a long series of trials, and in both cases subjects tended to see patterns in the random feedback. There is a problem with this research, though; the very nature of the tasks may have led subjects to expect to see a pattern. After all, if psychologists are interested in topics such as perception and learning, why would they present people with random feedback? To give subjects a reasonable chance of recognizing that the feedback they are getting is random, subjects should at least be forewarned that random feedback is a possibility.

In 1980, Christopher Peterson published a study that used the same general procedure used by Hake and Hyman, except that subjects in some conditions were asked not only to predict which stimulus would be shown on the next trial, but to indicate whether the sequence "has been generated randomly or in accordance with some rule." Half the subjects were presented with a random sequence, and half were presented with a patterned sequence. Peterson found that when randomness was explicitly included as a legitimate possibility, subjects were usually able to recognize the series as random or close to random.

Of course, the recognition of randomness does not necessarily eliminate superstitious choices if similar choices have been correct on previous trials. Peterson did not find that superstitious behaviors went away if people were warned that a series might be random. He simply found that by including randomness as an explicit possibility, many people did in fact label a random series as random. As the next section shows, however, perceptions of what "randomness" means are not always accurate.

SEEING PATTERNS IN RANDOMNESS

In 1970, Dutch researcher Willem Wagenaar published an intriguing study on the perception of randomness. Wagenaar (1970a) presented subjects with a large set of slides that each contained seven series of white and black dots on a neutral grey background. For each slide, subjects were asked to indicate which of the seven series looked most random (i.e., most like it was produced by flipping a coin). On every slide, one series had a .20 probability of repetition (the probability of a black dot following a black dot, or a white dot following a white dot), one series had a .30 probability of repetition, one series had a .40 probability of repetition, and so on up to .80. In a random series with two equally likely alternatives, the probability of repetition is .50 (just like the probability of tossing Heads after already tossing Heads), so if subjects were able to detect which of the seven series on each slide was random, they should have chosen the one with a .50 probability of repetition.

Instead, Wagenaar found that subjects judged series with a .40 probability of repetition as most random. That is, people thought that the most random-looking series was the one in which there was a 40 percent chance of one kind of dot occurring right after it had already occurred.* People expected a random series to alternate between the two kinds of dots more often than a truly random series would. Wagenaar found that subjects were particularly biased against long runs of the same outcome—for example, strings of six or more dots of the same kind. Thus, people saw randomness when there was actually a pattern, and saw patterns when the sequence was actually random. As mentioned earlier, Thomas Gilovich et al. (1985) found similar results in their study of streak shooting. People judged a series as most random when its probability of alternation was about .70 (equivalent to a .30 probability of repetition).

CAN PEOPLE BEHAVE RANDOMLY?

The difficulty people have in judging randomness implies that they should also have difficulty generating random sequences—and indeed they do. The earliest discussion of this issue was published by Hans Reichenbach (1949), who claimed that people are simply unable to produce a random series of responses, even when motivated to do their best.

This inability was clearly illustrated in an experiment published by Paul Bakan (1960). Bakan asked 70 college students to "produce a series of 'heads' (H) and 'tails' (T) such as [would] occur if an unbiased coin were tossed in an unbiased manner for a total of 300 independent tosses." Random 300-trial sequences should have an average of 150 alternations between Heads and Tails, but Bakan found that nearly 90 percent of the students produced a sequence with too many alternations (the average was 175). These findings are consistent with what Wage-

---

*Peter Ayton, Anne Hunt, and George Wright (1989) have criticized this line of research for leading subjects to equate randomness with how "random looking" a sequence is. Randomly generated sequences of sufficient length always contain sections that do not seem random; hence, asking subjects to choose the sequence that *looks* most random may induce a bias against repetition. Other studies have found, however, that subjects underestimate the amount of repetition in random sequences even when they are merely asked to detect whether the sequences were randomly generated—with no mention of how the sequences look (Diener & Thompson, 1985; Lopes & Oden, 1987).

naar (1970a) found—people expect more alternations between two outcomes than would actually occur in a random sequence.

This tendency is even more pronounced when people are asked to alternate randomly among more than two choices (Wagenaar, 1970b, 1972). For example, when people are presented with panels of six or eight pushbuttons and asked to generate a random pattern of button pressing, the amount of excessive alternation is even greater than in the case when they are presented with only two pushbuttons. The implication here is that in daily life, when there are often more than two available outcomes (such as Heads and Tails, or Horizontal and Vertical), the repetition of any one outcome will often be viewed as a nonrandom sequence. People expect a random sequence to alternate much more than the sequence would by chance alone.

LEARNING TO ACT RANDOMLY

In 1986, Allen Neuringer published a study that showed how people can be trained to behave "randomly" over an extended time period. Neuringer devised a computer program that gave subjects feedback on 5 or 10 statistical measures of randomness, such as the number of runs, the percentage of trials in which a certain choice was made, and so on. Subjects were simply asked to press one of two keys on a computer keyboard at any speed they wished, and as they went along, the computer gave them feedback on how they were doing.

Neuringer observed that subjects began by generating nonrandom sequences, just as Wagenaar and other researchers had found. But after receiving feedback over the course of several thousand responses, subjects were able to generate long strings (of 6000 keystrokes) that were indistinguishable from random sequences according to all the statistical indices that Neuringer had used to give subjects feedback. So it appears that people *can* behave in a random-like way, but only when they are explicitly trained to do so. Although few of us will ever enroll in a training procedure designed to teach us how to behave randomly—and few of us would want to behave randomly even if we could—Neuringer's experiment is important because it underscores the fact that misperceptions of randomness are not immutable. With enough training, they can be unlearned.

CONCLUSION

What are the practical implications of research on perceived randomness? The outcomes most common in daily life are not Heads and Tails or Horizontal and Vertical; they are hirings and firings in the workplace, wins and losses on the playing field, gains and losses in stock prices, and so forth. Although it certainly makes sense to seek patterns in these outcomes, research on perceived randomness suggests that decision makers have a tendency to overinterpret chance events.

For example, despite evidence that stock market fluctuations approximate a "random walk" down Wall Street (Fama, 1965; Malkiel, 1985), thousands of people labor each day to predict the direction stock prices will go. Indeed, Baruch Fischhoff and Paul Slovic (1980) found that subjects who were given stock prices and trend information were roughly 65 percent sure they could predict the direction stocks would change, even though they were correct only 49 percent of the time and would have done about as well tossing a coin.

As the studies in this chapter show, it is easy to see patterns in random outcomes. After witnessing three or four similar outcomes, most people conclude that a pattern is present. Of course, if a certain outcome does not usually occur, then three or four occurrences of that outcome may indeed be informative (for example, three closely spaced job turnovers in a company that rarely has turnovers). If the situation involves independent events with equally likely outcomes, however, it is not unusual to see three or four occurrences of the same outcome. In such circumstances, decision makers should resist the temptation to view short runs of the same outcome as meaningful.

CHAPTER 15

CORRELATION, CAUSATION, AND CONTROL

Over the past month, your dizzy spells have been increasing. At first, you thought they were from being in love. Then you thought they might have been from reading too much psychology. Now, however, you have begun to worry—a friend of yours mentioned that dizziness might be the result of a brain tumor.

You decide to read about brain tumors. At the library, you locate a research article in which 250 hospitalized neurology patients were classified as follows:

		BRAIN TUMOR	
		Present	Absent
DIZZINESS	**Present**	160	40
	Absent	40	10

Take a good look at this table and answer the following two questions: (1) Which cells of the table are needed in order to determine whether dizziness is associated with brain tumors? (2) According to the data in the table, is dizziness associated with having a brain tumor?

The latter question is known in psychology as a problem in "covariation assessment," or the assessment of whether two variables are related (whether they "co-vary"). Although such judgments may seem relatively simple (everyone knows that, on the average, more clouds mean more rain, more height means more weight, and so on), it turns out that covariation assessments are often fairly difficult (Jenkins & Ward, 1965; Ward & Jenkins, 1965). To see how you did on the brain tumor problem, take a look at your answer to Item #14 of the Reader Survey (adapted from Nisbett & Ross, 1980, p. 91).

Many people report an association between dizziness and brain tumors because the present-present cell of the table contains the largest

162

number of patients. Others report a positive association because the sum of the present-present and absent-absent cells (the top left and lower right cells) is larger than the sum of the present-absent and absent-present cells (the top right and lower left). These decision rules do not always yield correct answers, though; two variables will only be related if the chances of one event (such as a brain tumor) differ depending on whether the other event (dizziness) occurs.

To determine whether dizziness is related to brain tumors, all four cells of the table are needed (that is, all four pieces of information in Item #14a). You have to compare the ratio of tumor-present versus tumor-absent when dizziness is present (160:40) and the same ratio when dizziness is absent (40:10). In this case, the ratio is 4-to-1 whether or not dizziness is present. Thus, because the neurology patients were four times more likely to have a brain tumor than not *regardless* of whether they experienced dizziness, the correct answer to Item #14b is that there is no association between the variables.

The difficulty most people have in covariation assessment raises the question of whether health professionals might mistakenly see a symptom and a disease as related. Norwegian researcher Jan Smedslund (1963) explored this issue in one of the earliest studies on covariation assessment. In one experiment, Smedslund presented nurses with 100 cards said to contain excerpts from patient files. Each card listed whether the patient showed a particular symptom (labeled +A when present and −A when absent) and a particular disease (labeled +F when present and −F when absent). In all, 37 cards contained +A and + F, 33 contained −A and +F, 17 contained +A and −F, and 13 contained −A and −F. The nurses were asked to state whether the symptom was related to the disease, and they were told that they could study and arrange the cards in any way that might facilitate an accurate judgment. According to Smedslund's results, 86 percent of the nurses incorrectly reported a positive association between A and F, 7 percent correctly reported no positive relationship, and 7 percent gave up and did not answer the question.

When asked to explain their answers, most of the nurses who saw a positive relationship justified their answer by observing that instances of +A and +F were most common. On the basis of these results, Smedslund (1963, p. 165) concluded that "adult subjects with no statistical training apparently have no adequate concept of correlation. . . . In so far as they reason statistically at all, they tend to depend exclusively on the frequency of ++ cases in judging relationship." Although subsequent studies have found that people take more into account than just the present-present cell (Arkes & Harkness, 1983; Beyth-Marom, 1982; Shaklee & Mims, 1982; Shaklee & Tucker, 1980), Smedslund's basic observations have stood the test of time: People often have difficulty assessing the covariation between two events, and they tend to rely heavily on positive occurrences of both events (Alloy & Tabachnik, 1984; Crocker, 1981).

DOES GOD ANSWER PRAYERS?

In their discussion of covariation assessment, Richard Nisbett and Lee Ross (1980) illustrated this reliance on positive events by considering the question of whether God answers prayers. Many people believe that God answers prayers because they have asked God for something and it has come about. This strategy corresponds to a reliance on the present-present cell of a 2 × 2 table labeled "Prayed" and "Didn't Pray" along the top, and "Event Came About" and "Event Did Not Come About" along the side. To accurately assess covariation, though, you would need to know three additional pieces of information: (1) How often things prayed for did not come about; (2) how often things not prayed for came about; and, believe it or not, (3) how often things not prayed for did not come about (which is, of course, incalculable).

Such an approach flies in the face of common sense. People seldom pay as much attention to events that do not occur as those that do (cf. Bourne & Guy, 1968; Nahinsky & Slaymaker, 1970). As Nisbett and Ross pointed out, this is why Sherlock Holmes seemed so brilliant when he solved "The Silver Blaze" mystery by considering "the curious incident of the dog in the night-time." When the inspector objected that "The dog did nothing in the night-time," Holmes replied triumphantly, "That *was* the curious incident." Although a dog barking at an intruder is not particularly informative, Holmes realized that the *failure* to bark meant that the intruder was someone the dog knew, and Holmes was thus able to reduce the list of suspects.

ILLUSORY CORRELATION

The mistaken impression that two unrelated variables are correlated is known as "illusory correlation," a phenomenon named and first systematically studied by Loren and Jean Chapman (1967; 1969; 1971, November). In the very first study of illusory correlation, Loren Chapman (1967) projected various word-pairs, such as *bacon-tiger*, on a large screen in front of subjects. The word on the left side of the screen was always *bacon, lion, blossoms,* or *boat,* and the word on the right side was always *eggs, tiger,* or *notebook.* Even though each left-side word was paired an equal number of times with each right-side word, on the average subjects later said that when *bacon* appeared on the left, *eggs* was paired with it 47 percent of the time, and when *lion* was on the left, *tiger* was the word that appeared most often on the right. People saw a positive correlation between semantically related words when no such correlation existed.

In another experiment, Chapman and Chapman (1967) surveyed clinicians who were active in diagnostic testing. Chapman and Chapman wrote brief descriptions of six types of patients and asked each clinician what characteristics the patient might display in the Draw-A-Person projective test (a widely used diagnostic test). In general, the clinicians showed strong agreement. For example, 91 percent said that a suspicious patient would draw large or atypical eyes, and 82 percent said that a person worried about her or his intelligence would draw a large or emphasized head. In fact, however, there is no solid evidence that answers to the Draw-A-Person test follow these patterns. Such correlations are purely illusory—the result of shared clinical stereotypes.

Chapman and Chapman (1967) also presented college students (who had never heard of the Draw-A-Person test) with randomly paired patient drawings and patient descriptions. Lo and behold, even though the drawings and descriptions were randomly paired, students reported the same illusory correlations found earlier with clinicians (for example, most students reported that the patients described as suspicious tended to draw a person with atypical eyes). In other experiments, Chapman and Chapman (1967) investigated whether illusory correlations disappeared if subjects were allowed to view the test materials over three consecutive days, or if subjects were offered $20.00 for accuracy. In both cases, illusory correlations remained just as strong as before. Other researchers have confirmed that even with training, illusory correlations are hard to eliminate (cf. Golding & Rorer, 1972).

Finally, in perhaps their most famous experiment of the series, Chapman and Chapman (1969) asked 32 clinicians about their use of the Rorschach inkblot test to "diagnose" male homosexuality (in the 1960s, many psychologists classified homosexuality as a form of psychopathology—a view that is no longer widely shared). These clinicians, who had all seen a number of Rorschach responses from male homosexuals, reported that homosexual men were more likely than heterosexual men to interpret the inkblots as: (1) a buttocks or anus, (2) genitals, (3) female clothing, (4) human figures of indeterminate sex, and (5) human figures with both male and female features. In reality, none of these responses were empirically linked with homosexuality. Furthermore, only 2 of the 32 clinicians mentioned either of the two inkblot interpretations which *did* covary with homosexuality (a tendency to see monster figures or part-human, part-animal figures). From these results, Chapman and Chapman (1969) argued that most of the clinicians had formed illusory correlations based on their stereotypes of homosexual men. You can check whether you fell prey to the same illusory correlation by looking at your answer to Item #18 of the Reader Survey.

Although the causes of illusory correlation are not entirely clear, most theories focus on the availability and representativeness heuristics. The availability explanation runs like this: Illusory correlations arise because distinctive or salient pairings (such as bacon-eggs) are highly "available" in memory and are therefore overestimated in frequency (McArthur, 1980). The representativeness theory explains illusory correlation as a function of one event appearing typical of another (for example, certain inkblot interpretations seeming representative of male homosexuality). Both of these explanations have a great deal of support (Mullen & Johnson, 1990), and together, they account for a wide variety of illusory correlations.

INVISIBLE CORRELATIONS

The opposite of seeing a correlation that doesn't exist is *failing* to see one that does—what might be called an "invisible correlation." Whereas illusory correlations often arise because people expect two variables to be related (Hamilton & Rose, 1980), invisible correlations frequently result from the absence of such an expectation. In the absence of an expectation that two variables will be related, even strong associations may go undetected.

As with illusory correlations, invisible correlations are common and can lead to profound consequences. For example, until recent history, the correlation between smoking and lung cancer was largely invisible, and to many Americans, the link between meat consumption and colon cancer is still invisible.

One of the most comprehensive studies documenting the difficulty people have in detecting positive correlations was published by Dennis Jennings, Teresa Amabile, and Lee Ross (1982). Jennings, Amabile, and Ross gave college students three sets of paired data to examine. The first set contained 10 pairs of numbers, the second set contained drawings of 10 men of different heights with walking sticks of different lengths, and the third set contained audiotapes of 10 people saying a letter of the alphabet and singing a musical note (in the last set, the two variables of interest were the alphabetical position of the letter and the duration of the musical note). Within each set of data, the paired variables were correlated between 0 (no linear relationship) and 1.00 (a perfect positive association). Students were asked whether the relationship between the variables was positive or negative, and they were asked to rate how strong the relationship was (using a scale from 0 to 100, rather than 0 to 1.00).

The results showed that students did not reliably detect a positive relationship in the three data sets until the actual correlation reached .60 or .70 (a relatively strong association). When the variables were correlated between .20 and .40 (similar in size to the correlations typically found between personality traits and behavior in a specific situation), students estimated the relationship at an average of 4 to 8 points on the 100-point scale—barely above zero. Only when the variables were correlated more than .80 did student ratings average 50 on the 100-point scale, and correlations of 1.00 elicited average ratings of less than 85. In other words, moderately strong positive correlations were invisible to many students, and very strong correlations were often perceived as moderate in size.

GETTING BY

Why is it that people have so much trouble telling whether two variables are related? Consider the complexity of a typical problem in covariation assessment. Suppose you wanted to determine whether creativity is correlated with intelligence. What steps would you have to take in order to arrive at an accurate judgment? In her literature review of research on covariation assessment, Jennifer Crocker (1981) outlined six separate steps that are involved in judging covariation:

- First, you need to decide what kind of information is relevant. For example, will you examine only those cases in which intelligence and creativity are present, or will you also look at cases in which they are absent? Will your assessment be restricted to adults? Americans? Famous artists?
- Next, you need to sample cases from the population under consideration (randomly, if possible). This is the observation, or "data collection," phase.
- Third, you must interpret and classify your observations. What will count as creativity? As intelligence? Will people be classified along a continuum or placed in separate categories?
- Fourth, you need to remember the classifications long enough to estimate the frequency of confirming and disconfirming cases.
- Fifth, the estimates must be integrated in a meaningful way. There are statistical formulas that integrate frequency estimates, but as Smedslund (1963) and others have shown, people usually rely on more informal strategies.
- And finally, you need to use the integrated estimate to make a judgment about covariation.

Given the possibilities for bias at each of these stages, it is not surprising that people often have difficulty assessing covariation. For example, decision makers rarely collect random samples of observations. Instead, they make highly selective observations. As discussed in Chapter 3, decision makers also show a range of biases in memory, many of which complicate the task of covariation assessment. Indeed, with all the opportunities for bias, it is remarkable that people get along as well as they do. After all, most people *do* manage to detect the important covariations in their lives—covariations between studying and exam performance, over-eating and weight gain, racist remarks and social ostracism, and so forth.

How can these daily successes in covariation assessment be reconciled with the pessimistic results of laboratory research? Nisbett and Ross (1980) have offered the following explanation. First, many day-to-day associations are observed in situations that greatly facilitate the accurate recognition of covariation. For example: (1) covariations that are perfect or nearly perfect, such as putting a hand over a flame and feeling heat, or flicking a switch and seeing the lights come on; (2) covariations based on very distinctive, salient, or motivationally relevant stimuli, such as storm clouds and rain; (3) covariations in which the stimuli are close together in time or space, such as petting a dog and noticing that the dog's tail is wagging; and (4) covariations that can easily be tested, such as eating certain foods and getting indigestion.

Second, people are often able to assess covariation by using nonstatistical approximations based on a few cases, such as choosing the most representative or extreme instances of A and watching what happens to B. For example, you might assess the covariation between a friend's movie recommendations and your enjoyment of the films by considering how much you enjoyed the most enthusiastically recommended movies in the past. Or you might assess the general cost of living in different cities by looking at what it costs to rent a typical two-bedroom apartment in each locale.

Third, and importantly, people do not have to rediscover all covariations anew. Most covariations—whether detected by others or through one's own experience—become part of an enduring body of recognized covariations. For example, people do not have to keep discovering that sexual intercourse can lead to pregnancy; the covariation between intercourse and pregnancy was detected by other people long ago and has become part of an inherited corpus of well-recognized covariations.

The significance of this legacy becomes clear if you imagine the difficulty faced by a person trying to discover whether sexual intercourse leads to pregnancy. Many aspects of a romantic relationship covary with sexual intimacy, any of which might appear to cause pregnancy (thereby masking the connection with intercourse). For example, kissing might be mistaken as the cause of pregnancy, as might holding hands, sleeping together, or feeling euphoric. Many of the physical changes that accompany pregnancy might also be interpreted as causal, such as nausea, weight gain, emotional lability, and so on. In fact, because romantic relationships often end within the first few months, a *cessation* in sexual intercourse might be mistaken as the cause of pregnancy. Think of the havoc this belief would wreak!*

---

*This type of confusion is not so far-fetched as it may seem. In earlier times, women who gave birth to twins were sometimes thought to have engaged in adultery, and women who gave birth to severely deformed children were suspected of bestiality (Ives, 1970).

CAUSALATION

The presence of a correlation between two variables does not necessarily mean that one variable causes another—if it did, kissing would lead to dramatic overpopulation. Nonetheless, correlation is often equated with causation. For example, the advertisement in Figure 15.1 implies that buying a typewriter will lead to an improvement in grades, but there are many other explanations for such a correlation (if indeed it exists). Students with typewriters may receive higher grades because they come from families that have more money or care more about writing. Or students who buy a typewriter may be more motivated than other students. There are endless explanations for why typing might be correlated with scholastic performance.

The same inferential leap was made in a recent campaign to promote the advertising industry itself. In a full-page ad in the *New York Times*

FIGURE 15.1

Let the buyer beware: Correlation ≠ Causation. *(Courtesy Smith-Corona)*

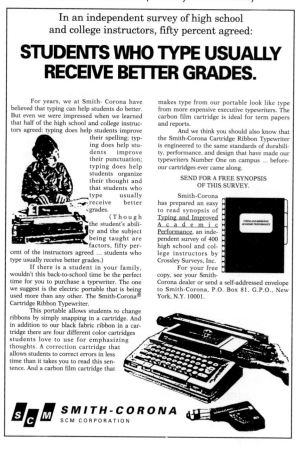

(August 26, 1990), the American Association of Advertising Agencies declared that "Advertising almost doubles your return-on-investment." Yet the evidence for this claim consisted of the following correlation: "Brands that advertise much more than their competitors average returns-on-investment of 32 percent, while brands that advertise much less than their competitors average only 7 percent return-on-investment." Even if true, such a finding need not imply that advertising increases return-on-investment. Perhaps only high-profit companies can *afford* to advertise, in which case financial success leads to advertising rather than the other way around.

Just as correlation need not imply a causal connection, causation need not imply a strong correlation. Hillel Einhorn and Robin Hogarth (1986) have called the belief that causation implies correlation "causalation." In their discussion of causalation, Einhorn and Hogarth asked readers to consider the following hypothetical classification of 200 couples:

		PREGNANCY		
		Yes	No	Total
	Yes	20	80	100
REPORTED INTERCOURSE	No	5	95	100
	Total	25	175	200

It may seem odd to see five pregnancies without reported intercourse, but this small number of cases might represent people who do not remember their activities accurately, who lie about their activities, and so forth.

The correlation between reported intercourse and pregnancy in this table is quite modest (only .34). On the basis of this correlation, covariation assessors who didn't know better might infer that intercourse does not cause pregnancy. Instead, they might infer that pregnancy is caused by more highly correlated factors. The logical flaw here is that intercourse need not be *perfectly* correlated with pregnancy in order to cause pregnancy. Causation does not imply that two variables are strongly correlated.

HEADS I WIN, TAILS IT'S CHANCE

The most fundamental covariation assessments people make—the ones most critical to survival and most significant personally—are probably judgments about behavior and its effects. In one form or another, the relation between actions and outcomes has occupied a central position in psychological theory, whether the focus has been on covariations in causal attribution (Kelley, 1967, 1973), the perception of self-efficacy

(Bandura, 1982, 1986), locus of control (Lefcourt, 1982), or other psychological constructs. One of the most interesting findings to emerge from this literature is that people often believe they have more control over chance outcomes than they actually do. This belief, known as the "illusion of control," was first empirically documented by psychologist Ellen Langer.

In one of her earliest studies, called "Heads I Win, Tails It's Chance," Langer found that in certain situations, people believed they could predict and control the outcome of a coin toss (Langer & Roth, 1975). Under the guise of a pilot test on "social cues," subjects were asked to predict the outcome of 30 coin tosses by the experimenter. In reality, the accuracy of subjects' predictions was rigged so that everyone guessed correctly on 15 trials, but roughly one-third of the subjects began by doing very well (guessing correctly on the first four tosses), roughly one-third began poorly (missing four of the first five tosses), and roughly one-third met with "random" success. Then, after the 30 coin tosses, subjects answered a number of questions concerning their performance.

The results showed that subjects who began by doing well rated their performance more highly than did other subjects. This is a "primacy effect" similar to the effects discussed in Chapter 4. In fact, these subjects actually recalled having made more successful predictions than did the other subjects, and when asked how they would do in predicting another 100 tosses, they expected to make significantly more accurate predictions. Langer and her co-author, Jane Roth, also noted that 40 percent of all subjects believed their performance would improve with practice, and 25 percent felt their performance would be hampered by distraction—even though the task was to predict a chance outcome. This finding is consistent with reports of gamblers who roll dice softly for low numbers and hard for high numbers, or the observation that people often concentrate when they roll the dice (Henslin, 1967). Langer and Roth (1975, p. 954) concluded that: "An early, fairly consistent pattern of successes leads to a skill attribution, which in turn leads subjects to expect future success."

In another study by Langer (1975), office workers participated in a lottery in which the tickets contained either familiar letters or unfamiliar symbols and the workers were either allowed to choose their tickets or were simply given a ticket. Once the workers had their tickets, they were then given the opportunity to hold on to them or trade them in for a ticket from another lottery with better chances of winning. What Langer found is that workers who had chosen their own tickets or who had tickets with familiar letters preferred to keep their tickets relatively more often than did other workers. Based on these results, Langer argued that familiarity and choice lead to an illusion of control. Similar findings have been reported by Camille Wortman (1975).

THE KIND OF HELP THAT DOESN'T HELP

The perception of control, even when largely an illusion, plays an important role in health. For example, Ellen Langer and Judith Rodin (1976) published a field study showing that small changes in the choices and responsibilities given to senior citizens can have dramatic health consequences. The study involved 91 ambulatory adults who ranged in age from 65 to 90 and who lived in a nursing home in Connecticut. On one floor of the nursing home, an administrator reminded the residents that they had control over their lives: how they spent their time, how the furniture in their rooms was arranged, whether they wanted anything changed in the nursing home, and so on. The administrator also gave each resident a small plant to care for. On another floor, the administrator reminded residents that the staff was there to take care of them and to make their lives as rich as possible. The administrator then gave each of these residents a small plant that the *nurses* would care for.

Three weeks after these communications, 71 percent of the residents who were told that the staff was there to "help" them were rated as having become more debilitated. In contrast, of the residents who were encouraged to make decisions for themselves, 93 percent showed an overall improvement in functioning. Based on their own judgments and the judgments of staff nurses (who were not told about the experiment), these residents were happier and more active. They were also judged to be more mentally alert than the other residents, and they spent relatively more time visiting with other residents and outside guests. Langer and Rodin (1976, p. 197) observed: "That so weak a manipulation had any effect suggests how important increased control is for these people, for whom decision making is virtually nonexistent."

One of the problems with this study, as with many field studies, is the difficulty in knowing which of the experimental changes, if any, were responsible for producing the end result. Was it the administrator's speech about having control? Was it the gift of a plant to care for? Or was it a function of preexisting differences between residents living on the two floors? There is no way to know for sure. Since the original study was conducted, however, there have been a number of other research projects that support the link between health and a sense of control, particularly among older people (Rodin, 1986). These studies highlight the central role of covariation judgments in daily life.

CONCLUSION

One of the most common judgments people make is the judgment of whether two variables are related. In many cases, these assessments are simply generalizations based on previously established relationships. In other situations, though, generalizations are not enough; the decision maker must weigh new and conflicting information in order to arrive at a fresh assessment. As the research in this chapter has shown, these can be dangerous waters for the decision maker.

Several recommendations emerge from research on covariation assessment. First, decision makers should focus on more than the positive and confirming cases of a relationship. In judgments of contingency, what did *not* take place is often as significant as what did. Second, before deciding whether a relationship exists, decision makers should ask themselves whether their judgment rests primarily on observations or expectations. If the former, covariation may have been underestimated; if the latter, it may have been overestimated. This difference, while very general, is consistent with research on illusory and invisible correlations (e.g., Jennings, Amabile, & Ross, 1982). Finally, decision makers should carefully distinguish between correlation and causation. Not only can two events covary without a causal connection, but two events can be causally connected with only a weak correlation. Chapter 16 is devoted to a detailed examination of one of the most important judgments of causation—judgments concerning the causes of behavior.

CHAPTER 16

ATTRIBUTION THEORY

You meet a friend who compliments you on your appearance. You go out on a date and it goes badly. You give an important talk in front of a group and the audience reacts negatively. If these situations happened to you, how would you explain them?

Attribution theory is a psychological theory about how people make "causal attributions," or explanations for the causes of actions and outcomes. The theory was first systematically developed in a paper by UCLA psychologist Harold Kelley (1967) that drew heavily from the classic works of Fritz Heider (1958) and Ned Jones and Keith Davis (1965). As in the case of expected utility theory, attribution theory was proposed as a normative theory of judgment (an idealized theory of how people should behave), but unlike expected utility theory, it was also offered as a descriptive model of everyday behavior.

In his original formulation, Kelley devised an attribution model which he called the "analysis of variance framework" (named after a statistical technique known as analysis of variance, or ANOVA). According to this model, people generally explain behavior in terms of three possible causes: (1) *the person*—something about the person in question may have caused the behavior; (2) *the entity*—some enduring feature of the situation may have caused the behavior; or (3) *the time*—something about the particular occasion may have caused the behavior. Kelley argued that these three attributions are based largely on three sources of information:

1. *Consensus:* Do other people respond similarly in the same situation?
2. *Distinctiveness:* Do other situations or stimuli elicit the same behavior?
3. *Consistency:* Does the same thing happen every time?

Table 16.1 contains some of the predictions from Kelley's attribution theory. In this table, "high consensus" means that most people behave similarly in the same situation, "high distinctiveness" means that the behavior is evoked only by distinctive stimuli or entities, and "high consistency" means that much the same thing happens each time the circumstance arises. To illustrate, suppose you were the only examinee (low consensus) who performed well on a variety of tests (low distinc-

174

TABLE 16.1
PREDICTIONS FROM ATTRIBUTION THEORY

Predicted Attribution	PATTERN OF INFORMATION		
	Consensus	Distinctiveness	Consistency
Person	Low	Low	High
Stimulus (entity)	High	High	High
Circumstance (time)	Low	High	Low

Note: This table is adapted from an article by Bruce Orvis, John Cunningham, and Harold Kelley (1975).

tiveness) over a range of occasions (high consistency). Kelley would predict a "person attribution"—an explanation of your behavior in terms of personal abilities (Explanation C in Item #24 of the Reader Survey). Indeed, the very idea of grading is based on the premise that the most accurate way to make person attributions is to measure behavior across time and situations. Using the ANOVA framework, this type of attribution can be represented with a band that cuts across time and entities but is limited to only one person (see Figure 16.1).

On the other hand, if the band cuts across time and people but is limited to only one entity, Kelley would predict an "entity attribution." For example, if one (highly distinctive) test were administered every year and students always performed well on it (with high consensus and high consistency), people should explain high scores as a function of the test (entity) rather than the person taking the test (see Table 16.1 and Figure 16.2).

According to Kelley, causal attributions are based on judgments of *covariation* (discussed in detail in Chapter 15). This link is embodied in

FIGURE 16.1
According to Harold Kelley's ANOVA model, this pattern of information should lead to a person attribution (an explanation based on factors specific to the person). *(Reprinted from Kelley, 1973.)*

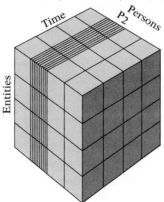

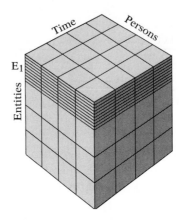

FIGURE 16.2

According to Harold Kelley's ANOVA model, this pattern of information should lead to an entity attribution (an explanation based on factors specific to the entity, or stimulus, in question). (Reprinted from Kelley, 1973.)

Kelley's (1973, p. 108) "covariation principle," which states that "an effect is attributed to the one of its possible causes with which, over time, it covaries."

Kelley realized how oversimplified this principle was, but he offered it as a general guideline to think about how people make causal attributions. Since the time attribution theory was first developed, it has stimulated hundreds of studies aimed at discovering whether Kelley's predictions are accurate. In fact, more than 900 articles appeared in the first 10 years of attribution research alone (Kelley & Michela, 1980). There have also been several notable refinements and extensions of the original theory (Cheng & Novick, 1990; Försterling, 1989; Hewstone & Jaspars, 1987; Hilton & Slugoski, 1986; Orvis, Cunningham, & Kelley, 1975).

Does attribution theory capture how people explain their behavior and the behavior of others? For the most part the answer is yes, but there are several important exceptions.

A LACK OF CONSENSUS

In certain situations, people deviate from the predictions of attribution theory by disregarding consensus information (Nisbett, Borgida, Crandall, & Reed, 1976). The underutilization of consensus information is essentially a case of base rate neglect, since consensus information is equivalent to the base rate of behavior in a given situation. For example, in his famous research on obedience to authority, Stanley Milgram (1963) found that a 65 percent "consensus" of subjects obeyed the experimenter fully. Yet, when Günter Bierbrauer (1973) reenacted

Milgram's experiment in front of observers, this base rate was all but ignored. Observers attributed the behavior of obedient subjects primarily to their personal characteristics rather than situational factors common to all subjects in the experiment.

Richard Nisbett and Eugene Borgida (1975) have argued that people often ignore base rates like this when making causal attributions. Nisbett and Borgida noted that, while there is considerable evidence that consistency information and distinctiveness information affect causal attributions, very little evidence suggests that consensus information plays a major role. One of the earliest experiments testing Kelley's ANOVA model, a study published by Leslie McArthur (1972), lends support to their argument. McArthur found that consistency and distinctiveness information each affected causal attributions several times more than did consensus information.

Additional support for their thesis comes from a pair of experiments Nisbett and Borgida (1975) conducted. In these experiments, college students were told about two previously published studies—one by Richard Nisbett and Stanley Schachter (1966), and the other by John Darley and Bibb Latané (1968). Some students were given consensus information describing how subjects behaved in the earlier studies, and others were given no consensus information.

Both of the earlier studies were chosen because they had yielded surprising consensus information. Nisbett and Schachter (1966) found that 32 of 34 subjects willingly received electric shocks in an experiment purporting to be on "skin sensitivity" (and nearly half withstood jolts so strong that their arms jerked). Even more startling, Darley and Latané (1968) found that 11 of 15 subjects failed to help an apparent seizure victim until the person began choking (and six never helped the victim at all). According to the ANOVA model, this consensus information should lead people to make situational attributions, because most subjects in the earlier studies behaved identically when confronted with the same situation.

Nisbett and Borgida (1975) asked their students a variety of questions, but two items are of particular interest. First, students were asked to rate how much the behavior of a specific subject—Bill J. in the shock experiment, who willingly received the most extreme shock, or Greg R. in the seizure experiment, who failed to help at all—was due to the subject's personality (as opposed to features of the situation). Second, students were asked to guess how *they* would have behaved if they had been subjects in the experiment.

Nisbett and Borgida found that consensus information was "virtually without effect." Students who were told that most subjects in the earlier experiments behaved similarly did *not* make significantly more situational attributions for the behavior of Bill J. and Greg R. Consensus information also failed to affect students' judgments of how they would have acted had they been in the original studies. How other people behaved simply did not matter.

Although some researchers have disputed the conclusions of Nisbett and Borgida (e.g., Ruble & Feldman, 1976; Wells & Harvey, 1977), their basic observation has been replicated by other investigators. When trends in behavior are presented as statistical base rates, people often discount or ignore consensus information (Fiske & Taylor, 1991; Kassin, 1979; Nisbett, Borgida, Crandall, & Reed, 1976). Nisbett and Borgida (1975) explained this tendency as a result of the abstract, pallid, and remote quality of base rate information. According to their explanation, consistency information and distinctiveness information are seen as more causal than consensus information because they are usually more concrete, vivid, and salient. As the next section shows, salient factors—that is, factors which command attention—are typically seen as more causal than less prominent factors.

SALIENCE

Salience is, in many respects, similar to availability and vividness. Information that is salient, available, or vivid tends to have more impact than information which is not. In very general terms: (1) The more *available* an event is, the more frequent or probable it will seem; (2) the more *vivid* a piece of information is, the more easily recalled and convincing it will be; and (3) the more *salient* something is, the more likely it will be to appear causal. Perceptions of causality are partly determined by where one's attention is directed within the environment, and attention is in turn a function of salience.

The link between salience and causal attribution was first proposed by Heider (1958) and was conclusively documented in a seminal review by Shelley Taylor and Susan Fiske (1978). Taylor and Fiske discussed a wide variety of evidence, including results from several of their own studies. For example, Taylor and Fiske (1975) conducted a study in which six observers watched a two-man conversation from one of three vantage points: seated behind one of the men who was talking, seated behind the other man who was talking, or seated on the sidelines equidistant from the two men (see Figure 16.3). All observers watched the dialogue simultaneously, so the only systematic difference among them was the visual salience of the men holding the conversation. Nonetheless, Taylor and Fiske found that observers tended to rate the man in their visual field as having set the tone of the conversation, having determined the type of information exchanged, and having caused the other person to respond as he did (sideline observers tended to rate the two men as equally influential).

In another study, subjects were shown a coordinated slide and tape presentation of six men brainstorming about a publicity campaign

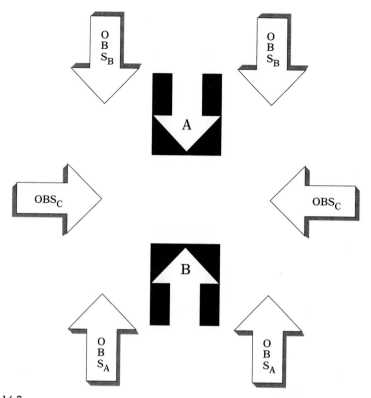

FIGURE 16.3

This diagram shows the seating arrangement in an experiment by Shelley Taylor and Susan Fiske (1975). Two observers faced Person A, two observers faced Person B, and two observers in the control group sat equidistant between Person A and Person B. Taylor and Fiske found that observers rated the person they faced as most influential.

(Taylor, Fiske, Close, Anderson, & Ruderman, 1977). In one experimental condition, each of the voices on the tape was paired with the photograph of a white male; in a second condition, three voices were paired with white males and three with black males; and in a third condition, the voices were paired with five whites and one black (the same soundtrack was used in all three conditions). In line with the hypothesis that salient individuals are perceived as more influential, Taylor and her colleagues found that the lone black in the third condition was perceived as talking more, being more influential, and giving a clearer impression than the same person in the context of other blacks (when he was less salient). Thus, the very same person saying the very same thing was perceived as talking more and being more influential when he was the only black in the group.

Additional studies have manipulated the salience of observed people in other ways—by having them wear a boldly patterned shirt as opposed to a grey shirt, by having them rock in a rocking chair instead of sitting motionless, or by having them sit under a bright light versus a dim light—and the results have tended to be the same (McArthur & Post, 1977). Salient people are perceived as relatively causal. In fact, one study even found that when people were seated in front of a large mirror, they tended to view themselves as more causal (Duval & Wicklund, 1973).

THE FUNDAMENTAL ATTRIBUTION ERROR

In his landmark work *The Psychology of Interpersonal Relations*, Heider (1958) observed that "behavior engulfs the field." What he meant by this statement is that the most salient thing in a social setting is behavior (and, by implication, the "actors" who are behaving). Situational factors, such as room temperature or the time of day, are generally secondary. People are in the foreground; most everything else is in the background.

In 1977, Lee Ross argued that this focus on actors and their behavior leads observers to overattribute behavior to dispositional factors—such as abilities, traits, and motives—and underestimate the influence of situational factors. In fact, Ross contended that this overreadiness to explain behavior in terms of dispositional factors is so widespread and universal that it should be called "the fundamental attribution error." The reason for labeling this tendency as an *error*, rather than simply an attributional bias or difference of opinion, is that dispositional attributions are often patently incorrect (Reeder, 1982). For example, Arthur Miller and his colleagues (1973) found that people judged highly obedient subjects in Milgram's (1963) study to be relatively cold, maladjusted, and aggressive, even though this was clearly not the case.

Additional evidence of overattribution comes from the first attitude attribution study ever published. In this experiment, conducted by Ned Jones and Victor Harris (1967), subjects were presented with an essay written by someone who was either explicitly forced to take a particular position or someone who had "free choice" in selecting a position. Even when subjects were expressly told that an essay's author was forced to take a particular position, they tended to attribute that position to the author. This finding is very robust and has been replicated in a number of different studies (Jones, 1979; Snyder & Jones, 1974).

The fundamental attribution error can be extremely persistent, as Paula Pietromonaco and Richard Nisbett (1982) illustrated in their study "Swimming Upstream Against the Fundamental Attribution Error." Pietromonaco and Nisbett presented roughly half their subjects with an abridged version of the Darley and Batson (1973) study of seminary students who failed to help a man in need because they were late to give a lecture on the parable of the Good Samaritan (discussed in Chapter 5). In that study, helping behavior depended on the situational factor of hurriedness rather than the dispositional factor of religiosity (63 percent of the students helped when they were under no time pressure, compared with only 10 percent when they were extremely rushed). The rest of Pietromonaco and Nisbett's subjects were not told about the results of Darley and Batson's experiment. All subjects were then given two scenarios similar to the one in Darley and Batson's study, and they were asked to estimate the percentage of people who would stop to help the victim in each scenario.

Pietromonaco and Nisbett (1982) found that subjects who were unaware of the study by Darley and Batson (1973) fell prey to the fundamental attribution error. They tended to predict helping behavior on the basis of religiosity (a dispositional factor that was actually unrelated to helping). By itself, this finding is unremarkable; not knowing the outcome of Darley and Batson's study, most people would assume that helping is a function of dispositional factors. More surprising is the finding that subjects who read about Darley and Batson's study *also* relied on religiosity to predict helping behavior. Indeed, they were not significantly less inclined to rely on dispositional factors than subjects who knew nothing about the study by Darley and Batson.

These results show once again that base rate information is often ignored, and they suggest that the fundamental attribution error may be very resistant to change. Even when people are explicitly told about the pressures present in one situation, they make dispositional attributions for behavior in related situations. Although some researchers have argued that the fundamental attribution error is not as "fundamental" as originally suspected (Harvey, Town, & Yarkin, 1981; Quattrone, 1982; Tetlock, 1985a), there is no question that observers frequently overattribute behavior to dispositional factors.

MY SITUATION IS YOUR DISPOSITION

If the behavior of an actor engulfs the observer's field, what engulfs the actor's field? The answer seems to be that actors focus on the situation at hand. Only in rare situations do actors watch themselves behave in the same way observers do.

As a consequence of this difference in focus, actors tend to explain their behavior as a function of situational factors more often than do observers. According to Ned Jones and Richard Nisbett (1971, p. 2), who first noted this difference between actors and observers: "The actor's view of his behavior emphasizes the role of environmental conditions at the moment of action. The observer's view emphasizes the causal role of stable dispositional properties of the actor. We wish to argue that *there is a pervasive tendency for actors to attribute their actions to situational requirements, whereas observers tend to attribute the same actions to stable personal dispositions.*"

One of the best known studies on actor-observer differences in attribution was published in 1973 by Richard Nisbett, Craig Caputo, Patricia Legant, and Jeanne Marecek. Nisbett and his colleagues conducted three separate experiments, each of which found significant attributional differences between actors and observers. In one experiment, for example, Nisbett and his associates asked male college students to write four brief paragraphs explaining (1) why they liked the woman they had dated most frequently during the past year or so, (2) why they had chosen their college major, (3) why their best male friend liked the woman he had dated most regularly in the past year or so, and (4) why their best friend had chosen his major. These paragraphs were then scored as to how much they stressed situational factors versus dispositional factors. For instance, statements such as "She's a relaxing person" or "Chemistry is a high-paying field" were scored as situational reasons, whereas "I need someone I can relax with" or "I want to make a lot of money" were scored as dispositional reasons.

Nisbett and his colleagues found that, when students explained why they liked their girlfriend, they gave more than twice as many situational reasons (reasons that referred to characteristics of the woman) than dispositional reasons (reasons that referred to their own needs, interests, and traits). On the other hand, when they explained why their best friend liked his girlfriend, they gave almost equal numbers of situational and dispositional reasons. Similarly, when students explained why they had chosen their major, they listed roughly the same number of situational and dispositional factors. Yet they gave almost four times as many dispositional reasons as situational reasons when explaining their best friend's choice of major.

Averaging over the dating question and college major question, students tended to give more situational reasons than dispositional reasons for their own behaviors, but more dispositional than situational reasons for the behavior of others. Or, putting the results another way, they made nearly the same number of dispositional attributions for their own behavior and the behavior of others, but made nearly twice as many situational attributions for themselves as others. Nisbett and his colleagues explained this discrepancy largely in terms of differences between the information that is salient to actors and observers.

In 1982, David Watson published a review article closely examining this issue. Watson wanted to know whether actor-observer differences were due mainly to a difference in making dispositional attributions, a difference in making situational attributions, or both. What he found was that in most studies, actors and observers both ascribed more causal importance to people's dispositions than to situational factors. As in the study by Nisbett et al. (1973), though, actors and observers differed in their tendency to make situational attributions. People were much more willing to invoke situational explanations for their own behavior than for the behavior of others.

TRADING PLACES

If actor-observer differences in attribution are largely a function of perspective, it should be possible to reverse these differences by swapping the perspectives of actors and observers. This was the logic behind a study by Michael Storms (1973), in which actors and observers were given an opportunity to trade places. Storms filmed a get-acquainted conversation that two "actor-subjects" had in the presence of two off-camera "observer-subjects." Each observer was assigned to watch a different actor, and two videotapes were made—one shot essentially from Actor 1's perspective looking at Actor 2, and another from Actor 2's perspective looking at Actor 1. Thirty foursomes, or 120 subjects in all, participated in the experiment.

After the get-acquainted conversation, subjects were assigned to one of three experimental conditions: (1) the *same orientation* condition, in which observers viewed a videotape of the same actor they had been watching, and actors viewed a videotape of their conversation partner; (2) the *new orientation* condition, in which observers viewed a videotape of the actor they had not been watching (thereby adopting their assigned actor's perspective), and actors viewed a videotape of themselves (adopting their observer's orientation); and (3) the *no videotape* condition, in which subjects did not watch a videotape of the conversation.

Storms then asked subjects to rate the degree to which personal characteristics and characteristics of the situation had been responsible for various aspects of the actors' behavior. Actors rated themselves, and observers rated the actor they had been assigned to watch during the get-acquainted conversation. What Storms found is that subjects who either watched a videotape from the same orientation or watched no videotape at all displayed actor-observer differences in attribution, but subjects who viewed a videotape shot from the opposite perspective showed a reversal of actor-observer differences in attribution (see Figure 16.4). From these results, Storms concluded that visual orientation powerfully influences the causal attributions people make.

CLINICAL IMPLICATIONS

Most of the research reviewed thus far points in the same direction: When explaining the causes of behavior, people rely heavily on factors that are salient at the time. For observers, the actor is most salient; for the actor, situational demands are salient. This seemingly minor distinction has profound implications. The difference between interpreting behavior as situationally caused or dispositionally caused is critical in a wide array of social judgments, including jury and parole board decisions, perceptions of battered wives, and explanations for scholastic failure (Frieze, Bar-Tal, & Carroll, 1979).

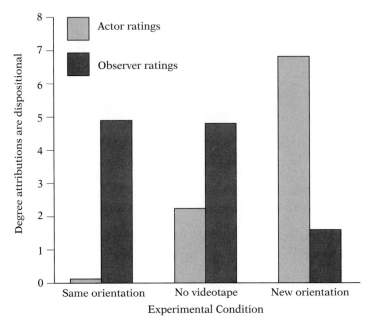

FIGURE 16.4

Attributional differences are reversed when actors and observers exchange perspectives. *(Results from a study by Michael Storms, 1973.)*

One area in which causal attributions are particularly critical is psychotherapy (Batson & Marz, 1979; Ross, Rodin, & Zimbardo, 1969; Shenkel, Snyder, Batson, & Clark, 1979; Snyder, 1977; Valins & Nisbett, 1971). Therapy is a special topic of interest because treatment recommendations often depend directly on whether a client's problem is attributed to situational factors or to the client's disposition (Batson, 1975). If situational factors are responsible for the problem, then efforts are frequently aimed at changing the situation. On the other hand, if dispositional factors are to blame, then an effort is usually made to change the individual. Unfortunately, this determination may have more to do with a therapist's orientation and training than the circumstance in question. As a study I conducted with Philip Zimbardo shows, attributional biases strongly color clinical inferences.

In this study, we used a mail survey to assess the attributional style of prominent psychoanalysts, behavior therapists, and a nontherapist control group. Respondents were asked to explain three hypothetical problems experienced by themselves, their closest same-sex friend, or a client. For instance, respondents were asked how they would explain the onset of a sleep disturbance with recurrent nightmares. These answers were then rated along dimensions such as situational-dispositional and physical-psychological.

The results showed a number of interesting patterns. First, psychoanalysts tended to explain problems in terms of the sufferer's personality, whereas behavior therapists and nontherapists tended to explain problems in terms of situational factors or a mixture of situational and dispositional causes. Second, when hypothetical problems were experienced by their friends or clients, psychoanalysts tended to see the problems as psychological in origin, but when the same problems were experienced by themselves, psychoanalysts explained them as physical. Behavior therapists and nontherapists showed no such tendency. Finally, clinicians holding medical degrees made more physical attributions and fewer psychological attributions than did clinicians with nonmedical degrees. These findings led us to conclude that "the selection of a therapist may be an important factor in determining inferred etiology and recommended treatment, independent of the actual problem" (Plous & Zimbardo, 1986, p. 570).

OTHER ATTRIBUTIONAL BIASES

In addition to actor-observer differences in attribution, the fundamental attribution error, and the tendency to ignore consensus information, there are a number of other attributional biases that influence social judgments. For example, people are more likely to accept responsibility for successes than for failures (Miller, 1976; Mullen & Riordan, 1988; Schlenker & Miller, 1977). Dale Miller and Michael Ross (1975) have referred to this tendency as a "self-serving" bias in attribution, and research suggests that it arises from a complex combination of cognitive and motivational factors (e.g., false expectations, the desire to look good, and the need to protect self-esteem).

A related class of biases, known as "egocentric" biases in attribution, have also been amply documented. Egocentric biases are those in which people accept more responsibility for joint outcomes than other contributors attribute to them. Michael Ross and Fiore Sicoly (1979) conducted the first empirical investigation of egocentric biases. In this research, Ross and Sicoly asked 37 married couples to complete a questionnaire about their relationship. Each member of the couple was asked to estimate how responsible she or he was for 20 different activities, such as making breakfast, cleaning dishes, demonstrating affection, and so on. In 16 of these activities, egocentric biases were evident (i.e., when ratings from each member of the couple were added together, the total exceeded more than 100 percent of the rating scale).

Although egocentric biases are sometimes simply a matter of claiming undue credit for positive outcomes and behavior, Ross and Sicoly also found that they occur for undesirable actions. They discovered, for example, that marriage partners tended to report *causing* as well as resolving the majority of conflicts in their relationship. These findings suggest that egocentric biases are more than attempts at self-enhancement. In some cases, they may arise because one's own actions are more available (more easily retrieved from memory) than the actions of other people (Thompson & Kelley, 1981).

Another closely related bias is what Shelley Taylor and Judy Koivumaki (1976) have called the "positivity effect." The positivity effect is a tendency to attribute positive behaviors to dispositional factors and negative behaviors to situational factors. In their research, Taylor and Koivumaki presented married people with a list of positive and negative behaviors committed by themselves, their spouse, a friend, or an acquaintance. For example, positive behaviors included paying a compliment to someone, talking cheerfully to another person, and having fun. Negative behaviors included having a heated argument with someone, being rude to someone, and forgetting to do something. Taylor and Koivumaki asked subjects to rate the degree to which these behaviors were due to situational or dispositional factors. What they found—regardless of who committed the behavior—was that positive behaviors were attributed primarily to dispositional factors, and negative behaviors were attributed mainly to situational factors.

Of course, Taylor and Koivumaki did not ask subjects to explain the behavior of people whom they disliked; if they had, an opposing "negativity effect" might have been observed (see, for example, Regan, Straus, & Fazio, 1974). Indeed, Thomas Pettigrew (1979) has called a negativity effect for disliked others the "ultimate attribution error." Pettigrew, a widely respected expert on racial prejudice, warned: "When race and ethnicity are involved, these attributions will take the form of believing the actions to be a result of immutable, genetic characteristics of the derogated people in general—the bedrock assumption of racist doctrine" (p. 465).

Pettigrew's warning is based on more than hollow speculation. In 1976, Birt Duncan linked attributional biases with racial prejudice. In this experiment, white college students were asked to watch a videotaped discussion between two people who eventually had a heated argument. Toward the end of the videotape, one of the discussants shoved the other. The experiment had four conditions: (1) black shover and white shovee; (2) white shover and black shovee; (3) both discussants white; and (4) both discussants black. Not only did subjects rate the shove as more violent when it came from a black person than a white person, but they tended to make dispositional attributions for black shoving and situational attributions for white shoving.

One additional form of attributional bias—a bias that often reinforces prejudicial judgments—is the tendency to ascribe less variability to others than to oneself. This bias was first documented in Germany by Daniele Kammer (1982) and was subsequently replicated in the United

States by Terri Baxter and Lewis Goldberg (1987). Kammer presented subjects with 20 different bipolar trait scales, such as quiet-talkative and cautious-bold, and asked them to rate how much they and their friends varied along these dimensions from situation to situation. Kammer found that people viewed their own behavior as more variable across situations than their friends' behavior. Research also suggests that people see themselves as more multifaceted and less predictable than others (Sande, Goethals, & Radloff, 1988), and that they are more willing to ascribe temporary states—moods, thoughts, and feelings—to themselves than others (White & Younger, 1988). As a result of this relatively undifferentiated view of others, racial, ethnic, and gender stereotypes flourish.

CONCLUSION

How do you explain the things that happen to you? Do you usually attribute them to your personal abilities, interests, and traits, or do you attribute them to outside factors? Are the causes typically specific to a particular situation, or are they fairly global and stable over time?

This chapter opened with three brief scenarios: (1) You meet a friend who compliments you on your appearance; (2) you go out on a date and it goes badly; and (3) you give an important talk in front of a group and the audience reacts negatively. Each of these scenarios was taken from the Attributional Style Questionnaire developed by Martin Seligman and his colleagues (Peterson, Semmel, von Baeyer, Abramson, Metalsky, & Seligman, 1982). Seligman and his associates have used this questionnaire to see whether depressed people display a different attributional style than nondepressed people. In an early paper, Lyn Abramson, Martin Seligman, and John Teasdale (1978) hypothesized that depressed people tend to attribute negative events to stable, global, and internal causes (e.g., "As usual, the date went badly because I stuck my foot in my mouth"). Research by Seligman and his colleagues supports this hypothesis (Seligman, Abramson, Semmel, & von Baeyer, 1979), as do the results of a statistical "meta-analysis" based on more than 100 studies (Sweeney, Anderson, & Bailey, 1986). Attributional style is directly related to mental health and emotional well-being.

Fortunately, it is possible to avoid many of the attributional pitfalls outlined in this chapter. For example, one way of reducing the fundamental attribution error is to pay close attention to consensus information. If most people behave similarly when confronted by the same situation, a dispositional explanation is probably unwarranted. Instead, observers should look to situational factors for an explanation of behavior.

Another "debiasing" technique is to ask how you would have behaved if thrust into the same circumstance. Research suggests that perspective-taking can reverse actor-observer differences in attribution (Galper, 1976; Regan & Totten, 1975). This technique will be discussed further in the Afterword.

Because causal attributions often depend on whatever factors happen to be most salient, it is also important to look for hidden causes. John Pryor and Mitchell Kriss (1977) found that even minor changes in wording can influence salience and, in turn, alter causal attributions. For example, statements such as "Fred likes the car" are more likely to elicit dispositional explanations than "The car is liked by Fred," because Fred is more salient in the former sentence than the latter. This sensitivity to question wording is consistent with the research reviewed in Chapters 5 and 6, and it suggests that causal attributions are "plastic" in much the same way as are other judgments.

THE SOCIAL SIDE OF JUDGMENT AND DECISION MAKING

Previous sections of this book have focused mainly on the behavior of lone decision makers, but in many cases, decision makers are strongly influenced by other people. This section covers some of the ways that social factors affect judgment and decision making (Chapter 17), and it compares the behavior of groups with the behavior of individuals (Chapter 18).

CHAPTER 17

SOCIAL INFLUENCES

Seeing ourselves as others see us would probably confirm our worst suspicions about them.

—Franklin P. Jones (cited in Peter, 1977)

As Chapter 16 showed, people frequently discount or ignore consensus information when making causal attributions. Does this mean, then, that decision makers are unconcerned with the behavior and attitudes of other people? Far from it. Even the most independent decision makers are strongly affected by social factors.

Indeed, Philip Tetlock (1985b) has argued that social factors play a pivotal role in judgment and decision making. According to Tetlock (p. 325): "Experimental cognitive research on judgment and decision-making has adopted a misleadingly narrow focus on its subject matter and needs to be broadened to take into consideration the impact of social and organizational context." Tetlock has proposed that decision makers be regarded as "politicians" who are accountable to their "constituents" (e.g., friends, family members, and co-workers), and who are constantly concerned with questions such as "How will others react if I do this?" and "How can I justify my views to others if challenged?" The importance of outside evaluations—and their ability to influence how people behave—is one of the oldest findings in experimental social psychology.

SOCIAL FACILITATION

In his history of social psychology, Gordon Allport (1954, p. 46) wrote that: "The first experimental problem—and indeed the only problem for the first three decades of experimental research—was formulated as follows: What change in an individual's normal solitary performance occurs when other people are present?" Although work on this question began in the latter part of the nineteenth century, it was not until 1965 that a comprehensive answer was given. In that year, Robert Zajonc made the case that the performance of simple, well-learned responses is usually enhanced by the presence of onlookers, but the performance of complex, unmastered skills tends to be impaired by the presence of others. Zajonc speculated that this effect, known as "social facilitation,"

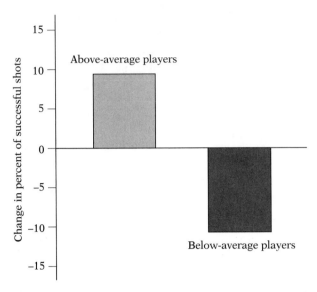

FIGURE 17.1
Above-average pool players benefit from being watched, whereas below-average players grow worse in the presence of an audience. *(Adapted from Michaels et al., 1982.)*

was at least partly due to arousal from the physical presence of others. Later research showed that this enhancement or impairment takes place even when the prospect of being evaluated by others does not involve their physical presence (Henchy & Glass, 1968).

Although social facilitation has been found with a variety of verbal and mathematical tasks, one of the most straightforward demonstrations of the effect was conducted in a college pool hall (Michaels, Blommel, Brocato, Linkous, & Rowe, 1982). In this study, unobtrusive observers classified pool players as above or below average in ability, and they recorded the percentage of successful shots made by these players in the presence or absence of onlookers. As Figure 17.1 shows, the presence of an audience improved the performance of above-average players and hurt the performance of below-average players. Charles Bond and Linda Titus (1983) found similar, though less dramatic, results in a statistical meta-analysis that covered more than 200 studies and 20,000 subjects. The presence of an audience impaired accuracy in complex tasks and slightly improved accuracy in simple tasks.

SOCIAL LOAFING

Social facilitation is not the only way that performance is influenced by the presence of others. Roughly 30 years after social facilitation effects were first documented, Walther Moede (1927) reported an experiment showing that people do not work as hard in groups as they work alone. In this experiment, conducted by a student of Moede's named Ringelmann, people were found to pull harder on a rope when tugging alone than in groups of two, three, or eight. On the average, individual subjects performing in twosomes pulled only 93 percent as hard as subjects working alone, subjects in threesomes pulled only 85 percent as hard, and subjects in groups of eight pulled only 49 percent as hard. In a clever replication of this study, Alan Ingham, George Levinger, James Graves, and Vaughn Peckham (1974) found the same drop in performance even when people pulled alone but were blindfolded and led to believe that others were pulling with them. Bibb Latané, Kipling Williams, and Stephen Harkins (1979) referred to this effect as "social loafing," and they found that it also occurs when people are asked to shout or clap as loudly as possible (see Figure 17.2).

What causes social loafing? The answer is unclear. Latané, Williams, and Harkins proposed that social loafing arises because people in groups do not feel the link between their effort and the final outcome as directly as people working alone. Related to this difference, responsibility for the final outcome is diffused among members of a group, whereas individuals working alone bear sole responsibility for the outcome. Dif-

FIGURE 17.2

This figure illustrates social loafing. On the average, as the size of a group increases, the contribution of each individual declines. Here, the average noise created by an individual shouting or clapping alone (measured in dynes per square centimeter) is roughly twice that of individuals working in groups of six. *(Adapted from Latané, Williams, and Harkins, 1979.)*

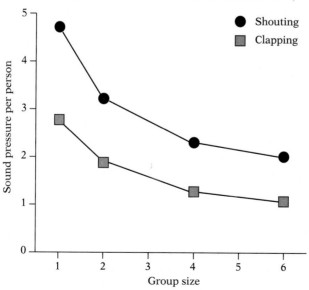

fusion of responsibility can have a powerful influence on judgment and decision making, as the following three scenes illustrate.

SCENE 1: "LET THAT GIRL ALONE!"

It is 3:20 in the morning, March 13, 1964. The setting is a parking lot next to the Kew Gardens Railroad Station in New York. Kitty Genovese, a 28-year-old bar manager, has just returned home from work. She parks her red Fiat, turns off the lights, locks the door, and walks toward her apartment 100 feet away.

Then, suddenly, she notices a man on the other side of the parking lot.

Kitty heads toward a police call box located on a nearby boulevard, but she does not make it there in time. The man grabs her under a street light, and she lets out a scream. Lights go on in the 10-story apartment building across the street, windows slide open, and Kitty cries out, "Oh, my God, he stabbed me! Please help me! Please help me!"

A man in one of the apartments calls down, "Let that girl alone!"

The assailant complies, and Kitty is left there to bleed. Soon the apartment lights go out. Kitty tries to reach her apartment, but the man reappears and stabs her again. This time she shrieks, "I'm dying! I'm dying!" Apartment lights come on once again, neighbors open their windows, and the man gets into his car and drives off.

After a short time, Kitty struggles to her feet. A city bus passes by on its way to Kennedy Airport. It is now 3:35 AM.

Kitty finally manages to get to her apartment entrance, where she slumps over at the foot of the stairs. Then the man returns and stabs her a third time—fatally.

Now for the unnerving epilogue to this story: When the murder first occurred, its coverage in the *New York Times* consisted of only five sentences buried on page 26. Two weeks later, though, the story appeared in a large front-page article. Why? Because a police investigation found that no less than 38 "respectable, law-abiding citizens" had witnessed the killing, but "not one person telephoned the police during the assault" (Gansberg, 1964, March 27, p. 1). The police received their first call 30 minutes *after* Kitty Genovese had initially been attacked. In other words, the assailant attacked her on and off for half an hour while she cried for help, but none of the 38 neighbors who witnessed her murder came to her assistance or even called the police from their apartment.

SCENE 2: TUNNEL VISION

It is Saturday, July 14, 1990. The setting is a highway near Florence, Italy. Marco Moretti is driving his six-year-old daughter, Vanessa, to the beach when suddenly, just as he enters a tunnel, Marco suffers a massive heart attack. Marco manages to pull the car over and tell Vanessa to make her way home. Then, at the age of 33, Marco dies.

Vanessa slips out of the car into onrushing traffic and tries to get help. Cars shoot by so fast that gusts of wind knock her to the ground, but she continues—scratched, bleeding, and in tears—desperately seeking help. During the next 30 minutes, Vanessa walks more than a mile as hundreds of cars streak by, but no one stops to help her. Finally a motorist pulls over to help, and soon afterward the police are summoned.

This story, like the story of Kitty Genovese, made the front page of national newspapers. Italians asked themselves how this event could have happened, and they took it as a sign that Italy was no longer the warm, compassionate place it once was. For example, one Italian sociologist was widely quoted as saying that Vanessa was "a symbol of an Italy that we would like to ignore—a cold Italy, at times glacial, where in the best of cases each one thinks only about himself and a few others more or less close to him" (Haberman, 1990, July 19, p. A11).

SCENE 3: PICKING UP THE PIECES

It is now the early 1970s. The setting is an elevator in one of three American cities: Columbus, Seattle, or Atlanta. Just after the elevator doors close, a person in the back "accidentally" drops 8 to 10 pencils (or, in some cases, pennies or nickels—the object doesn't matter).

The event, part of a field experiment conducted by Bibb Latané and James Dabbs (1975), is repeated on 1497 separate occasions with 145 different people dropping objects in front of a total of 4813 bystanders. Latané and Dabbs are interested in the following question: "Who will help the person pick up the objects?" One of the things they discover is that individuals are less likely to help as the number of people in the elevator increases.

BYSTANDER INTERVENTION

The common thread running through each of the preceding scenes is that the responsibility to help was *diffused* in relatively large groups. When individuals were faced with a decision about whether to intervene, they were influenced by the presence of other people. This relationship between intervention and diffusion of responsibility was first documented by Bibb Latané and John Darley (1969, 1970) in a brilliant series of experiments on bystander intervention.

In one of these experiments, Latané and Darley invited students to come for an interview on "some of the problems involved in life at an urban university." When students arrived, they were seated in a waiting room either alone, with two confederates (i.e., assistants of the experimenter) who had been instructed to remain passive, or with two other actual subjects. Then, as subjects sat in the waiting room, a stream of white smoke began pouring into the room through a vent in the wall.

Latané and Darley wanted to see whether students would be less inclined to report the smoke in the presence of other bystanders than when they were waiting alone.

What Latané and Darley found was that three-quarters of the students who waited alone reported the smoke, half of them within two minutes. In contrast, only 1 subject in 10 ever reported the smoke in the presence of two confederates who remained inactive. They coughed, rubbed their eyes, and opened the window—but never reported the smoke!

As for the three students who waited together, it is not really appropriate to compare them directly with students who waited alone. If students waiting alone reported the smoke 75 percent of the time, then a group of three independent people should report the smoke 98 percent of the time (because the probability of all three students *not* reporting the smoke is $.25 \times .25 \times .25 = .02$, and $1.00 - .02 = .98$). Instead, three-person groups reported the smoke only 38 percent of the time.

Just to make sure these findings were not the result of extraneous factors, such as fear of fires alone versus in groups, Latané and Darley decided to replicate the experiment in a different context. In an experiment ostensibly on "market research," they had students wait alone, with a friend, with a stranger, or with a passive confederate. Then, while subjects waited, they were led to believe that someone in the room next door fell and injured herself. This was done by playing a high fidelity recording of a crash, followed by a woman crying out: "Oh, my God, my foot . . . I . . . I . . . can't move it . . . Oh, my ankle. I . . . can't . . . can't . . . get . . . this thing off . . . me."

In response to her cries, 70 percent of the students who waited alone offered help. This means that if members of a pair were behaving independently of one another, at least one of them should have helped the woman 91 percent of the time (because again, the chances of both subjects *not* helping are $.30 \times .30 = .09$, and $1.00 - .09 = .91$). In contrast, pairs of unacquainted subjects helped the woman only 40 percent of the time, and pairs of friends helped only 70 percent of the time. Thus, even though paired friends were more likely to intervene than paired strangers, they still exerted an inhibiting effect on each other when compared to subjects who waited alone. The inhibiting effect of others is also clear when subjects who waited alone are contrasted with subjects who waited with a passive confederate. In the latter case, only 7 percent of the subjects intervened.

Latané and Darley found similar results in several additional studies, and since the time of their initial work, many other researchers have confirmed that helping is inhibited by the presence of others. In fact, in the decade following the first study by Latané and Darley, 48 of 56 experiments found that bystanders helped less often when someone else was present (Latané & Nida, 1981). Averaging over these 56 studies, people who were alone intervened 75 percent of the time, whereas those in groups helped out only 53 percent of the time.

Is there any group of people who are immune from the inhibiting effects of other bystanders? According to the results of a review by Bibb Latané and Steve Nida (1981), there is only one such group in American society: children under the age of nine. After that, the decision to intervene is heavily influenced by the presence of others.

SOCIAL COMPARISON THEORY

Research on social facilitation, social loafing, and diffusion of responsibility tends to support Tetlock's notion of decision makers as finely tuned politicians. People often take their cues directly from others, and they are very concerned about the opinions others have of them. Research also suggests that people evaluate their opinions and abilities by comparing themselves with others (Suls & Miller, 1977). The most elaborate theory of how they make these judgments is known as "social comparison theory."

Social comparison theory was proposed in 1954 by Leon Festinger—the same person who developed cognitive dissonance theory. Festinger postulated that people have a need to evaluate their ability levels and the appropriateness of their opinions, and that, in the absence of objective nonsocial standards, they compare themselves with others. In defining social comparison theory, Festinger tried to be as specific and as rigorous as possible. The theory contained nine hypotheses, eight corollaries, and eight derivations, or a total of 25 formal propositions.

In rough paraphrase, the most central of these propositions were the following:

> **Hypothesis I:**   People have a natural tendency to evaluate their opinions and abilities.
> **Hypothesis II:**   To the extent that objective, nonsocial information is unavailable, people evaluate their opinions and abilities by comparison with the opinions and abilities of others.
> **Corollary IIIA:**   Given a choice, people prefer to compare themselves with others who are close to them in opinions and abilities.

This last statement has been the subject of particularly intense scrutiny, and for the most part, research has supported Festinger's (1954) assertion. People usually compare themselves to others who are similar to them rather than to those who are dissimilar. For example, if you are a college student, chances are good that you measure your academic achievement against the performance of other college students, rather than graduate students or professors. Likewise, assistant professors normally compare themselves to other assistant professors, not to senior professors.

TAKING CUES FROM THOSE WHO ARE SIMILAR

The role of similarity in social comparison was demonstrated in an entertaining field experiment published by Harvey Hornstein, Elisha Fisch, and Michael Holmes (1968). In this study, more than 100 pedestrians in midtown Manhattan came across an addressed but unstamped envelope containing a lost wallet and a letter to the wallet's owner. Among other things, the wallet contained $2.00 in cash, a check made out to E.M.H. Co. (the initials of the investigators' first names!), a scrap of paper with someone's phone number, and an identification card with the owner's name, phone number, and address. The owner's name was Michael Erwin—carefully chosen to avoid any ethnic or religious connotations—and in all cases, the wallet and its contents were the same.

What varied was the letter to the wallet's owner. In some experimental conditions, the letter was from someone similar to the pedestrian-subject (i.e., someone fluent in English who seemed to be a fellow citizen), and in other conditions, the letter was from someone dissimilar (i.e., a foreigner who barely knew English). Also, the author of the letter struck a positive tone in one-third of the letters, a neutral tone in another third, and a negative tone in the remaining third. For example, the negative letter from a fluent English speaker (the "similar other") went as follows:

> Dear Mr. Erwin:
> I found your wallet which I am returning. Everything is here just as I found it.
> I must say that taking responsibility for the wallet and having to return it has been a great inconvenience. I was quite annoyed at having to bother with the whole problem of returning it. I hope you appreciate the efforts that I have gone through.

On the other hand, the negative letter from a dissimilar person was worded:

> Dear Mr Erwin:
> I am visit your country finding your ways not familiar and strange. But I find your wallet which here I return. Everything is here just as I find it.
> To take responsibility for wallet and necessity to return it is great inconvenience. Is annoyance to bother with whole problem of return and hope you appreciate effort I went to.

Hornstein, Fisch, and Holmes (1968) hypothesized that people would be affected by the tone of the letter more often when the writer was sim-

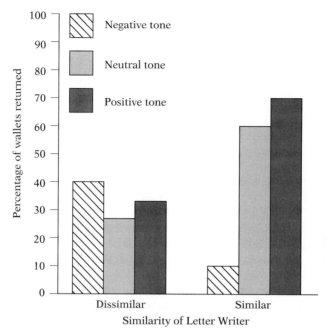

FIGURE 17.3

These percentages represent the number of people returning lost wallets in a study by Harvey Hornstein, Elisha Fisch, and Michael Holmes (1968).

ilar to them than when the writer was dissimilar (that is, they predicted that when the writer was similar, positive letters would lead to a higher return rate than negative letters, but when the writer was dissimilar, the letter's tone would not matter). As shown in Figure 17.3, this is exactly what happened. When the writer was a fellow citizen, a positive letter led people to return the wallet seven times more often than did a negative letter. In contrast, the return rate for positive, negative, and neutral letters was virtually identical when the letter was written by a foreigner. Although these results cannot, by themselves, be considered conclusive, they support Festinger's (1954) conjecture that people take their cues from others who are similar.

SOCIAL ANALGESIA

In 1978, Kenneth Craig and Kenneth Prkachin showed how strongly social comparisons can influence perceptions. These authors found that social comparisons with someone who has a high pain tolerance can actually lead people to experience less pain than they would otherwise.

Subjects in this study were given electric shocks to their left forearm. At first the shocks were barely detectable, but as the experiment continued, the shocks increased by small increments (0.25 milliampere). After each shock, subjects indicated on a scale from 0 to 100 how uncomfortable they felt, and when they rated a shock as 100, the experiment was ended.

There were two experimental conditions: the *tolerant modeling* condition and the *control* condition. In the tolerant modeling condition, each subject was paired with a confederate who posed as another subject and who consistently rated the shocks as 25 percent less painful than did the actual subject (the true subject always rated the shock first). In the control condition, the confederate simply observed the subject, and the subject was the only one who rated the electric shocks (this controlled for the presence of another person).

Craig and Prkachin found that subjects who were paired with a tolerant confederate not only rated the shocks as less painful; they actually seemed to experience less pain. Subjects in the tolerant model condition responded to increases in shock intensity with less heart rate reactivity and lower forearm skin potential (two measures of physical arousal) than subjects in the control condition. Thus, social comparisons affected bodily processes as well as pain ratings.

CONFORMITY

Take a close look at Lines 1, 2, and 3 in Item #32 of the Reader Survey. Which one is equal in length to Line A? If you are like most people, you see Line 3 as equal in length to Line A, and you have very little doubt that you are right.

But what if you were in a room with seven other people, each of whom declared Line 1 equal to Line A? Would you hold fast to your judgment, or would you bend in the face of a unanimous majority?

This is essentially the situation that Solomon Asch (1951; 1955, November; 1956) created in his classic experiments on conformity. In most of these experiments, 7 to 9 male college students were seated around a table and were asked to match the length of a "standard" line shown on one card with one of three "comparison" lines shown on another card. The experiment ran for 18 trials, and on every trial the judgments were very easy to make; a control group of independent raters averaged more than 99 percent correct. What subjects did not know is that the people seated around them were confederates. In most experimental sessions, the group contained only one real subject.

On the first trial of the experiment, the standard line was 10 inches long and the three comparison lines were 8¾ inches, 10 inches, and 8 inches. Students gave their judgments in clockwise order around the table, and everyone indicated that the 10-inch comparison line was equal to the standard line. No problem so far.

On the second trial, students were shown a standard line 2 inches long and comparison lines that were 2 inches, 1 inch, and 1½ inches in length. Again, students matched the comparison and standard lines without difficulty.

On the third trial, though, something strange happened. Instead of identifying a 3-inch standard line as equal in length to a 3-inch comparison line, the confederates chose a 3³/4-inch comparison line. Unbeknownst to the subject—who was always seated near the end of the group—Asch had instructed the confederates to unanimously give an incorrect answer on 12 of the 18 trials. Asch wanted to see whether subjects would succumb to the pressure to conform.

Under these conditions, Asch found that subjects conformed to the incorrect majority view on roughly one-third of the 12 critical trials. Three-fourths of the subjects conformed on at least one trial, and one-third of the subjects conformed on half or more of the critical trials. In other words, most people rendered at least some judgments that contradicted the evidence of their senses, and many conformed on the majority of trials.

Asch also conducted several variations of the experiment. For example, in one set of studies, he varied the size of the group (see Figure 17.4). When subjects were paired with only one confederate who contradicted their views, they were hardly affected at all. Most subjects

FIGURE 17.4

In his experiments on conformity, Solomon Asch found that unanimous majorities of three were just as effective in producing conformity as groups five times larger. *(Asch, 1951.)*

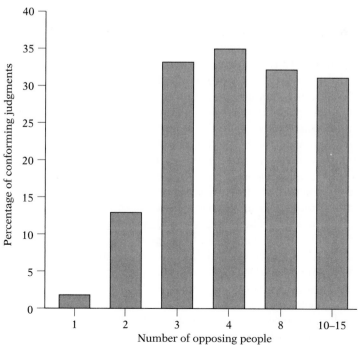

answered correctly on nearly all trials. When subjects were opposed by two people, they conformed to the majority view 13 percent of the time. And when subjects were opposed by three confederates, they conformed on 33 percent of the critical trials. Beyond this point, Asch found no further increases in conformity, although later work by other researchers suggests that conformity may increase somewhat with majorities larger than three (Latané & Wolf, 1981). Regardless of how this question is eventually settled, however, it is clear that small majorities are sufficient to elicit a substantial degree of conformity.

In another set of experiments, Asch broke the unanimity of the majority by adding either a second subject who was seated in the fourth position and usually offered correct judgments, or a confederate in the fourth position who was instructed to give correct answers. Asch wanted to see what would happen when the majority was no longer unanimous.

What he found was a huge effect. Conformity was cut to about one-fourth of previous levels—that is, when the majority was not unanimous, subjects conformed on roughly one-fourth as many critical trials as when the majority was unanimous. In fact, Asch found that a unanimous majority of three was far more powerful than a majority of eight with one dissenter. These results show that in situations where there are strong pressures to conform, lone dissenters can have a major effect.

MINORITY INFLUENCE

In 1969, Serge Moscovici and two colleagues turned Asch's experimental paradigm on its head to study the influence of minorities on majorities (Moscovici, Lage, & Naffrechoux, 1969). Instead of observing the influence of a majority of confederates on one or two subjects, Moscovici examined the effect of a few confederates on a larger group of subjects. Moscovici and his coauthors showed that a consistent minority can have a significant influence even when the minority is not particularly powerful or prestigious.

In the original set of experiments conducted by Moscovici, the group consisted of two confederates and four subjects. Everyone was seated in front of a blank screen and was told that the experiment was on color perception. A series of slides was then shown, and on each trial, members of the group were asked for their opinion as to the color and light intensity of the slide. The slides were all varying intensities of blue, but the confederates were instructed to judge them as green on certain critical trials. What Moscovici and his associates found was that subjects agreed with the confederates on an average of 8 percent of the critical trials, and that 32 percent of the subjects judged the slides as green at least once. In contrast, a control group of uninfluenced subjects mistook the slides for green only twice in 792 judgments.

Thus, Moscovici and his colleagues found that a minority was able to exert a significant degree of influence on the majority. There was one qualification, though—the minority had to be consistent. If the two confederates waffled between blue and green, randomly identifying the slides as blue one-third of the time, subjects judged the slides as green on only 1 percent of the trials. The minority only had a significant influence when the confederates took a consistent position (for reviews and extensions of this work, see Maass & Clark, 1984; Nemeth, 1986; Nemeth & Chiles, 1988).

GROUPTHINK

When groups are cohesive and relatively insulated from the influence of outsiders, group loyalty and pressures to conform can lead to what Irving Janis (1982) called "groupthink." As defined by Janis, groupthink "refers to a deterioration of mental efficiency, reality testing, and moral judgment that results from in-group pressures" (p. 9). The most famous example of groupthink leading to a poor decision is the Bay of Pigs fiasco, in which the presidential cabinet of John F. Kennedy recommended an ill-conceived invasion of Cuba. More recently, James Esser and Joanne Lindoerfer (1989) found evidence of groupthink in the fateful 1986 decision to launch the U.S. space shuttle Challenger during unsafe weather conditions.

According to Janis, there are eight common symptoms of groupthink:

- An illusion of invulnerability, shared by most or all group members, that leads to overoptimism and excessive risk taking
- Collective efforts to rationalize or discount warnings
- An unquestioned belief in the group's inherent morality
- Stereotyped views of adversaries as too evil to make negotiating worthwhile, or too weak and stupid to pose a serious threat
- Pressure directed at any group member who dissents from the majority view
- A shared illusion of unanimity
- Self-censorship of deviations from the apparent group consensus
- Self-appointed "mindguards" who protect the group from information that might challenge the group's complacency

If a group shows these warning signs, it stands a good chance of suffering from groupthink. To protect against groupthink, Janis recommended several preventive measures. First and foremost, group leaders should explicitly encourage dissent and criticism—including criticism of their own positions. Second, group leaders should refrain from stating any personal preferences at the outset. Jay Russo and Paul Schoemaker (1989) have observed that certain Japanese companies adopt this rule by allowing the lowest-ranking member of a group to speak first, followed by the next-to-lowest, followed by the next in line, and so on. That way, no one is afraid to differ with an opinion expressed by someone higher up in the company.

A third preventive measure is for groups to set up other groups—with other leaders—to consider the same question (thereby allowing for a comparison of different answers). Fourth, group members should periodically discuss the group's deliberations with trusted associates, and should report these discussions to the group. Fifth, groups should invite outside experts or qualified colleagues to attend the group meetings, and should encourage them to challenge the group's consensus. In fact, Janis proposed that one of the best ways to avoid groupthink is to officially appoint someone in the group to be a devil's advocate. Each of these measures legitimizes disagreement and capitalizes on the fact that dissenting minorities reduce conformity.

CONCLUSION

The theme of this chapter is a simple one: Because people are social by nature, their judgments and decisions are subject to social influences. Even when decision makers operate alone, they often tailor their behavior in anticipation of how it will be evaluated by others. Consequently, any comprehensive account of judgment and decision making must include social factors.

In some cases, these factors influence decisions without affecting underlying judgments. For example, many people respond to conformity pressures and groupthink by advocating a choice that they do not agree with personally. In other instances, judgments may be distorted. Asch found, for example, that a handful of his subjects actually experienced a distortion in perception and were unaware that the majority had influenced them. Similarly, Latané and Darley found that many unresponsive bystanders altered their perception of the situation when responsibility was diffused. As Latané and Darley (1970, p. 65) put it: "[These] subjects almost uniformly claimed that in a 'real' emergency, they would be among the first to help the victim."

The social influences discussed in this chapter are only a few of hundreds that hold sway in daily life. They are meant to be illustrative, not exhaustive, and as in the case of social facilitation effects, they show that social factors can improve performance as well as hinder it. Chapter 18 continues this discussion by comparing group performance with the performance of individuals.

CHAPTER 18

GROUP JUDGMENTS AND DECISIONS

If a group succeeds in avoiding groupthink, will it make better judgments and decisions than an individual would? Do groups operate with the same heuristics and biases as individuals?

Relatively few studies have compared individual-level heuristics and biases with group-level heuristics and biases, and as of yet, there have been no major reviews contrasting the two. Of the studies that have been published, however, most suggest that biases in attribution and judgment are similar in individuals and groups. The first part of this chapter discusses several of these parallels, and the second part focuses on how groups and individuals differ.

GROUP ERRORS AND BIASES

As mentioned in Chapter 16, the fundamental attribution error is a tendency to overattribute an individual's behavior to dispositional causes. For example, people interpret an essay as reflecting its author's personal position even when they are told that the author was forced to take that position (Jones & Harris, 1967). The tendency to make unwarranted dispositional attributions about a group is known as the "group attribution error." According to Scott Allison and David Messick (1985, p. 564), who first documented the group attribution error, "Both the fundamental attribution error and the group attribution error share a common ground, and that is our tendency to ignore external determinants of behavior and to assume a correspondence between behavior and some underlying attitude." In their research, Allison and Messick found that subjects inferred greater public support for water conservation when a city manager enacted conservation measures than when no measures were adopted, even though there was little reason to suppose that public opinions mirrored the decision of a single government employee. Similar findings have been reported by Diane Mackie and Scott Allison (1987).

Another attributional parallel exists between "self-serving" biases and "group-serving" biases. In the former, individuals make dispositional attributions for their successes and situational attributions for their failures. In the latter, group members make dispositional attributions for group successes and situational attributions for group failures. Donald Taylor and Janet Doria (1981) compared self-serving and group-serving biases among intercollegiate athletes and found that group-serving biases were at least as strong as self-serving biases. Specifically, athletes exhibited group-serving biases by attributing their team's success to good team play more often than they attributed failures to bad team play.

Still another group-level attributional bias is known as the "outgroup homogeneity bias." Just as individuals perceive themselves as more varied than other people, groups perceive their own members as more varied than members of other groups (Mullen & Hu, 1989). For instance, in one experiment, members of four different student clubs at Princeton rated members of their own group and members of three other groups on personality dimensions such as introverted/extroverted, arrogant/humble, and laid-back/uptight (Jones, Wood, & Quattrone, 1981). The results showed that students rated members of their own group as more varied in personality than members of the outgroups, regardless of which club students were in.

Now you might say, "Sure they thought their group was more varied—they knew more members of their own club than the other club." As it turned out, though, outgroup homogeneity biases were unrelated to the number of ingroup or outgroup members that students knew. Furthermore, outgroup homogeneity biases occur in groups that have quite a bit of contact with each other, such as females and males (Park & Rothbart, 1982). Thus, outgroup homogeneity biases are not simply the result of differences in familiarity.

One serious consequence of outgroup homogeneity biases is that they help to perpetuate stereotypes. Because outgroup members are perceived as relatively homogeneous, their individuality is undermined. Unfortunately, the tendency to perceive outsiders as homogeneous is particularly common in international relations. For example, when Soviet leader Yuri Andropov came to power, former U.S. National Security Advisor Zbigniew Brzezinski wrote: "It's wrong to divide these people into conservatives or liberals, hawks and doves, Stalinists or non-Stalinists. The point is that they're all tough and brutal" (Schmemann, 1985, March 3, p. 55). Later events proved how mistaken Brzezinski was.

Very few studies have looked at whether heuristics such as availability and representativeness operate in group judgments. In one rare exception, Linda Argote, Mark Seabright, and Linda Dyer (1986) presented individual subjects and five-person groups with variants of the lawyer-engineer problem discussed in Chapter 10. Argote, Seabright, and Dyer found that groups relied on the representativeness heuristic even more than did individuals. Scott Tindale, Susan Sheffey, and

Joseph Filkins (1990) also found that four-person groups were more likely than individuals to commit the conjunction fallacy when presented with problems similar to Item #1 of the Reader Survey (another result of representativeness).

What does all this mean? Although more research is certainly needed, these preliminary findings suggest that individual-level heuristics and biases continue to operate in group judgment and decision making. Indeed, these biases are sometimes stronger in groups than individuals. In the case of representativeness, for example, Argote, Seabright, and Dyer (1986, p. 74) concluded that: "Group discussion appears to amplify the inclination of individuals to judge by representativeness when assessing category membership."

GROUP POLARIZATION

The tendency for group discussion to amplify the inclinations of group members is known as "group polarization" (Moscovici & Zavalloni, 1969). This phenomenon was first documented by James Stoner (1961), who found that subjects were more willing to advocate risky actions after they had participated in a group discussion. Stoner referred to this change as the "risky shift," and since the time of his initial experiment, hundreds of studies have explored the topic. After all, if group polarization leads to greater risk taking on the part of groups than individuals, Stoner's findings have profound implications for national security, business, and other areas in which groups make important decisions.

In roughly four out of every five risky shift experiments, the procedure goes something like this: First, subjects are given a questionnaire in which their tendency to take risks is assessed. This questionnaire is usually the "choice-dilemmas" survey developed by Nathan Kogan and Michael Wallach (1964), which describes 12 hypothetical situations involving a person who has to choose between a risky or conservative course of action. For example, in one item, a 45-year-old accountant has to decide whether to risk heart surgery or live with a debilitating heart condition (see Figure 18.1).

In the choice-dilemmas survey, subjects are asked to indicate what the odds of success would have to be before they would advise the person to choose the risky alternative. This administration of the questionnaire is known as the pretest. Then groups of five or so subjects discuss the 12 problems and reach a consensus on what level of risk to advocate for each hypothetical situation. This phase is known as the treatment test. The risky shift is simply measured by subtracting average scores on the pretest from average scores on the treatment test.

Although there are dozens of variations on this theme, research results have been fairly consistent. Group discussion usually leads people to advocate riskier courses of action than they would otherwise.

Mr. B, a 45-year-old accountant, has recently been informed by his physician that he has developed a severe heart ailment. The disease would be sufficiently serious to force Mr. B to change many of his strongest life habits -- reducing his work load, drastically changing his diet, giving up favorite leisure-time pursuits. The physician suggests that a delicate medical operation could be attempted which, if successful, would completely relieve the heart condition. But its success could not be assured, and in fact, the operation might prove fatal.

Imagine that you are advising Mr. B. Listed below are several probabilities or odds that the operation will prove successful.

Please check the lowest probability that you would consider acceptable for the operation to be performed.

_____ Place a check here if you think Mr. B should not have the operation no matter what the probabilities.
_____ The chances are 9 in 10 that the operation will be a success.
_____ The chances are 7 in 10 that the operation will be a success.
_____ The chances are 5 in 10 that the operation will be a success.
_____ The chances are 3 in 10 that the operation will be a success.
_____ The chances are 1 in 10 that the operation will be a success.

FIGURE 18.1

This is an item from the Choice-Dilemmas questionnaire developed by Nathan Kogan and Michael Wallach (1964, pp. 256–257).

When the initial inclination is toward caution, however, group discussion can sometimes lead to a "cautious shift." Consequently, many researchers now adopt the more general term "choice shift" to describe the basic phenomenon.

As popular as choice shift research has been, group polarization extends far beyond the issue of risk taking. For example, David Myers and George Bishop (1970) found that highly prejudiced students became even more prejudiced after discussing racial issues with one another, whereas relatively unprejudiced students became even less so after discussing the same issues. Similarly, Myers (1975) found that the gap between "chauvinists" and "feminists" widened after members of each group discussed women's issues among themselves. This type of research is based on a "group composition" paradigm, in which groups are composed of people with the same inclination (an inclination that becomes amplified through group discussion).

Another type of group polarization research uses a paradigm in which the problem itself produces an inclination that becomes polarized. David Myers and Martin Kaplan (1976) found, for instance, that simulated juries presented with weak incriminating evidence became even more lenient following group discussion, whereas juries given strong evidence became even harsher. Thus, initial leanings based on legal evidence became polarized through group discussion (for overviews on group polarization and its causes, see Myers, 1982; Myers & Lamm, 1976).

HORSE SENSE

"A man bought a horse for $60 and sold it for $70. Then he bought it back for $80 and again sold it for $90. How much money did he make in the horse business?"

This problem—which appears as Item #20 of the Reader Survey—made its research debut in a classic study by Norman Maier and Allen Solem (1952). Maier and Solem found that only 45 percent of the college students they asked could solve the problem when working alone. When students worked in five- or six-person groups, however, they did considerably better. Students who worked in groups with an "inactive" leader (a person who simply observed the conversation) answered correctly 72 percent of the time, and students who worked in groups with a "permissive" leader (who encouraged all group members to express an opinion) answered correctly 84 percent of the time.

To see how an effective group might solve the problem, let's step through the mists of time and listen to an imaginary group discussion taking place in Maier and Solem's laboratory:

WENDY [The group leader]:   I'm suspicious of the problem—it seems deceptively simple, and I don't trust psychologists. Let's each share what we think the answer is, and say a few words about why we think our answer is right.

BENNETT: I'm pretty sure the answer is $10. The way I solved the problem was to think in terms of a stock exchange. If I buy a share of stock for $60 and sell at $70, I'm up $10. Then, if I change my mind and buy the same stock at $80, I've just paid $10 more than $70 and erased my earlier earnings. Selling the stock at $90 leaves me $10 ahead, though, so I come out okay.

JILL: My answer was $20, because the man makes $10 the first time he buys the horse and $10 the second time. After hearing Ben, though, I'm not sure whether this answer is correct.

WENDY: Don't worry about whether you're right—we're just trying to lay out all the possibilities. What about you, Steven?

STEVEN: I think the right answer is $30. The man starts with $60 and ends up with $90, so how can his profits be anything other than $30?

AMY: His profits would be $30 if he never had to borrow any money, but after selling the horse for $70, he had to come up with an extra $10 to buy the horse for $80. This leaves $20 profits—$30 minus the extra $10 he borrowed.

WENDY: So you agree with Jill?

AMY: Yes. In fact, I think the only reason this problem seems confusing is that the same horse is being bought and sold. If the problem involved two separate horses, the answer would be obvious.

BENNETT: What do you mean?

AMY: Well, suppose the man bought Horse A for $60 and sold the horse for $70. How much profit would he have made?

BENNETT: $10.

AMY: Now suppose the man buys a second horse—Horse B—for $80 and sells the horse for $90. How much has he gained?

BENNETT: Another $10.

AMY: Exactly, so the man ends up $20 ahead. His profits don't depend on whether one horse is traded or two horses are traded—he gains $20 either way. If you like to think of the problem in terms of stocks, imagine trading two separate stocks rather than one. It's a mistake to think that buying the second stock for $80 represents a loss of $10— to lose money, the man would have had to sell a stock for less than he bought it for.

Now freeze the scene, and imagine that you are a member of this group. Amy concludes her explanation, and your turn comes to explain why you answered the problem as you did. After you finish speaking, the group spends a few more minutes discussing the problem. Then the experimenter asks each member of the group to record a final answer. You have a choice: You can either maintain the answer you gave to Item #20 of the Reader Survey, or you can change your answer. What would you do?

Most people in this situation give the correct answer—$20. Group members who begin with the correct answer rarely change following discussion, and others usually answer correctly after group discussion. Although Maier and Solem (1952) found that groups outperformed individuals regardless of whether group leaders were inactive or permissive, accuracy was highest when group leaders actively encouraged all group members to share their point of view.

The benefits of permissive leadership were particularly apparent when groups began with only one member who had the correct answer. In such cases, 76 percent of the students in permissive groups answered correctly, compared with only 36 percent of the students whose group leaders had been inactive. This finding is consistent with two points made in the last chapter: (1) The best way to avoid groupthink is to explicitly encourage dissenting viewpoints (Janis, 1982), and (2) under the right conditions, minorities can dramatically improve the accuracy of group judgments (Nemeth, 1986).

Maier and Solem (1952) showed that open discussion can lead to large increases in accuracy. Despite the advantages of group discussion, however, it is worth noting that not all group members in Maier and

Solem's experiment solved the problem. Even though 63 of 67 groups contained at least one member who knew the correct answer at the outset, roughly one out of every five subjects answered incorrectly after group discussion. Edwin Thomas and Clinton Fink (1961) found similar results using the same horse-trading problem. In their experiment, 29 of 44 groups contained at least one member who knew the correct answer before group discussion, but only 15 groups turned in unanimously correct answers afterward. Thus, group discussion led to a significant improvement in accuracy, but it did not ensure that *all* group members answered accurately.

ARE SEVERAL HEADS BETTER THAN ONE?

Group judgments tend to be somewhat more accurate than individual judgments, though this is not always the case. Group accuracy depends on a variety of factors, including the nature and difficulty of the task, the competence of group members, the way that group members are allowed to interact, and so forth. Reid Hastie (1986) published a review that looked at many of the factors which affect group judgment, and he compared groups and individuals on three different types of judgment tasks: (1) judgments of quantities and magnitudes, such as the number of beans in a jar; (2) judgments of the logically correct answer to brain teasers, such as the horse-trading problem; and (3) judgments in response to general knowledge questions, such as "Is absinthe a liqueur or a precious stone?"

With respect to quantitative judgments, Hastie concluded that groups are usually slightly more accurate than individuals (for readers acquainted with statistics, Hastie estimated this difference to be roughly one eighth of a standard deviation unit). More recent research by Janet Sniezek and Becky Henry (1989, 1990) suggests that, in some cases, this advantage may be larger than Hastie estimated. Using a measure known as "standardized bias," Sniezek and Henry found that three-person groups were 23 to 32 percent more accurate than individuals—two or three times the margin typically found in the studies reviewed by Hastie.

As for brain teasers and other problems of logic, Hastie found that groups usually outperformed individuals, but that the best member of a group, working alone, tended to do better than the group as a whole. Likewise, he concluded that groups usually outperformed the average individual at answering general knowledge questions, but that the best member of a group tended to equal or surpass the performance of the group. Thus, across all three types of judgment he examined, Hastie found that groups made more accurate judgments than average individuals, though the best individual in a group often outperformed the group as a whole.

Similar results were found by Gayle Hill (1982) in a major review entitled "Group versus Individual Performance: Are $N + 1$ Heads Better Than One?" In this article, Hill reviewed 50 years of research on individual and group performance. Although she looked at many types of performance other than judgment and decision making, part of her review focused on creativity and problem solving. What she found was that groups were often superior to average individuals, but groups frequently performed worse than the best individual in a statistical aggregate of people (a noninteracting group of the same size). Hill found that, for easy tasks, enlarging the size of a group simply increased the chances that it would contain at least one member who could solve the problem. For difficult tasks, the main advantage of teamwork seemed to be that group members could pool their resources and correct each other's errors.

Hill also looked at brainstorming. In particular, she compared the number of ideas generated in group sessions with the number of ideas generated when the same number of people brainstormed alone and later added their ideas together. Hill found that brainstorming was more effective when ideas were generated independently and later combined than when it was conducted in a group session.* She concluded that the superiority of group performance was mainly a function of aggregation (i.e., of simply having more people working on the problem) rather than group interaction per se. From a practical perspective, this means that the best way to generate solutions to a difficult problem is by having several people work on it independently and later share their ideas.

THE BENEFITS OF DICTATORSHIP

Although group judgments tend to be more accurate than individual judgments, accuracy depends in part upon how group members combine their answers (Davis, 1973). A study that illustrates this point was published by Janet Sniezek (1989). Sniezek compared five types of group decision techniques: (1) "consensus," in which face-to-face discussions led to one judgment accepted by all group members; (2) the "dialectic" technique, in which group members were required to discuss factors that might be biasing their judgments; (3) the "dictator" technique (a.k.a. the best member technique), in which face-to-face discussions led to the selection of one group member whose judgments represented the group; (4) the "Delphi" technique, in which group members

---

*Although Hill did not explicitly mention the possibility, social loafing may be partly responsible for this finding. Elizabeth Weldon and Gina Gargano (1985, 1988) have found that social loafing occurs when people work together on complex judgment tasks.

did not meet face to face, but instead, provided answers anonymously in a series of "rounds" until a consensus was reached or until the median judgment stabilized (the advantage of this technique is that the group is protected from members who might monopolize the discussion or who are unduly confident of their judgments); and (5) the "collective" technique, which prohibited any interaction among group members and simply averaged individual judgments together in order to arrive at a "group" judgment (in Sniezek's study, the collective technique established a baseline level of accuracy for aggregation without social interaction).

Each group was made up of five college students, and each group used all five decision techniques. Groups began by using the collective technique, after which they adopted the other decision techniques in various orders. The judgment task was for students to estimate how much merchandise a campus bookstore would sell in the coming month—how many dollars of clothing, magazines, cards and gifts, and health and beauty items. Sniezek measured judgment accuracy in terms of a reduction in "absolute percent error" from actual sales figures.

What she found was that each of the first four techniques (consensus, dialectic, dictator, and Delphi) yielded more accurate judgments than simple aggregation (the collective technique), but the largest improvement was produced by the dictator technique, which reduced absolute percent error by three times the amount of any other technique. Interestingly, though, in every case the "dictator" of a group changed her or his final judgment in the direction of the collective mean, thereby *increasing* the amount of error. In other words, groups were able to select a highly accurate dictator, but the dictator invariably became democratic, and in so doing, reduced final accuracy.

Of course, Sniezek's findings are specific to groups of a particular size (five) from a particular population (college students) working on a particular judgment task (sales forecasting). It would be foolish to assume that the dictator technique works best in all situations. Nonetheless, Sniezek's experiment shows that group accuracy depends partly on the decision rules that groups adopt. Her results also demonstrate that, in some cases, interacting groups perform better than statistical aggregates of people who do not interact with one another. Thus, at least in certain situations, the superior performance of groups is a function not only of having "more heads than one," but of "putting heads together."

CONCLUSION

Because group performance depends on so many different factors, it is difficult to make broad generalizations (Tindale, 1989). For much the same reason, it is also difficult to reconcile mixed or contradictory results from group research. Are discrepancies due to differences in the task? In group size? In the decision rules used? Ironically, the very richness of group research complicates the interpretation of experimental findings.

It is also the case that group judgment and decision making has not received as much attention as individual judgment and decision making, despite the ubiquity of committees, panels, boards, juries, and other decision making bodies. Furthermore, the line between individual and group research is often blurred by the fact that groups are, ultimately, comprised of individuals. For example, research on the group attribution error is really research on how *individuals* make attributions about groups. Similarly, choice shifts can be measured by comparing group decisions and individual decisions, or by comparing individual decisions made before and after group discussion. Only in the former case are *group* decisions actually made.

Notwithstanding these complications, research on group judgment and decision making suggests the following tentative conclusions:

- Many individual-level heuristics and biases appear to operate with equal force in groups.
- Group discussion often amplifies preexisting tendencies.
- Groups usually perform somewhat better than average individuals, particularly if an appointed leader encourages all group members to express an opinion.
- The best member of a group often outperforms the group (a fact that can sometimes be exploited by using the dictator decision technique).
- Brainstorming is most effective when conducted by several people independently, rather than in a group session.

Each of these conclusions is supported by a good deal of research, but because group performance is affected by so many factors, care should be exercised in applying such general conclusions to particular situations. Although decision makers are usually best off pooling their efforts, collaboration is no guarantee of a successful outcome.

COMMON TRAPS

This section of the book focuses on three common problems that beset decision makers. Chapter 19 addresses the issue of overconfidence, Chapter 20 discusses self-fulfilling prophecies, and Chapter 21 examines a special kind of predicament known as the "behavioral trap." Each chapter concludes by suggesting practical tips on how to avoid these problems.

CHAPTER 19

OVERCONFIDENCE

The odds of a meltdown are one in 10,000 years.

—Vitali Skylarov, Minister of Power and Electrification in
the Ukraine, two months before the Chernobyl accident
(cited in Rylsky, 1986, February)

No problem in judgment and decision making is more prevalent and
more potentially catastrophic than overconfidence. As Irving Janis
(1982) documented in his work on groupthink, American overconfidence enabled the Japanese to destroy Pearl Harbor in World War II.
Overconfidence also played a role in the disastrous decision to launch
the U.S. space shuttle Challenger. Before the shuttle exploded on its
twenty-fifth mission, NASA's official launch risk estimate was 1 catastrophic failure in 100,000 launches (Feynman, 1988, February). This
risk estimate is roughly equivalent to launching the shuttle once per day
and expecting to see only one accident in three centuries.

THE CASE OF JOSEPH KIDD

Was NASA genuinely overconfident of success, or did it simply need to
appear confident? Because true confidence is hard to measure in such
situations, the most persuasive evidence of overconfidence comes from
carefully controlled experiments.

One of the earliest and best known of these studies was published by
Stuart Oskamp in 1965. Oskamp asked 8 clinical psychologists, 18 psychology graduate students, and 6 undergraduates to read the case study
of "Joseph Kidd," a 29-year-old man who had experienced "adolescent
maladjustment." The case study was divided into four parts. Part 1
introduced Kidd as a war veteran who was working as a business assistant in a floral decorating studio. Part 2 discussed Kidd's childhood
through age 12. Part 3 covered Kidd's high school and college years.
And Part 4 chronicled Kidd's army service and later activities.

Subjects answered the same set of questions four times—once after
each part of the case study. These questions were constructed from factual material in the case study, but they required subjects to form clinical judgments based on general impressions of Kidd's personality. Ques-

217

tions always had five forced-choice alternatives, and following each item, subjects estimated the likelihood that their answer was correct. These confidence ratings ranged from 20 percent (no confidence beyond chance levels of accuracy) to 100 percent (absolute certainty).

Somewhat surprisingly, there were no significant differences among the ratings from psychologists, graduate students, and undergraduates, so Oskamp combined all three groups in his analysis of the results. What he found was that confidence increased with the amount of information subjects read, but accuracy did not.

After reading the first part of the case study, subjects answered 26 percent of the questions correctly (slightly more than what would be expected by chance), and their mean confidence rating was 33 percent. These figures show fairly close agreement. As subjects read more information, though, the gap between confidence and accuracy grew (see Figure 19.1). The more material subjects read, the more confident they became—even though accuracy did not increase significantly with additional information. By the time they finished reading the fourth part of the case study, more than 90 percent of Oskamp's subjects were over-confident of their answers.

FIGURE 19.1

Stuart Oskamp (1965) found that as subjects read more information from a case study, the gap between their estimated accuracy (confidence) and true accuracy increased.

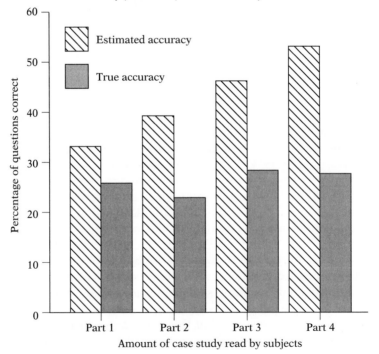

In the years since this experiment, a number of studies have found that people tend to be overconfident of their judgments, particularly when accurate judgments are difficult to make. For example, Sarah Lichtenstein and Baruch Fischhoff (1977) conducted a series of experiments in which they found that people were 65 to 70 percent confident of being right when they were actually correct about 50 percent of the time.

In the first of these experiments, Lichtenstein and Fischhoff asked people to judge whether each of 12 children's drawings came from Europe or Asia, and to estimate the probability that each judgment was correct. Even though only 53 percent of the judgments were correct (very close to chance performance), the average confidence rating was 68 percent.

In another experiment, Lichtenstein and Fischhoff gave people market reports on 12 stocks and asked them to predict whether the stocks would rise or fall in a given period. Once again, even though only 47 percent of these predictions were correct (slightly less than would be expected by chance), the mean confidence rating was 65 percent.

After several additional studies, Lichtenstein and Fischhoff drew the following conclusions about the correspondence between accuracy and confidence in two-alternative judgments:

- Overconfidence is greatest when accuracy is near chance levels.
- Overconfidence diminishes as accuracy increases from 50 to 80 percent, and once accuracy exceeds 80 percent, people often become *under*confident. In other words, the gap between accuracy and confidence is smallest when accuracy is around 80 percent, and it grows larger as accuracy departs from this level.
- Discrepancies between accuracy and confidence are not related to a decision maker's intelligence.

Although early critics of this work claimed that these results were largely a function of asking people questions about obscure or trivial topics, recent studies have replicated Lichtenstein and Fischhoff's findings with more commonplace judgments. For example, in a series of experiments involving more than 10,000 separate judgments, Lee Ross and his colleagues found roughly 10 to 15 percent overconfidence when subjects were asked to make a variety of predictions about their behavior and the behavior of others (Dunning, Griffin, Milojkovic, & Ross, 1990; Vallone, Griffin, Lin, & Ross, 1990).

This is not to say that people are *always* overconfident. David Ronis and Frank Yates (1987) found, for instance, that overconfidence depends partly on how confidence ratings are elicited and what type of judgments are being made (general knowledge items seem to produce relatively high degrees of overconfidence). There is also some evidence that expert bridge players, professional oddsmakers, and National Weather Service forecasters—all of whom receive regular feedback following their judgments—exhibit little or no overconfidence (Keren, 1987; Lichtenstein, Fischhoff, & Phillips, 1982; Murphy & Brown, 1984; Murphy & Winkler, 1984). Still, for the most part, research suggests that overconfidence is prevalent.

EXTREME CONFIDENCE

What if people are virtually certain that an answer is correct? How often are they right in such cases? In 1977, Baruch Fischhoff, Paul Slovic, and Sarah Lichtenstein conducted a series of experiments to investigate this issue. In the first experiment, subjects answered hundreds of general knowledge questions and estimated the probability that their answers were correct. For example, they answered whether absinthe is a liqueur or a precious stone, and they estimated their confidence on a scale from .50 to 1.00 (this problem appears as Item #21 of the Reader Survey). Fischhoff, Slovic, and Lichtenstein then examined the accuracy of only those answers about which subjects were absolutely sure.

What they found was that people tended to be only 70 to 85 percent correct when they reported being 100 percent sure of their answer. How confident were you of your answer to Item #21? The correct answer is that absinthe is a liqueur, though many people confuse it with a precious stone called amethyst.

Just to be certain their results were not due to misconceptions about probability, Fischhoff, Slovic, and Lichtenstein (1977) conducted a second experiment in which confidence was elicited in terms of the odds of being correct. Subjects in this experiment were given more than 100 items in which two causes of death were listed—for instance, leukemia and drowning. They were asked to indicate which cause of death was more frequent in the United States and to estimate the odds that their answer was correct (i.e., 2:1, 3:1, etc.). This way, instead of having to express 75 percent confidence in terms of a probability, subjects could express their confidence as 3:1 odds of being correct.

What Fischhoff, Slovic, and Lichtenstein (1977) found was that confidence and accuracy were aligned fairly well up to confidence estimates of about 3:1, but as confidence increased from 3:1 to 100:1, accuracy did not increase appreciably. When people set the odds of being correct at 100:1, they were actually correct only 73 percent of the time. Even when people set the odds between 10,000:1 and 1,000,000:1—indicating virtual certainty—they were correct only 85 to 90 percent of the time (and should have given a confidence rating between 6:1 and 9:1).*

---

*Although these results may seem to contradict Lichtenstein and Fischhoff's earlier claim that overconfidence is minimal when subjects are 80 percent accurate, there is really no contradiction. The fact that subjects average only 70 to 90 percent accuracy when they are highly confident does not mean that they are always highly confident when 70 to 90 percent accurate.

Finally, as an added check to make sure that subjects understood the task and were taking it seriously, Fischhoff, Slovic, and Lichtenstein (1977) conducted three replications. In one replication, the relation between odds and probability was carefully explained in a twenty-minute lecture. Subjects were given a chart showing the correspondence between various odds estimates and probabilities, and they were told about the subtleties of expressing uncertainty as an odds rating (with a special emphasis on how to use odds between 1:1 and 2:1 to express uncertainty). Even with these instructions, subjects showed unwarranted confidence in their answers. They assigned odds of at least 50:1 when the odds were actually about 4:1, and they gave odds of 1000:1 when they should have given odds of 5:1.

In another replication, subjects were asked whether they would accept a monetary bet based on the accuracy of answers that they rated as having 50:1 or better odds of being correct. Of 42 subjects, 39 were willing to gamble—even though their overconfidence would have led to a total of more than $140 in losses. And in a final replication, Fischhoff, Slovic, and Lichtenstein (1977) actually played subjects' bets. In this study, 13 of 19 subjects agreed to gamble on the accuracy of their answers, even though they were incorrect on 12 percent of the questions to which they had assigned odds of 50:1 or greater (and all would have lost from $1 to $11, had the experimenters not waived the loss). These results suggest that (1) people are overconfident even when virtually certain they are correct, and (2) overconfidence is not simply a consequence of taking the task lightly or misunderstanding how to make confidence ratings. Indeed, Joan Sieber (1974) found that overconfidence *increased* with incentives to perform well.

WHEN OVERCONFIDENCE BECOMES A CAPITAL OFFENSE

Are people overconfident when more is at stake than a few dollars? Although ethical considerations obviously limit what can be tested in the laboratory, at least one line of evidence suggests that overconfidence operates even when human life hangs in the balance. This evidence comes from research on the death penalty.

In a comprehensive review of wrongful convictions, Hugo Bedau and Michael Radelet (1987) found 350 documented instances in which innocent defendants were convicted of capital or potentially capital crimes in the United States—even though the defendants were apparently judged "guilty beyond a reasonable doubt." In five of these cases, the error was discovered prior to sentencing. The other defendants were not so lucky: 67 were sentenced to prison for terms of up to 25 years, 139 were sentenced to life in prison (terms of 25 years or more), and 139 were sentenced to die. At the time of Bedau and Radelet's review, 23 of the people sentenced to die had been executed.

CALIBRATION

"Calibration" is the degree to which confidence matches accuracy. A decision maker is perfectly calibrated when, across all judgments at a given level of confidence, the proportion of accurate judgments is identical to the expected probability of being correct. In other words, 90 percent of all judgments assigned a .90 probability of being correct are accurate, 80 percent of all judgments assigned a probability of .80 are accurate, 70 percent of all judgments assigned a probability of .70 are accurate, and so forth.

When individual judgments are considered alone, it doesn't make much sense to speak of calibration. How well calibrated is a decision maker who answers ".70" to Item #21b of the Reader Survey? The only way to reliably assess calibration is by comparing accuracy and confidence across hundreds of judgments (Lichtenstein, Fischhoff, & Phillips, 1982).

Just as there are many ways to measure confidence, there are several techniques for assessing calibration. One way is simply to calculate the difference between average confidence ratings and the overall proportion of accurate judgments. For instance, a decision maker might average 80 percent confidence on a set of general knowledge items but be correct on only 60 percent of the items. Such a decision maker would be overconfident by 20 percent.

Although this measure of calibration is convenient, it can be misleading at times. Consider, for example, a decision maker whose overall accuracy and average confidence are both 80 percent. Is this person perfectly calibrated? Not necessarily. The person may be 60 percent confident on half the judgments and 100 percent confident on the others (averaging out to 80 percent confidence), yet 80 percent accurate at both levels of confidence. Such a person would be underconfident when 60 percent sure and overconfident when 100 percent sure.

A somewhat more refined approach is to examine accuracy over a range of confidence levels. When accuracy is calculated separately for different levels of confidence, it is possible to create a "calibration curve" in which the horizontal axis represents confidence and the vertical axis represents accuracy. Figure 19.2 contains two calibration curves—one for weather forecasters' predictions of precipitation, and the other for physicians' diagnoses of pneumonia. As you can see, the weather forecasters are almost perfectly calibrated; on the average, their predictions closely match the weather (contrary to popular belief!). In contrast, the physicians are poorly calibrated; most of their predictions lie below the line, indicating overconfidence.

There are additional ways to assess calibration, some of them involving complicated mathematics. For instance, one of the most common techniques is to calculate a number known as a "Brier score" (named after statistician Glenn Brier). Brier scores can be partitioned into three

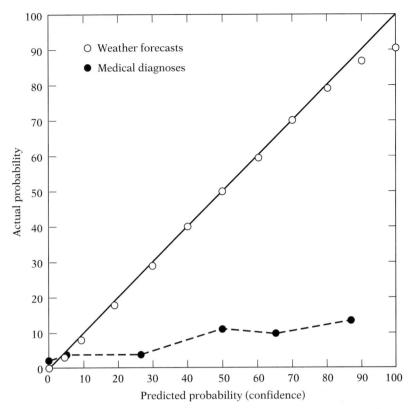

FIGURE 19.2

This figure contains calibration curves for weather forecasters' predictions of precipitation (hollow circles) and physicians' diagnoses of pneumonia (filled circles). Although the weather forecasters are almost perfectly calibrated, the physicians show substantial overconfidence (i.e., unwarranted certainty that patients have pneumonia). The data on weather forecasters comes from a report by Allan Murphy and Robert Winkler (1984), and the data on physicians comes from a study by Jay Christensen-Szalanski and James Bushyhead (1981).

components, one of which corresponds to calibration. The Brier score component for calibration is a weighted average of the mean squared differences between the proportion correct in each category and the probability associated with that category (for a good introduction to the technical aspects of calibration, see Yates, 1990).

One of the most interesting measures of calibration is known as the "surprise index." The surprise index is used for interval judgments of unknown quantities. For example, suppose you felt 90 percent confident that the answer to Item #12 of the Reader Survey was somewhere between an inch and a mile (see Item #12b for your true 90 percent confidence interval). Because the correct answer is actually greater than a mile, this answer would be scored as a surprise. The surprise index is simply the percentage of judgments that lie beyond the boundaries of a confidence interval.

In a major review of calibration research, Sarah Lichtenstein, Baruch Fischhoff, and Lawrence Phillips (1982) examined several studies in which subjects had been asked to give 98 percent confidence intervals (i.e., intervals that had a 98 percent chance of including the correct answer). In every study, the surprise index exceeded 2 percent. Averaging across all experiments for which information was available—a total of nearly 15,000 judgments—the surprise index was 32 percent. In other words, when subjects were 98 percent sure that an interval contained the correct answer, they were right 68 percent of the time. Once again, overconfidence proved the rule rather than the exception.

Are *you* overconfident? Edward Russo and Paul Schoemaker (1989) developed an easy self-test to measure overconfidence on general knowledge questions (reprinted in Figure 19.3). Although a comprehensive assessment of calibration requires hundreds of judgments, this test will

FIGURE 19.3

This test will give you some idea of whether you are overconfident on general knowledge questions *(reprinted with permission from Russo and Schoemaker, 1989)*.

SELF-TEST OF OVERCONFIDENCE

For each of the following ten items, provide a low and high guess such that you are 90 percent sure the correct answer falls between the two. Your challenge is to be neither too narrow (i.e., overconfident) nor too wide (i.e., underconfident). If you successfully meet this challenge you should have 10 percent misses -- that is, exactly one miss.

	90% Confidence Range	
	LOW	HIGH
1. Martin Luther King's age at death	———	———
2. Length of the Nile River	———	———
3. Number of countries that are members of OPEC	———	———
4. Number of books in the Old Testament	———	———
5. Diameter of the moon in miles	———	———
6. Weight of an empty Boeing 747 in pounds	———	———
7. Year in which Wolfgang Amadeus Mozart was born	———	———
8. Gestation period (in days) of an Asian elephant	———	———
9. Air distance from London to Tokyo	———	———
10. Deepest (known) point in the ocean (in feet)	———	———

ANSWERS: (1) 39 years; (2) 4187 miles; (3) 13 countries; (4) 39 books (5) 2160 miles; (6) 390,000 pounds; (7) 1756; (8) 645 days; (9) 5959 miles; (10) 36,198 feet.

give you a rough idea of what your surprise index is with general knowledge questions at one level of confidence. Russo and Schoemaker administered the test to more than 1000 people and found that less than 1 percent of the respondents got nine or more items correct. Most people missed four to seven items (a surprise index of 40 to 70 percent), indicating a substantial degree of overconfidence.

THE CORRELATION BETWEEN CONFIDENCE AND ACCURACY

*Over*confidence notwithstanding, it is still possible for confidence to be correlated with accuracy. To take an example, suppose a decision maker were 50 percent accurate when 70 percent confident, 60 percent accurate when 80 percent confident, and 70 percent accurate when 90 percent confident. In such a case, confidence would be perfectly correlated with accuracy, even though the decision maker would be uniformly overconfident by 20 percent.

The question arises, then, whether confidence is correlated with accuracy—regardless of whether decision makers are overconfident. If confidence ratings increase when accuracy increases, then accuracy can be predicted as a function of how confident a decision maker feels. If not, then confidence is a misleading indicator of accuracy.

Many studies have examined this issue, and the results have often shown very little relationship between confidence and accuracy. To illustrate, consider the following two problems concerning military history:

Problem 1. The government of a country not far from Superpower A, after discussing certain changes in its party system, began broadening its trade with Superpower B. To reverse these changes in government and trade, Superpower A sent its troops into the country and militarily backed the original government. *Who was Superpower A—the United States or the Soviet Union? How confident are you that your answer is correct?*

Problem 2. In the 1960s Superpower A sponsored a surprise invasion of a small country near its border, with the purpose of overthrowing the regime in power at the time. The invasion failed, and most of the original invading forces were killed or imprisoned. *Who was Superpower A, and again, how sure are you of your answer?*

A version of these problems appeared as Items #9 and #10 of the Reader Survey. If you guessed the Soviet Union in the first problem and the United States in the second, you were right on both counts. The first problem describes the 1968 Soviet invasion of Czechoslovakia, and the second describes the American invasion of the Bay of Pigs in Cuba.

Most people miss at least one of these problems, despite whatever confidence they feel.

In the November 1984 issue of *Psychology Today* magazine, Philip Zimbardo and I published the results of a reader survey that contained both of these problems and a variety of others on superpower conflict. The survey included 10 descriptions of events, statements, or policies related to American and Soviet militarism, but in each description, all labels identifying the United States and Soviet Union were removed. The task for readers was to decide whether "Superpower A" was the United States or the Soviet Union, and to indicate on a 9-point scale how confident they were of each answer.

Based on surveys from 3500 people, we were able to conclude two things. First, respondents were not able to tell American and Soviet military actions apart. Even though they would have averaged 5 items correct out of 10 just by flipping a coin, the overall average from readers of *Psychology Today*—who were more politically involved and educated than the general public—was 4.9 items correct. Only 54 percent of the respondents correctly identified the Soviet Union as Superpower A in the invasion of Czechoslovakia, and 25 percent mistook the United States for the Soviet Union in the Bay of Pigs invasion. These findings suggested that Americans were condemning Soviet actions and policies largely because they were *Soviet*, not because they were radically different from American actions and policies.

The second thing we found was that people's confidence ratings were virtually unrelated to their accuracy (the average correlation between confidence and accuracy for each respondent was only .08, very close to zero). On the whole, people who got nine or ten items correct were no more confident than less successful respondents, and highly confident respondents scored about the same as less confident respondents.

This does not mean that confidence ratings were made at random; highly confident respondents differed in a number of ways from other respondents. Two-thirds of all highly confident respondents (i.e., who averaged more than 8 on the 9-point confidence scale) were male, even though the general sample was split evenly by gender, and 80 percent were more than 30 years old. Twice as many of the highly confident respondents wanted to increase defense spending as did less confident respondents, and nearly twice as many felt that the Soviet government could not be trusted at all. Yet the mean score these respondents achieved on the survey was 5.1 items correct—almost exactly what would be expected by chance responding. Thus, highly confident respondents could not discriminate between Soviet and American military actions, but they were very confident of misperceived differences and advocated increased defense spending.

As mentioned earlier, many other studies have found little or no correlation between confidence and accuracy (Paese & Sniezek, 1991;

Ryback, 1967; Sniezek & Henry, 1989, 1990; Sniezek, Paese, & Switzer, 1990). This general pattern is particularly apparent in research on eyewitness testimony. By and large, these studies suggest that the confidence eyewitnesses feel about their testimony bears little relation to how accurate the testimony actually is (Brown, Deffenbacher, & Sturgill, 1977; Clifford & Scott, 1978; Leippe, Wells, & Ostrom, 1978). In a review of 43 separate research findings on the relation between accuracy and confidence in eye- and earwitnesses, Kenneth Deffenbacher (1980) found that in two-thirds of the "forensically relevant" studies (e.g., studies in which subjects were not instructed in advance to watch for a staged crime), the correlation between confidence and accuracy was not significantly positive. Findings such as these led Elizabeth Loftus (1979, p. 101), author of *Eyewitness Testimony,* to caution: "One should not take high confidence as any absolute guarantee of anything."

Similar results have been found in clinical research. In one of the first experiments to explore this topic, Lewis Goldberg (1959) assessed the correlation between confidence and accuracy in clinical diagnoses. Goldberg was interested in whether clinicians could accurately detect organic brain damage on the basis of protocols from the Bender-Gestalt test (a test widely used to diagnose brain damage). He presented 30 different test results to four experienced clinical psychologists, ten clinical trainees, and eight nonpsychologists (secretaries). Half of these protocols were from patients who had brain damage, and half were from psychiatric patients who had nonorganic problems. Judges were asked to indicate whether each patient was "organic" or "nonorganic," and to indicate their confidence on a rating scale labeled "Positively," "Fairly certain," "Think so," "Maybe," or "Blind guess."

Goldberg found two surprising results. First, all three groups of judges—experienced clinicians, trainees, and nonpsychologists—correctly classified 65 to 70 percent of the patients. There were no differences based on clinical experience; secretaries performed as well as psychologists with four to ten years of clinical experience. Second, there was no significant relationship between individual diagnostic accuracy and degree of confidence. Judges were generally as confident on cases they misdiagnosed as on cases they diagnosed correctly. Subsequent studies have found miscalibration in diagnoses of cancer, pneumonia (see Figure 19.2), and other serious medical problems (Centor, Dalton, & Yates, 1984; Christensen-Szalanski & Bushyhead, 1981; Wallsten, 1981).

HOW CAN OVERCONFIDENCE BE REDUCED?

In a pair of experiments on how to improve calibration, Lichtenstein and Fischhoff (1980) found that people who were initially overconfident could learn to be better calibrated after making 200 judgments and receiving intensive performance feedback. Likewise, Hal Arkes and his

associates found that overconfidence could be eliminated by giving subjects feedback after five deceptively difficult problems (Arkes, Christensen, Lai, & Blumer, 1987). These studies show that overconfidence
can be unlearned, although their applied value is somewhat limited.
Few people will ever undergo special training sessions to become well
calibrated.

What would be useful is a technique that decision makers could carry
with them from judgment to judgment—something lightweight,
durable, and easy to apply in a range of situations. And indeed, there
does seem to be such a technique. The most effective way to improve
calibration seems to be very simple:

Stop to consider reasons why your judgment might be wrong.

The value of this technique was first documented by Asher Koriat,
Sarah Lichtenstein, and Baruch Fischhoff (1980). In this research, subjects answered two sets of two-alternative general knowledge questions,
first under *control* instructions and then under *reasons* instructions.
Under control instructions, subjects chose an answer and estimated the
probability (between .50 and 1.00) that their answer was correct. Under
reasons instructions, they were asked to list reasons for and against
each of the alternatives before choosing an answer.

Koriat, Lichtenstein, and Fischhoff found that under control instructions, subjects showed typical levels of overconfidence, but after generating pro and con reasons, they became extremely well calibrated
(roughly comparable to subjects who were given intensive feedback in
the study by Lichtenstein and Fischhoff). After listing reasons for and
against each of the alternatives, subjects were less confident (primarily
because they used .50 more often and 1.00 less often) and more accurate (presumably because they devoted more thought to their answers).

In a followup experiment, Koriat, Lichtenstein, and Fischhoff found
that it was not the generation of reasons per se that led to improved calibration; rather, it was the generation of *opposing* reasons. When subjects listed reasons in support of their preferred answers, overconfidence was not reduced. Calibration improved only when subjects
considered reasons why their preferred answers might be wrong.
Although these findings may be partly a function of "social demand
characteristics" (i.e., subjects feeling cued by instructions to tone down
their confidence levels), other studies have confirmed that the generation of opposing reasons improves calibration (e.g., Hoch, 1985).

These results are reminiscent of the study by Paul Slovic and Baruch
Fischhoff (1977) discussed in Chapter 3, in which hindsight biases were
reduced when subjects thought of reasons why certain experimental
results might have turned out differently than they did. Since the time
of Slovic and Fischhoff's study, several experiments have shown how

FIGURE 19.4

The difficult task of considering multiple perspectives. (Calvin and Hobbes *copyright 1990 Watterson. Dist. by Universal Press Syndicate. Reprinted with permission. All rights reserved.*)

various judgment biases can be reduced by considering the possibility of alternative outcomes or answers (Griffin, Dunning, & Ross, 1990; Hoch, 1985; Lord, Lepper, & Preston, 1984).

As Charles Lord, Mark Lepper, and Elizabeth Preston (1984, p. 1239) pointed out: "The observation that humans have a blind spot for opposite possibilities is not a new one. In 1620, Francis Bacon wrote that 'it is the peculiar and perpetual error of human intellect to be more moved and excited by affirmatives than by negatives.'" In Chapter 20, this blind spot—and some of its consequences—will be explored in detail.

CONCLUSION

It is important to keep research on overconfidence in perspective. In most studies, average confidence levels do not exceed accuracy by more than 10 to 20 percent. Consequently, overconfidence is unlikely to be catastrophic unless decision makers are nearly certain that their judgments are correct. As the explosion of the space shuttle illustrates, the most devastating form of miscalibration is inappropriate certainty.

Taken together, the studies in this chapter suggest several strategies for dealing with miscalibration:

- ✔ First, you may want to flag certain judgments for special consideration. Overconfidence is greatest when judgments are difficult or confidence is extreme. In such cases, it pays to proceed cautiously.
- ✔ Second, you may want to "recalibrate" your confidence judgments and the judgments of others. As Lichtenstein and Fischhoff (1977) observed, if a decision maker is 90 percent confident but only 70 to 75 percent accurate, it is probably best to treat "90 percent confidence" as though it were "70 to 75 percent confidence."
- ✔ Along the same lines, you may want to automatically convert judgments of "100 percent confidence" to a lesser degree of confidence. One hundred percent confidence is especially unwarranted when predicting how people will behave (Dunning, Griffin, Milojkovic, & Ross, 1990).
- ✔ Above all, if you feel extremely confident about an answer, consider reasons why a different answer might be correct. Even though you may not change your mind, your judgments will probably be better calibrated.

CHAPTER 20

SELF-FULFILLING PROPHECIES

Suppose each of the cards in Figure 20.1 has a number on one side and a letter on the other, and someone tells you: "If a card has a vowel on one side, then it has an even number on the other side." Which of the cards would you need to turn over in order to decide whether the person is lying? (See Item #39 of the Reader Survey for your answer.)

When Peter Wason and Phil Johnson-Laird (1972) put this type of question* to 128 university students, they found that "E and 4" was the

FIGURE 20.1

---

*Some versions of the question used symbols other than E, K, 4, and 7, but the logical structure of the problem was always the same.

most common response (given by 59 students), and "E" was the next most common (given by 42). In other words, most students chose to turn over cards capable of *confirming* the statement. Only five students gave the correct answer: "E and 7."

If this answer seems surprising, think of the problem as follows. The rule being tested is "If vowel, then even number," or more basically, "If X, then Y." The only way to falsify an if-then statement is to find an instance of "X and *not* Y" (i.e., vowel and *odd* number). Thus, the only cards capable of disconfirming the rule are those with vowels or odd numbers ("E and 7"). Cards with even numbers or consonants are simply not relevant.

Despite its seeming simplicity, this problem is extremely difficult for most people. Robyn Dawes (1975) even found that four of five "highly regarded" mathematical psychologists could not solve the problem. The focus of this chapter is on why such problems are difficult, and what the implications are for decision makers.

GUESS AGAIN

> "You will be given three numbers which conform to a simple rule that I have in mind. This rule is concerned with a relation between any three numbers and not with their absolute magnitude, i.e. it is not a rule like all numbers above (or below) 50, etc.
>
> Your aim is to discover this rule by writing down sets of three numbers. . . . After you have written down each set, I shall tell you whether your numbers conform to the rule or not. . . . There is no time limit but you should try to discover this rule by citing the minimum sets of numbers.
>
> Remember that your aim is not simply to find numbers which conform to the rule, but to discover the rule itself. When you feel highly confident that you have discovered it, and not before, you are to write it down. . . . Have you any questions?"

Wason (1960) gave these instructions—along with the sample set of numbers 2, 4, 6—to 29 college students in an experiment on hypothesis testing. The rule he had in mind was always "Three Numbers in Increasing Order of Magnitude," but he found that only six subjects discovered the correct rule without first naming an incorrect one. In rough paraphrase, the transcript of a typical subject follows:

SUBJECT NO. 4 (a 19-year-old female):   8, 10, 12.
EXPERIMENTER: Those numbers conform to the rule.
SUBJECT: 14, 16, 18.
EXPERIMENTER: Those numbers conform to the rule.
SUBJECT: 20, 22, 24.
EXPERIMENTER: Those numbers conform to the rule.

SUBJECT: 1, 3, 5.

EXPERIMENTER: Those numbers conform to the rule.

SUBJECT: *The rule is that by starting with any number, two is added each time to form the next number.*

EXPERIMENTER: That is not the correct rule. Please continue. . . .

As with the four-card problem, Wason found that subjects tried to confirm the rule (e.g., 8, 10, 12) more often than disconfirm the rule (e.g., 12, 10, 8). This tendency is known as a "confirmation bias." Although the term "confirmation bias" has been used as something of a catch-all phrase (Fischhoff & Beyth-Marom, 1983), it usually refers to a preference for information that is consistent with a hypothesis rather than information which opposes it.

In an incisive analysis of how people test hypotheses (hunches, rules, theories, and so on), Josh Klayman and Young-Won Ha (1987, pp. 220) argued that confirmation biases are the result of a "positive test strategy" which serves as a useful heuristic, but which, "like any all-purpose heuristic . . . is not always optimal and can lead to serious difficulties in certain situations." One set of difficulties was already discussed in Chapter 15—problems that arise in covariation assessment when decision makers focus mainly on positive co-occurrences (e.g., the study of nurses by Jan Smedslund, 1963). Another example is given in the next section.

SELF-PERPETUATING SOCIAL BELIEFS

In 1979, Mark Snyder and Nancy Cantor published three experiments on confirmation biases in social perception. In the first of these experiments, all subjects were given the same account of a woman named Jane—someone who was extroverted in some situations and introverted in others. For example, Jane spoke freely with strangers when jogging, but she felt shy and timid at the supermarket. Two days after reading the account, subjects were asked to assess one of two propositions: (1) that Jane was well-suited for a job normally associated with extroversion (real estate sales), or (2) that Jane was well-suited for a job associated with introversion (research librarianship). Some subjects were told that Jane was applying for the job, and others were told that she had already taken the job. For simplicity, we will focus on subjects who thought she was applying for the job.

These subjects were asked to list all facts from the account relevant to whether Jane was well-suited for the job, and to decide how suitable she would be for the job. What Snyder and Cantor found was that subjects who considered Jane for a real estate sales position tended to list evidence of her extroversion as relevant, and subjects who considered her for a library position tended to list evidence of her introversion as relevant. In other words, subjects in both conditions saw confirming evidence as more relevant than disconfirming evidence. Moreover, this confirmation bias was correlated with judgments about Jane's suitability for the job under consideration. The more subjects favored confirming evidence over disconfirming evidence, the more suitable they judged Jane to be—regardless of what position she applied for.

The second experiment replicated the first one with a few minor changes (e.g., replacing the term "well-suited" with "suitability" to avoid emphasizing confirmation), and in the third experiment, subjects simply listed what they would want to know about a job candidate in order to assess how suitable the person was for a position in real estate sales or library research. As before, confirming information was listed more frequently than disconfirming information. For example, when considering candidates for a real estate position, subjects asked "How outgoing is the candidate?" far more often than "How shy is the candidate?" Similar findings were obtained in several experiments by Mark Snyder and William Swann (1978).

The implications of these results extend well beyond employment situations. As Snyder and Swann (1978, pp. 1211–1212) observed:

> [People] may create for themselves a world in which hypotheses become self-confirming hypotheses and beliefs become self-perpetuating beliefs. . . . From this perspective, it becomes easier to understand why so many popular beliefs about other people (in particular, clearly erroneous social and cultural stereotypes) are so stubbornly resistant to change. Even if one were to develop sufficient doubt about the accuracy of these beliefs to proceed to test them actively, one nevertheless might be likely to "find" all the evidence one needs to confirm and retain these beliefs. And, in the end, one may be left with the secure (but totally unwarranted) feeling that these beliefs must be correct because they have survived (what may seem to the individual) perfectly appropriate and even rigorous procedures for assessing their accuracy.

THE PYGMALION EFFECT

Treat people as if they were what they ought to be and
you help them to become what they are capable of being.

—Johann W. von Goethe (cited in Peter, 1977)

The term "self-fulfilling prophecy" was coined in 1948 by Robert Merton. In the words of Merton (1948, pp. 195–196): "The self-fulfilling prophecy is, in the beginning, a *false* definition of the situation evoking a new behavior which makes the originally false conception come *true*. The specious validity of the self-fulfilling prophecy perpetuates a reign of error. For the prophet will cite the actual course of events as proof that he was right from the beginning. . . . Such are the perversities of social logic." In short, self-fulfilling prophecies are misconceptions, but they are misconceptions that ultimately prove true.

In 1968, Robert Rosenthal and Lenore Jacobson published what is now the most famous study ever conducted on self-fulfilling prophecies. In this study, grade school teachers were given diagnostic information indicating that some 20 percent of their students would "bloom" academically in the coming year. As measured by IQ tests eight months later, these students did indeed improve more than other students.

What makes this finding noteworthy is that the high achievers were selected at *random*. Apparently, teachers gave the bloomers more praise and attention than other students, and as a result, bloomers actually improved more than others. Rosenthal and Jacobson called this phenomenon the "Pygmalion effect" (after the George Bernard Shaw play *Pygmalion*, in which Professor Higgins turns a flower girl into a "lady" by teaching her to dress and speak in such a way that people expect her to be a lady).

Since the time of Rosenthal and Jacobson's study more than 400 experiments have investigated the self-fulfilling nature of interpersonal expectations, and more than 100 have specifically examined the effects of teacher expectations (Brophy, 1983; Jussim, 1986; Rosenthal, 1987, December). On the whole, these studies suggest that teacher expectations significantly influence student performance, though the effect is often modest (Brophy, 1983). Interestingly, there is also evidence of "the student as Pygmalion." Robert Feldman and his colleagues have found that student expectations—both of their own performance and of their teacher's performance—can influence student-teacher relations and student performance just as strongly as teacher expectations (Feldman & Prohaska, 1979; Feldman & Theiss, 1982).

IN THE MINDS OF MEN

Although Rosenthal and Jacobson (1968) investigated student-teacher interactions, Pygmalion effects are not limited to the classroom. One of the most dramatic illustrations of the Pygmalion effect was a study by Mark Snyder, Elizabeth Tanke, and Ellen Berscheid (1977) that explored how male stereotypes of female attractiveness can be self-fulfilling.

In the first part of this experiment, randomly paired men and women were audiotaped for ten minutes while they got acquainted with each other via the telephone. Unbeknownst to the women, however, male subjects were first informed by the experimenter that "other people in the experiment have told us they feel more comfortable when they have a mental picture of the person they're talking to." The men were then photographed with a Polaroid camera, and they were given a snapshot of a woman (ostensibly their partner). In reality, the snapshot was randomly selected from a pool of eight photographs that had been prepared in advance. Four of these photographs were of women who had been rated as highly attractive, and four were of women who had been rated as unattractive. In this way, male subjects were led to believe that their counterpart was either physically attractive or physically unattractive. The Polaroid snapshots taken of male subjects were simply discarded, and female subjects were never told anything about forming mental pictures.

After the get-acquainted conversation, each male subject completed a questionnaire concerning his impressions of the woman he spoke with. Included in this questionnaire were many of the stereotypic characteristics associated with an attractive person—sociability, poise, humor, and so on. Not surprisingly, male subjects who thought they had talked with a physically attractive woman later judged her to be more sociable, poised, humorous, and socially adept than did male subjects who thought they had talked with an unattractive woman. This is an example of the halo effect discussed in Chapter 4.

More important are the judgments of several independent raters who listened to clips of the audiotaped conversation. One set of raters listened only to the male voice in each conversation, and one set listened only to the female voice (each set of raters contained both males and females, though there were no significant gender differences in ratings). According to judgments made by these raters—who knew nothing of the experimental hypotheses or the actual physical attractiveness of subjects—male subjects who thought they were interacting with an attractive woman sounded more sociable, sexually warm and permissive, interesting, bold, outgoing, humorous, and socially adept than males who thought they were talking with an unattractive woman. And presumably in response, female subjects who were initially perceived as physically attractive actually sounded more stereotypically attractive (in terms of sociability, poise, and so forth) than female subjects who were originally thought to be unattractive—even though subjects were randomly assigned to experimental conditions, and male preconceptions had nothing to do with how physically attractive the women actually were.

As Snyder, Tanke, and Berscheid (1977, pp. 661, 663) put it: "What had initially been reality in the minds of the men had now become reality in the behavior of the women with whom they had interacted—a behavioral reality discernible even by naive observer judges, who had access *only* to tape recordings of the women's contributions to the conversations. . . . The initially erroneous attributions of the perceivers had become real: The stereotype had truly functioned as a self-fulfilling prophecy."

SELF-FULFILLING RACIAL STEREOTYPES

This kind of self-fulfilling prophecy—the kind that perpetuates stereotypes—plays a critical role in racial discrimination. A study on this topic was published by Carl Word, Mark Zanna, and Joel Cooper (1974).

Word, Zanna, and Cooper prefaced their report by noting that people often reveal their attitudes toward others through nonverbal cues. For example, when people have a positive attitude toward someone, they usually position themselves fairly close to the person, show a relatively high degree of eye contact, more direct shoulder orientation, and more forward lean. On the other hand, people tend to avoid stigmatized individuals. For instance, they terminate interviews with such people sooner, and they maintain a greater physical distance from them. Word, Zanna, and Cooper investigated these biases in two experiments—one in which white subjects interviewed white and black experimental confederates, and one in which a white experimental confederate interviewed white subjects. All subjects and confederates were male.

In the first experiment, subjects were met at the laboratory by what appeared to be two other subjects (but were in fact two confederates of the experimenter). Another confederate then arrived, and soon afterward, the experimenter walked in. The experimenter told the four "subjects" that they would compete against four other teams in a marketing campaign. The experimenter explained, however, that their team needed one more person, and that one team member would need to interview four applicants to select a fifth team member. A rigged drawing was then held in which the subject was chosen as interviewer.

The reason for scheduling four interviews was to disguise the true purpose of the study (i.e., a direct comparison of how white and black interviewees are treated by white interviewers). The first interview (always with a white applicant) was simply regarded as a warmup interview, and the last interview never took place (subjects were told that the applicant had called to cancel his appointment). The interviews of interest to Word, Zanna, and Cooper (1974) were the second and third interviews. Half the subjects interviewed a white applicant first and a black applicant second, and half interviewed a black applicant first and a white applicant second (though order was later found to make no difference). In these interviews, the applicants—who were also confederates of the experimenter—were trained to behave in a standardized way, and they were not told anything about what the experiment was designed to test.

Word, Zanna, and Cooper (1974) measured several characteristics of the interviews, including: (1) interview length, (2) number of speech errors made by the interviewer (which was assumed to reflect discomfort), and (3) physical distance between the interviewer and the applicant. The first variable was measured by the experimenter, and the second was scored by independent raters who listened to an audiotape of the interview and recorded instances of stuttering, word repetition, and so on. The third variable, physical distance, was measured in a particularly creative way. When subjects were brought into the interviewing room, the applicant was already seated and the experimenter pretended to discover that there was no chair for the interviewer. Subjects were then asked to wheel in a chair from an adjoining room, and their placement of the chair provided a measure of physical distance from the applicant.

What Word, Zanna, and Cooper (1974) found was that subjects spent about 35 percent more time interviewing white applicants than black applicants, made about 50 percent more speech errors interviewing blacks than whites, and positioned their chairs about 7 percent further away from blacks than whites. All differences were statistically significant.

But that's not all. After documenting these differences, Word, Zanna, and Cooper ran a second experiment to assess the effects of such discrimination on job interview performance. In the second experiment, white subjects were interviewed by a white confederate who treated them either as blacks had been treated in the first experiment or as whites had been treated. That is, in the former experimental condition, the interviewer sat further from the applicant, made more speech errors, and terminated the interview earlier.

Word, Zanna, and Cooper (1974) found that subjects who were treated as black interviewees had been treated in the first experiment performed more poorly in the interview (as rated by independent judges who viewed videotapes of the interviews), made 50 percent more speech errors, and later rated the interviewer as less friendly. Thus, the same treatment that black subjects experienced in the first experiment led white subjects to perform poorly in the second experiment—a powerful demonstration of how racial stereotypes can become self-fulfilling.

CONCLUSION

Although research on self-fulfilling stereotypes has been limited mainly to studies of male subjects (Christensen & Rosenthal, 1982), other self-fulfilling prophecies and confirmation biases have been amply documented with both male and female subjects (for three excellent reviews, see Darley & Fazio, 1980; Miller & Turnbull, 1986; and Snyder, 1984). The tendency people have to seek confirming evidence—whether in logical problem solving tasks, job interviews, classroom settings, or otherwise—is widespread and well-established.

Moreover, two experiments by Clifford Mynatt, Michael Doherty, and Ryan Tweney suggest that confirmation biases may be difficult to eliminate. In the first experiment, Mynatt, Doherty, and Tweney (1977) created a simulated research environment in which subjects had to discover certain laws governing "particle motion" on a computer screen. Subjects randomly received one of three instructions: (1) *instructions to confirm*, in which they were told that the basic job of a scientist was to confirm theories and hypotheses; (2) *instructions to disconfirm*, in which they were told that the basic job of a scientist was to disprove or disconfirm theories and hypotheses; or (3) *instructions to test*, in which they were simply told that the job of a scientist was to test theories and hypotheses.

Mynatt and his colleagues found that instructions to disconfirm had virtually no effect on confirmation biases. Regardless of what instructions subjects were given, they sought confirming evidence on roughly 70 percent of all experimental trials.

In a second experiment, Mynatt, Doherty, and Tweney (1978) expanded the instructions to disconfirm. Using the same procedure as before, they randomly assigned subjects to one of two conditions: (1) a *no instructions control group*, or (2) a *strong inference group*, in which subjects received extensive instructions stressing the value of falsification and multiple hypothesis testing. Once again, however, instructions to disconfirm had little or no effect.

How can confirmation biases and self-fulfilling prophecies be avoided? Although research on this question is scant, one strategy may be to focus on motivational factors (Snyder, in press). For example, Mark Snyder, Bruce Campbell, and Elizabeth Preston (1982) eliminated confirmation biases by warning interviewers that the people they interview may see certain questions as indicative of closed-mindedness or prejudice (e.g., questions that are directed at confirming stereotypes). Once the interviewers in this study were sensitized to this possibility, they solicited confirming and disconfirming evidence in roughly equal measure.

Another valuable strategy may be to frame questions in a way that encourages disconfirming answers. Decision researchers Jay Russo and Paul Schoemaker (1989) tell the story of a former student of theirs, Jay Freedman, who used this strategy with great success. Freedman, a top analyst at the investment firm Kidder, Peabody and Company, made it a practice to solicit disconfirming evidence before making financial recommendations. Russo and Schoemaker (1989, pp. xiv–xv) describe Freedman's approach as follows:

> When gathering intelligence on a company he deliberately asks questions designed to "disconfirm" what he thinks is true. If Freedman thinks the disposable diaper business is becoming less price competitive, for example, he will ask executives a question that implies

the opposite such as, "Is it true that price competition is getting tougher in disposable diapers?" This kind of question makes him more likely than competing analysts to get the real story.

As mentioned in Chapter 19, decision makers can reduce overconfidence and improve the quality of their decisions by considering why their judgments might be wrong (Koriat, Lichtenstein, & Fischhoff, 1980; Lord, Lepper, & Preston, 1984). Such an approach may also reduce self-fulfilling prophecies and self-fulfilling stereotypes. At present, however, this possibility is speculative and has yet to be confirmed—or *disconfirmed*—by psychological research.

CHAPTER 21

BEHAVIORAL TRAPS

"Thank you for calling. All of our operators are temporarily busy. Please stay on the line and your call will be answered in the order received."

A minute passes. Two minutes. You begin to wonder whether you should hang up and redial. Maybe you got transferred to an empty line—a telephone twilight zone of some kind. If a call rings in the forest and no one is there to answer it. . . .

On the other hand, hanging up probably means starting over. Other people will advance in the queue, and you will lose whatever priority you had. Better to keep waiting. Who knows, you may even be next in line.

You wait awhile longer. Three minutes. Four minutes. *What is taking so long?*, you wonder.

Finally you make a decision. If an operator doesn't pick up the phone in the next sixty seconds, you will hang up. Thirty seconds goes by. Forty seconds. Fifty seconds and still no answer. As the deadline passes, you hesitate a few hopeful moments, then slam the receiver down in frustration.

Sound familiar? This situation has all the features of a "behavioral trap." A behavioral trap is a situation in which individuals or groups embark on a promising course of action that later becomes undesirable and difficult to escape from. This definition is similar to one developed by John Platt (1973) in his pioneering work on social traps, and the present chapter will borrow heavily from the analyses of Platt and his colleagues John Cross and Melvin Guyer (1980). Because traps can be nonsocial as well as social, however, the general term "behavioral trap" will be used rather than the more traditional "social trap."

A TAXONOMY OF TRAPS

In 1980, Cross and Guyer published a taxonomy of traps and countertraps. In the words of Cross and Guyer (1980, p. 18): "Countertraps (sins of omission) arise when we avoid potentially beneficial behavior, while traps (sins of commission) occur when we take potentially harmful courses of action." As mentioned above, one common trap involves waiting for a telephone operator. Ordinary countertraps include aversive cleaning chores (in which messes worsen with time) and overdue correspondence (in which embarrassment increases with the length of delay).

There are several distinct types of traps, each with a corresponding countertrap. Using the Cross-Guyer taxonomy as a departure point, we can divide traps into five general categories:

- Time delay traps
- Ignorance traps
- Investment traps
- Deterioration traps
- Collective traps

Although the elements of these five traps often combine to form hybrid traps, each trap works on somewhat different principles. The following sections therefore discuss each type of trap separately.

TIME DELAY TRAPS

If you find it hard to diet or exercise regularly, you know the power of time delay traps. In time delay traps, momentary gratification clashes with long-term consequences. What begins innocently enough with a favorite dessert or a few cigarettes ends up many years later in obesity or lung cancer. Or, in the countertrap version, the avoidance of what is momentarily unpleasant—aerobic exercise for some people, dental exams for others—eventually leads to a heart attack or periodontal disease. What is striking about these traps and countertraps is that relatively small pains and pleasures in the short run are sufficient to produce behavior that is devastating or even lethal in the long run.

Any situation in which short-term consequences run counter to long-term consequences has the potential for becoming a time delay trap. Prototypic conflicts include the euphoria of drinking versus the next day's hangover; the momentary pleasure of unprotected sex versus the deferred prospect of AIDS or unwanted pregnancy; the convenience of disposable products versus the long-range environmental consequences; the "buy now, pay later" option afforded by credit cards and layaway plans; and the quick but ultimately counterproductive results brought by corporal punishment. Even the apple in the Garden of Eden can be regarded as bait in a time delay trap—the ultimate symbol of temptation and its potentially entrapping consequences.

IGNORANCE TRAPS

People in time delay traps often realize the long-term consequences of their behavior. Overeaters are usually very aware of putting on weight, and smokers sometimes even refer to cigarettes as "cancer sticks." Warnings about weight gain or cancer are rarely effective against time delay traps.

Ignorance traps operate differently. In these traps, the negative consequences of behavior are not understood or foreseen at the outset. For example, smokers in the nineteenth century did not realize that smoking was related to lung cancer, and if this information had been available, many people would never have begun to smoke (of course, smoking still has the properties of a time delay trap, and millions of people continue to be trapped even though the link with lung cancer is now well known).

Ignorance traps are common when new life paths are taken. For example, college students sometimes end up majoring in a field that is not as exciting as initially imagined; workers sometimes find themselves trapped in a job that does not live up to expectations; and lovers sometimes get involved with partners who are less appealing than they first seemed to be. Such traps are an inevitable part of life, though there are ways to minimize the chances of being trapped (techniques to reduce or avoid entrapment are discussed later in the chapter).

One particularly tragic example of an ignorance trap is the story of insecticide dependence in American agriculture. When synthetic organic insecticides such as DDT were introduced in the 1940s, they appeared to be an effective way to protect crops against insect damage. Soon after these products became available, American farmers adopted them as the method of choice for insect control.

Then two unforeseen events occurred: (1) Birds and other insect predators began to die, and (2) insects developed a resistance to the chemicals that were used. Insect damage began to *increase*. New insecticides were invented, but resistant strains of insects emerged once again. After four hundred million years of evolution, the insects were not giving up without a fight.

For decades this battle has been fought on the farmlands of America, yet each new round of chemical weapons serves only to provoke further pestilence. The percentage of American crops lost to insects doubled between the years 1950 and 1974 (Robbins, 1987), and according to entomologists at the University of California, 24 of the 25 most serious agricultural pests in California are now insecticide-induced or insecticide-aggravated (Luck, van den Bosch, & Garcia, 1977). Each year, more than 100 million pounds of insecticides are used in the United States, much to the detriment of wildlife, vegetation, waterways, and human safety.

INVESTMENT TRAPS

Cross and Guyer (1980) did not explicitly include investment traps in their taxonomy, but this type of trap has recently become the topic of a great deal of research. Investment traps occur when prior expenditures of time, money, or other resources lead people to make choices they would not otherwise make. In the parlance of decision research, these traps result in "sunk cost effects."

Hal Arkes and Catherine Blumer (1985) illustrated the effects of sunk costs in 10 different mini-experiments. In one of these experiments, a group of subjects were given the following problem:

> As the president of an airline company, you have invested 10 million dollars of the company's money into a research project. The purpose was to build a plane that would not be detected by conventional radar, in other words, a radar-blank plane. When the project is 90% completed, another firm begins marketing a plane that cannot be detected by radar. Also, it is apparent that their plane is much faster and far more economical than the plane your company is building. The question is: should you invest the last 10% of the research funds to finish your radar-blank plane?

You can check your answer to this problem by looking at Item #6 of the Reader Survey. Arkes and Blumer found that 85 percent of their subjects recommended completing the project, even though the finished aircraft would be inferior to another plane already on the market. When a second group of subjects were given a version of the problem that did *not* mention prior investments, however, only 17 percent opted to spend money on the project. A sunk cost of $10 million made the difference.

In another experiment, Arkes and Blumer (1985) showed that sunk costs can have long-lasting effects. The subjects in this study were 60 theater patrons who approached the ticket window to buy season tickets for the Ohio University Theater. Unbeknownst to these people, they were randomly sold one of three tickets: (1) a normal ticket for $15.00, (2) a ticket discounted by $2.00, or (3) a ticket discounted by $7.00. Subjects lucky enough to receive discounted tickets were told that the discounts were part of a promotion by the theater department.

Each type of ticket was a different color, so Arkes and Blumer (1985) were able to collect the stubs after each performance and determine how many subjects had attended each play. For purposes of analysis, the theater season was divided into two halves, each with five plays that ran over the course of six months. Although Arkes and Blumer did not find significant differences in the second half of the season, they found that, for the first six months, subjects who had paid the full ticket price attended more plays than those who had received a discount (regardless of the size of the discount). Thus, even a paltry $2.00 difference in investment continued to influence behavior for up to six months.

This study is important for two reasons. First, it shows that sunk cost effects are not limited to paper-and-pencil measures. Second, it shows that differences in investment can have relatively enduring effects on behavior. As Baruch Fischhoff and his colleagues (1981, p. 13) wrote in their book *Acceptable Risk*: "The fact that no major dam in the United States has been left unfinished once begun shows how far a little concrete can go in defining a problem."

DETERIORATION TRAPS

Deterioration traps are similar to investment traps, except that the costs and benefits of behavior change over time. These traps—which Cross and Guyer (1980) called "sliding reinforcer traps"—occur when initially rewarding courses of action gradually become less reinforcing and/or more punishing.

The emblematic example of a deterioration trap is heroin addiction (though heroin addiction can also be considered a time delay trap and an ignorance trap). At first, heroin users find the drug enjoyable. In time, however, they build up a tolerance. Larger doses are needed to achieve the same feeling, and eventually, heroin users end up taking the drug to avoid withdrawal symptoms rather than to experience euphoria. What begins as a pleasant experience turns into a nightmare of dependence.

Much the same process operates with "insecticide addiction." Although the use of insecticides may have begun as an ignorance trap, it continues in part as a deterioration trap. According to a report in *Bio-Science*, insecticide dependence works like this:

> There is first a period of variable duration, in which crop losses to insects are greatly reduced. . . . Eventually, however, resistance develops in one of the primary, occasional, or insecticide-induced pests. This problem is met by adding (diversifying) and changing insecticides, but the substituted materials . . . are generally more ephemeral and thus must be applied more frequently to effect the same degree of control. At this point, it also becomes difficult if not impossible for growers to extricate themselves from the strategy. As they continue to apply insecticides, their problems magnify (Luck, van den Bosch, & Garcia, 1977, p. 607).

Deterioration traps and countertraps often produce behavior which seems absurd or self-destructive to bystanders who have not watched the situation evolve. In his memoir *Notebooks*, B. F. Skinner (1980, pp. 150–151) described one example of such behavior:

> Bill's truck is his only means of support—like a fisherman's boat or a small farmer's cow and plow horse. The island salt air, badly maintained roads, and the abuse of a drunken driver have nearly finished it. The windshield is full of small holes with radiating cracks. The fenders are rusted to thin sheets, bent and torn. Only fragments of padding remain on the springs of the seat. . . .
>
> I asked Bill to help bring our boat down the hill. The truck was parked on a downgrade in front of the village store. I got in and sat on what was left of the right side of the seat. Bill gave the truck a push, jumped in, set the gear, and, as we picked up a little speed, let in the clutch. A violent jerk, and the motor began to cough. Bill . . . pumped the accelerator wildly, keeping his hand on the choke. Satisfied that the motor was started, he reversed and backed rapidly to the store to turn

around. The truck stalled, across the road. Three or four of us pushed, including two young men from a car whose way was blocked. . . . We went downgrade again, starting and stalling. From time to time Bill would jump out, open the hood, and adjust something with a wrench. We worked our way a tenth of a mile in the wrong direction, the engine coughing and exploding and refusing to race as Bill pumped gas. Eventually he explained that his starter was in for repairs. It might come back on the excursion boat. How would it be if he came up for the boat in a couple of hours? He did not come. Forty-eight hours later he was still parking his truck on downgrades. No one would tow him anymore.

Why does he go on? For one thing there is no alternative. He drinks away his income. . . . [But his] lack of alternatives is not the whole story. His zealous preoccupation with the truck is the result of a [shrinking ratio of reinforcement to effort]. . . . Bill will not take No from the truck. If it were a horse, he would have beaten it to death long ago, for it is also the lot of an aging horse to reinforce the behavior of its owner on a lengthening ratio of work per task. Bill's truck is being beaten to death, too.

To an outside observer who does not know Bill's history, his actions may seem ludicrous and bizarre. Yet the same dynamic operates routinely in deteriorating social or romantic relationships. When interpersonal relationships erode gradually over time, they create a countertrap in which exiting becomes extremely difficult.

COLLECTIVE TRAPS

Unlike the previous traps, collective traps involve more than one party. In collective traps, the pursuit of individual self-interest results in adverse consequences for the collective. A simple example is rush-hour traffic. Hundreds of people prefer to drive at the same time, but if each person operates according to self-interest, everyone suffers.

Collective traps—a close cousin of the "social dilemma" in mathematical game theory (Dawes, 1980)—have received more research attention than all other traps combined. The most celebrated example of a collective trap is the Prisoner's Dilemma, in which two prisoners are confined in separate jail cells and offered a deal such as the following:

DISTRICT ATTORNEY: Listen, Billy Boy. We've got enough evidence to send you and your partner up the river for a year if neither of you confesses. What we'd really like, though, is to get at least one confession. If you confess and your partner doesn't, we'll hit your partner with 10 years and let you go free. On the other hand, if you play it quiet and your partner comes clean, you'll be the one who gets 10 years.

WILD BILL: What if we *both* confess—will we both get 10 years?

DISTRICT ATTORNEY: No. In that case, we'll reward your honesty with a reduced sentence of 5 years.

In a standard Prisoner's Dilemma, both prisoners face the same choice—a choice in which they are better off confessing regardless of what their partner chooses. If their partner refuses to confess, they are set free; if not, they are at least protected against a 10-year sentence. The dilemma is that if both prisoners follow their self-interest and confess, they will each receive a sentence five times longer than if both keep quiet (see Figure 21.1).

Another famous collective trap is what biologist Garrett Hardin (1968) dubbed "the tragedy of the commons." In the classic version of this trap, a herding community uses common pasture land to graze cattle. At first there is no problem, but in time, the number of cattle reaches the carrying capacity of the land. At that point, the utility of adding another animal to the herd has two components—one positive and one negative. The positive utility consists of whatever profit can be made from raising one more animal. This profit belongs solely to the herder who adds the animal. The negative utility is a function of the additional overgrazing caused by a new animal. This cost is borne by all members of the community and is negligible to any one herder. The result is a dilemma in which each person benefits from adding another animal to the herd, but the pursuit of individual self-interest leads to an outcome that is less than ideal. Hardin likened the tragedy of the commons to problems such as overpopulation, pollution, global resource depletion, and the proliferation of nuclear weapons.

The tragedy of the commons is similar in many ways to the infamous "mattress problem," a collective countertrap first described by Thomas Schelling (1971). In the mattress problem, thousands of cars on a two-

FIGURE 21.1
An example of the Prisoner's Dilemma. The number above the diagonal in each cell indicates Prisoner A's sentence, and the number below the diagonal indicates Prisoner B's sentence.

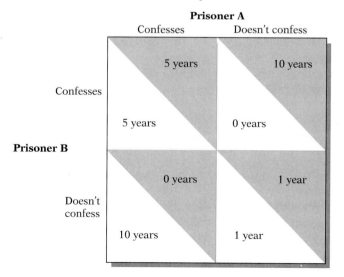

lane highway are returning from a weekend on Cape Cod when a mattress falls into the northbound lane, unnoticed, from the top of a station wagon. The question is: Who stops to move the mattress?

Oftentimes, the answer is that no one does. People far back in the stream of traffic don't know what the problem is and can't help. People who are passing the mattress have waited so long in line that all they can think of is how to get around it. After such a long wait, the last thing they want to do is spend another few minutes pulling a mattress out of the lane. And those who have already passed the mattress no longer have a direct stake in moving it.

The mattress problem resembles the type of collective countertrap found in emergency situations (in which responsibility is diffused and bystanders are slow to intervene). It may also provide a partial explanation for the political "apathy" so prevalent in the United States. Unfortunately, as Douglas Hofstadter (1985, p. 757) has succinctly observed, "Apathy at the individual level translates into insanity at the mass level."

HOW MUCH WOULD YOU PAY FOR A DOLLAR?

One of the best known behavioral traps in psychological research is the dollar auction game—a game that combines the features of a collective trap, an investment trap, and an ignorance trap. In this game, invented by Martin Shubik (1971), a dollar bill is auctioned to the highest bidder. As outlined by Platt (1973), the dollar auction game has four simple rules:

1. No communication is allowed among bidders while the auction is taking place.
2. Bids can be made only in multiples of 5 cents, beginning with a nickel.
3. Bids must not exceed $50.00 (to protect bidders from wild enthusiasm).
4. The two highest bidders *both* have to pay what they bid, even though the dollar goes only to the highest bidder (after all, the auctioneer has to recover losses somehow).

Although the game sounds innocent enough, there are two "points of no return" worth noting. The first one comes when the two highest bids cumulatively exceed $1.00, thereby assuring the auctioneer of a profit (e.g., when one person bids 50 cents and another bids 55 cents). At this point, the auction still seems attractive from a bidder's-eye-view (a dollar bill in return for 55 cents), but the pursuit of individual self-interest has already ensured a collective loss to the bidders.

The second slippery slope appears with the first bid above $1.00. To see why people might bid more than $1.00 for a dollar bill, consider the predicament of someone who has just bid 95 cents, only to have some-one else bid $1.00. What would you do in such a situation? If you quit at that point, you are sure to lose 95 cents. On the other hand, if you bid $1.05 and win the dollar, you lose only a nickel. The problem is that the person you are bidding against faces the same situation.

And as a result, the bidding often reaches a few dollars.

One reason the dollar auction game has received so much attention is that it resembles the nuclear arms race and other international conflicts (Costanza, 1984). In 1980, Allan Teger published *Too Much Invested to Quit*, an entire book devoted to research on the dollar auction game, and many of his conclusions are directly applicable to military conflict. According to Teger, subjects are usually motivated initially by personal gain, but in time their motivation changes. As the bidding continues, subjects become concerned with winning the competition, saving face, minimizing losses, and punishing their opponent for getting them into such a mess (typically, only two bidders remain active in late stages of the trap). Teger found that when the bidding approached $1.00, both sides felt they were being forced by the other bidder to continue, and many subjects thought the other person was crazy to continue—without seeing that identical forces were operating on both participants. This "mirror image" is strikingly reminiscent of the nuclear arms race.

KNEE DEEP IN THE BIG MUDDY

Once bidders in the dollar auction game are caught—"knee deep in the big muddy," as Barry Staw (1976) puts it—they usually continue clob-bering each other before someone finally gives up. Joel Brockner and Jeffrey Rubin (1985, p. 5) refer to this dynamic as "entrapment," defined as "a decision making process whereby individuals escalate their com-mitment to a previously chosen, though failing, course of action in order to justify or 'make good on' prior investments."

One of the first studies of entrapment was conducted by Staw (1976). Staw presented business students with a hypothetical but richly detailed scenario concerning a high-tech company that had begun to lose money, and he asked them to assume the role of Financial Vice Presi-dent. According to the scenario, the company's directors had decided to pump $10 million of additional research and development funds into one of the two largest divisions—Consumer Products or Industrial Prod-ucts. In Part I of the study, half the students were asked to choose which division should receive the additional funding (i.e., were highly respon-sible for the decision), and half were told that another financial officer of the company had already chosen a division to receive funding (i.e., were not responsible for the decision). Roughly half the students were then told that the chosen division outperformed the unchosen division

over the next five years (i.e., that the choice had yielded positive consequences), and roughly half were told the reverse (i.e., that the choice
had yielded negative consequences).

In Part II of the experiment, students learned that a re-evaluation by
company managers had led to the allocation of an additional $20 mil-
lion for research and development, and they were asked to split this
amount between the consumer and industrial divisions in any way they
saw fit. What Staw (1976) found was entrapment—the escalation of
commitment to a failing course of action. As shown in Figure 21.2, students who were personally responsible for an initially unsuccessful
choice allocated an average of approximately $13 million to the previ-
ously chosen division—about $4 million more than the allocation made
by other students. When responsibility was high, failure produced
greater investment, not lesser investment.

Staw's (1976) experiment stimulated a great deal of subsequent
research, and since the time of his study, several theoretical analyses of
entrapment have appeared (two of the best are Brockner & Rubin, 1985,
and Staw & Ross, 1987). Although research on entrapment is still relatively new, experimental evidence suggests that (1) situations in which

FIGURE 21.2

This figure shows an example of entrapment. Barry Staw (1976) found that business students
who fruitlessly devoted R&D funds to a failing company division later allocated more R&D money
to that division than did students who were not responsible for initial funding levels or whose earlier funding decision had turned out positively.

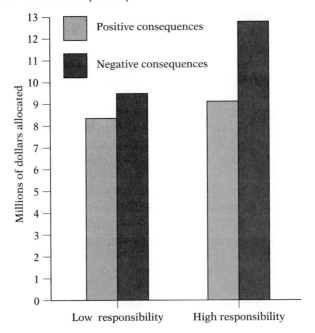

passivity maintains the status quo, such as automatic reinvestment plans, are more entrapping than situations in which decisions to continue must be made actively (Brockner, Shaw, & Rubin, 1979); (2) entrapment is greater in competitive social situations than in nonsocial situations, at least for men (Rubin, Brockner, Small-Weil, & Nathanson, 1980); and (3) entrapment occurs as readily with groups as with individuals (Bazerman, Giuliano, & Appelman, 1984), though this may be true only for women (Brockner & Rubin, 1985).

There is also some data on entrapment in romantic relationships. Caryl Rusbult (1980) found that college students in a role-playing experiment were more committed to a romantic partner—and less likely to date other people—when the relationship had lasted a year rather than a month. Thus, all things being equal, the amount of time students had already invested in the relationship was directly related to their degree of future commitment.

THE GREAT ESCAPE

As sticky as traps can be, they rarely last forever. Eventually, people waiting on hold hang up. Corporate officers stop throwing good money after bad. Romantic partners who are unhappy break up. Usually the problem is not that behavioral traps capture victims permanently, but that in retrospect, people wish they had exited the trap sooner than they did.*

Luckily, there are several ways that entrapment can be reduced or avoided (for reviews, see Brockner & Rubin, 1985; Cross & Guyer, 1980; Staw & Ross, 1987). One technique proposed by Barry Staw and Jerry Ross (1987) is to "bring phase-out costs forward" before a commitment is made—that is, to explicitly consider the costs of withdrawal before embarking on a long-term venture. Experimental evidence suggests that entrapment is reduced or eliminated when the costs of participation are made salient up front (Brockner, Rubin, & Lang, 1981; Nathanson et al., 1982).

In their book on entrapment, Brockner and Rubin (1985, p. 203) advise decision makers to set limits in advance whenever possible, and to use these limits in the following way:

> Rather than to quit automatically upon investing the amount specified by their limits, decision makers should use their limit point as a time to *reassess* whether persistence or withdrawal is wiser, *independent of the fact that prior investments have been made*. That is, if individuals decide to invest beyond their earlier set limit, this must be the result of a prospective, future (rather than past-oriented) cost-benefit analysis.

---

*Certain collective traps, such as those involving overpopulation, hunger, environmental degradation, and military conflict, may be exceptions to this rule. These problems have a disturbing air of permanence, and it remains to be seen whether humanity will be able to solve them.

In a business context, Staw and Ross (1987, March-April) recommend asking the question: "If I took over this job for the first time today and found this project going on, would I support it or get rid of it?" This question can easily be adapted for use in contexts other than business (e.g., "If I were meeting this person for the first time today, would I be attracted?").

One other technique is to have different people make initial and subsequent decisions (Bazerman, Giuliano, & Appelman, 1984; Staw & Ross, 1987). For example, a financial loan might be made by one bank officer and reviewed for renewal by another. The advantage of this technique is that later decisions are made by people who are not responsible for earlier blunders (and who therefore have little reason to escalate commitment). The disadvantage, however, is a disruption in continuity and a potential loss in "institutional memory."

CONCLUSION

Behavioral traps are a ubiquitous part of life, and if unchecked, they can lead to serious consequences. Staw (1981) has argued that many of the most damaging personal decisions and public policies arise from sequential and escalating commitments (such as those found in the Vietnam War). Platt (1973, p. 651) went even further, claiming that "traps represent all of our most intractable and large-scale urban, national, and international problems today."

Yet traps are not always bad. As Brockner and Rubin (1985) observed, there are many cases in which people deliberately attempt to trap themselves. For example, recovering alcoholics, ex-smokers, and dieters often "screw their courage to the sticking place" by intentionally trapping themselves in healthful patterns of living.

When entrapment is *desired*, decision makers should:

- ✔ Avoid information about the costs of entrapment.
- ✔ Refrain from setting limits or evaluating the costs of continuing.
- ✔ Make a public declaration of commitment.
- ✔ Compete with other people who are striving toward the same goal.

As with many of the heuristics and biases discussed in this book, behavioral traps are neither inherently good nor inherently bad, and it is not the purpose of psychological research to adjudge this issue. Rather, the purpose of entrapment research—and decision research in general—is more circumscribed. It is to further our understanding of how decision processes operate, and, in so doing, contribute to the quality of the decisions that are made.

AFTERWORD: TAKING A STEP BACK

After 21 chapters of mind-bending problems and counterintuitive results, it is time to take a step back and ask what it all means. Are decision makers fundamentally irrational? Do the strategies that reduce judgment and decision biases share any underlying principles? How are the conclusions in this book limited? And how do they apply to decision researchers themselves? This Afterword addresses each of these questions in turn.

BIASES ARE NOT NECESSARILY IRRATIONAL

As mentioned in Chapter 21, it is not the purpose of psychological research to determine whether biases are good or bad. Most findings discussed in this book have both positive and negative consequences. For example, there is a great deal of evidence suggesting that an inflated self-image actually promotes psychological health and well-being (Taylor & Brown, 1988). Although the chapters of this book reflect the "rhetoric of irrationality" that currently dominates decision research (Lopes, 1991), it is important to emphasize that biases in judgment and decision making are *not* necessarily detrimental or irrational. As Lola Lopes (1982) has pointed out, rationality means more than being "right" as often as possible. A rational strategy is one that is likely to produce the kind of results decision makers desire.

In some cases, decision makers may care more about avoiding disasters than maximizing utility. In other cases, they may choose an outcome that benefits friends and family members rather than themselves. And in still others, they may seek to maximize utility in much the same way that an idealized "rational actor" would according to expected utility theory. Decision makers may pursue any number of objectives, and it would be a mistake to define rationality in terms of a single normative standard.

Furthermore, even when decision makers are treated as rational actors in an expected utility framework, there is no reason to assume

253

that optimal accuracy always maximizes utility. Lopes has made this point with respect to the fundamental attribution error (discussed in Chapter 16). According to Lopes (1982, p. 633), the fundamental attribution error "is the predisposition of most of us to attribute the behavior of others to stable personality variables rather than to transient and often equivocal situational factors. But this may be no error at all. Both physical and social survival require that we learn as well as we can to predict and control the effects that other people have on us. Thus, if an effect is predictable, even weakly, by the presence of some individual, then it is important that we find this out." The tendency to overattribute behavior to dispositional causes may therefore constitute a rational approach to making attributions.

To see why this is so, consider the imaginary and highly oversimplified payoff scheme given in Figure A.1. If Lopes' conjecture about the importance of detecting dispositional causes is true, the payoff for accurately discerning dispositional causes would be relatively large (say, +3 in utility), and the payoff for failing to detect dispositional causes would be fairly low (−3). On the other hand, it may not make much difference whether situational causes are accurately detected (+1) or whether they are missed (−1).

FIGURE A.1

These numbers represent imaginary payoffs for four attributional outcomes. According to this scheme, the fundamental attribution error (upper right cell) is not as harmful as failing to detect a dispositional cause (lower left cell), and the reward for making an accurate dispositional attribution (upper left cell) is greater than the reward for accurately making a situational attribution (lower right cell). Under these circumstances, it may make sense for decision makers to overattribute behavior to dispositional causes.

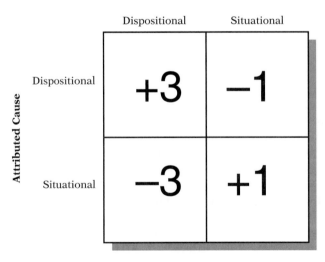

Actual Cause of Behavior

If we assume, for the sake of argument, that situational causes occur 60 percent of the time, and we further assume that a decision maker has no idea which type of attribution to make, what would a "rational" response be to the payoffs in Figure A.1?

In such a case, *dispositional* attributions yield the greatest average payoff. A decision maker who always attributed behavior to dispositional causes would average +.60 in utility (60 percent of the time the payoff would be −1, but 40 percent of the time it would be +3), whereas a decision maker who always attributed behavior to situational causes would average only −.60 in utility (usually +1, but sometimes −3). Even though situational attributions would be *correct* more often than dispositional attributions, the most *rewarding* strategy would be to over-attribute behavior to dispositional causes (i.e., commit the fundamental attribution error).

Of course, the payoffs in Figure A.1 are merely hypothetical. There is no way to determine the utility of hits and misses over a lifetime of attributions, and there is no way to assess the relative frequency of situational and dispositional causes. Computer simulations of decision heuristics suggest, however, that the cost of certain biases may often be rather low. For example, Warren Thorngate (1980) found that heuristics which ignored probability information performed almost as well as probability-based decision rules, and Don Kleinmuntz (1985) found that heuristics which neglected base rate information performed quite well when feedback was provided in a repeated judgment task. Thus, in cases when probability or base rate information is difficult to obtain or assimilate, heuristics may provide an attractive alternative to normative decision rules.

These results are not meant to suggest that decision makers are as well off being biased as unbiased. There are many instances in which biases in judgment and decision making lead to grievous problems (e.g., medical misdiagnoses). Rather, these findings are meant to place judgment and decision biases in proper perspective, and to demonstrate that biases need not imply irrationality.

A COMMON THREAD

Although there is more to rationality than being correct, in most cases decision makers strive to make accurate judgments. Accordingly, decision researchers have sought to develop effective "debiasing" techniques (i.e., techniques that reduce biases and errors in judgment). In some cases, simply learning about a potential problem is enough to avoid it. For example, people who learn about entrapment are less likely to become entrapped (Nathanson et al., 1982). Most of the time, however, warnings are not sufficient to eliminate biases and errors.

A variety of debiasing techniques have been discussed throughout the book—techniques to reduce overconfidence, hindsight biases, framing effects, groupthink, attributional biases, and so forth. It is natural to wonder whether these debiasing techniques have anything in common.

At the risk of oversimplification, and without intending to reduce all debiasing strategies to a common theme, there *does* seem to be an element of continuity:

> *Many of the most effective debiasing techniques involve the consideration of alternative perspectives.*

For instance, overconfidence is usually reduced by considering why answers might be wrong. Hindsight biases can be reduced or eliminated by considering reasons why a different outcome might have occurred. Framing effects are minimized when the same problem is framed in multiple ways. Groupthink can be avoided by having one member of the group play the role of devil's advocate. Actor-observer differences in attribution can be reversed by having actors and observers swap visual orientations. In all of these cases, "considering the opposite" leads to greater accuracy in judgment.

Consistent with this general theme, there is also evidence that empathy eliminates certain biases in social judgment. Two years after Michael Storms (1973) showed that actor-observer differences in attribution could be reversed by switching the visual orientation of actors and observers (discussed in Chapter 16), Dennis Regan and Judith Totten (1975) found that instructions to empathize had much the same effect. In this research, subjects were instructed either to simply observe one of two people having a get-acquainted conversation (someone named Margaret), or to empathize with her (to "imagine how Margaret feels as she engages in the conversation").

Regan and Totten (1975) found that subjects who simply observed Margaret gave more dispositional than situational attributions for her behavior, but subjects who empathized with her gave more situational than dispositional attributions for her behavior. In other words, instructions to empathize produced the same effect Storms had found earlier; it reversed actor-observer differences in attribution.

One year later, Ruth Galper published a similar study in which she found much the same thing. Galper (1976, p. 333) summarized her findings as follows:

> Subjects who had not been instructed to empathize with the actor displayed the typical "observer bias," rating personal factors as significantly more important than situational factors. Subjects under "empathy" instructions, on the other hand, displayed a reversal of this bias, and rated personal factors as significantly *less* important than situational factors. While Storms (1973) has demonstrated that a *literal* change of perspective can systematically affect the attributional biases of actors and observers, the present results demonstrate that a

figurative "change of perspective" can elicit "actor-like" causal attributions from observers.

These and other studies suggest the value of considering divergent
perspectives before making final judgments (Anderson, 1982; Lord, Lepper, & Preston, 1984). Although no single debiasing technique is a
panacea, the consideration of alternative viewpoints will often improve
the quality of judgment and decision making.

AND NOW FOR THE BAD NEWS . . .

Despite the usefulness of decision research on debiasing techniques and
other topics, the conclusions presented in this book suffer from several
limitations. Some limitations stem from the restricted coverage of topics in the book, and others reflect shortcomings in decision research
itself.

As mentioned in the Preface, the studies covered in this book do not
represent an exhaustive survey of all judgment and decision research.
Instead, they were specifically chosen to surprise, entertain, and
intrigue. Many important research areas have been discussed in only
the briefest way, and, of necessity, a number of fine studies have not
been discussed at all. The following two examples illustrate how these
limitations can affect the generality of research conclusions.

First, as mentioned briefly in Chapter 17, decision making is strongly
influenced by "accountability." Decision makers who feel accountable
for their actions show less overconfidence than those who do not (Tetlock & Kim, 1987), display less social loafing (Weldon & Gargano,
1988), and exhibit greater analytic complexity (Hagafors & Brehmer,
1983; Tetlock, 1983). As Philip Tetlock, Linda Skitka, and Richard
Boettger (1989, p. 640) have noted: "How people think depends in part
on why people think." Any complete picture of decision making must
take this relation into account, and research conclusions should be
qualified by the degree to which experimental subjects feel accountable
for their actions.

Second, judgment and decision making depends heavily on situation-
specific factors such as how much time a decision maker has available
and what mood the decision maker is in. When time pressure is high,
decision makers use simplifying strategies, attend to a small number of
cues, and choose relatively low-risk alternatives (Ben Zur & Breznitz,
1981; Rothstein, 1986; Wright, 1974). Also, decision makers who are in
a good mood tend to be more creative (Isen, Daubman, & Nowicki,
1987), perceive negative events as relatively infrequent and improbable
(Johnson & Tversky, 1983; Salovey & Birnbaum, 1989; Wright & Bower,
1992), and take certain low-level risks that others are unwilling to
accept (Isen & Geva, 1987; Isen & Patrick, 1983). Once again, these
findings suggest that conclusions from decision research should be carefully qualified so as to avoid overgeneralization.

The conclusions in this book are also limited by the nature of decision research itself, and it is worth noting some of these limitations. First, as might be expected from the research discussed in Chapters 4 through 6, many findings in judgment and decision research are context-dependent (Schum, 1990). This limitation was forcefully demonstrated by Richard Griggs and James Cox (1982), who randomly assigned college students to receive one of two problems: (1) the standard four-card problem discussed in Chapter 20, or (2) a version of the four-card problem in which "E," "K," "4," and "7" were replaced with the phrases "DRINKING A BEER," "DRINKING A COKE," "22 YEARS OF AGE," and "16 YEARS OF AGE" (with the rule "If a person is drinking a beer, then the person must be over 19 years of age"). When a beer-drinking context was used, roughly three-fourths of the students answered correctly, whereas none of the students solved the problem when it was cast in terms of letters and numbers. Changes in wording can also affect covariation judgments (Crocker, 1982) and the conjunction fallacy (Fiedler, 1988).

Another limitation of judgment and decision research is its reliance on laboratory experiments conducted with college students. As valuable as these studies are, laboratory tasks do not always involve the same decision processes found in naturalistic environments. For example, Ebbe Ebbesen and Vladimir Konečni (1975) found that municipal and superior court judges arrived at actual bail decisions very differently than they arrived at simulated bail decisions. And as pointed out in Chapter 19, the judgments of expert bridge players and professional weather forecasters tend to be far better calibrated than the judgments made by ordinary mortals (Keren, 1987; Murphy & Brown, 1984; Murphy & Winkler, 1984). On the other hand, several studies have found that experts display either roughly the same biases as college students (Dubé-Rioux & Russo, 1988) or the same biases at somewhat reduced levels (Christensen-Szalanski, Beck, Christensen-Szalanski, & Koepsell, 1983; Smith & Kida, 1991). Clearly, more research is needed on expert decision makers.

Still another shortcoming of decision research is that it lacks a cross-cultural orientation. Most decision research is conducted in North America and Europe. Relatively few empirical studies have been conducted on how the rest of the world makes decisions, and as a consequence, it is hard to determine how universal certain findings are (Fletcher & Ward, 1988). The following examples illustrate the difficulty of drawing firm conclusions:

- Donald Taylor and Vaishna Jaggi (1974) found that Hindu Indians displayed attributional biases similar to those found in the United States, but other researchers have found differences in attributional style between Americans and Indians. In contrast to Americans—who are prone to the "fundamental" attribution error—Indians attribute behavior to situational causes more often than dispositional causes (Miller, 1984).

- James Stoner (1968) reported that risky shifts had been documented among American, British, and Israeli subjects, but other researchers have found differences in how American, British, and Asian subjects think about probability (Wright et al., 1978; Yates et al., 1989).
- Taha Amir (1984) found that the Asch paradigm produced conformity levels in Kuwait comparable to those found in the United States, but Noriyuki Matsuda (1985) found higher levels of conformity in Japan than in the United States. Thus, findings that appeared general one year became culture-bound the next year.
- Research also suggests that Japanese subjects do not exhibit self-serving biases in attribution—unlike subjects from the United States, India, South Africa, and Yugoslavia (Chandler, Shama, Wolf, & Planchard, 1981).

These findings provide only a glimmer of the complexity that awaits cross-cultural decision researchers. Until a sizable body of such work is conducted, care should be exercised in applying the results of decision research to non-Western cultures.

THE FALLIBILITY OF DECISION RESEARCHERS

Research on judgment and decision making suffers from one other problem—a problem rarely mentioned, but one that has profound implications:

Judgment and decision research is conducted by human beings who are prone to many of the same biases and errors as their experimental subjects.

As a consequence of this inescapable fact, the conclusions of judgment and decision research—which are, after all, nothing more than a set of judgments and decisions—are vulnerable to a variety of biases and errors.

For example, just as experimental subjects are overconfident of their answers, decision researchers may be overconfident of their theories. Similarly, researchers are susceptible to cognitive dissonance and investment traps, and it is reasonable to assume that in many cases the sunk costs of past work lead researchers to become entrapped. As Joel Brockner and Jeffrey Rubin (1985, p. 260) warned in the closing lines of their book on entrapment: "Good entrapment researchers—like the very decision makers who have been the object of our experimental study—must know how to evaluate their actions in the larger scheme of things."

Baruch Fischhoff (1991) has further observed that researchers who want and expect to see a phenomenon are likely to overestimate its frequency (presumably because matches between theory and data are more salient than mismatches). As a consequence of the availability heuristic, the frequency and/or probability of matches are likely to be overestimated, and researchers may perceive an illusory—or at least inflated—correlation between theory and data. This possibility is consistent with research on selective perception, biased assimilation, and the perseverance of erroneous beliefs in the face of discrediting evidence (e.g., Lord, Ross, & Lepper, 1979; Ross, Lepper, & Hubbard, 1975).

Perhaps most serious of all, researchers are prone to confirmation biases and self-fulfilling prophecies (Jenkins, 1981; Rosenthal, 1976). One of the first studies on this topic, and one of the most dramatic, was an experiment by Robert Rosenthal and Kermit Fode (1963). Rosenthal and Fode led a dozen experimenters to believe that they would be working either with "maze-bright" rats or "maze-dull" rats, when in reality, these labels were assigned at random. Each experimenter was given five rats to work with and was asked to record how the rats performed on 50 trials of a maze-running task.

Averaging over all 50 trials, Rosenthal and Fode found that "maze-bright" rats were correct 50 percent more often than "maze-dull" rats. Thus, even though expectations had been induced at random, experimenters found the results they had expected to find.

In conclusion, judgment and decision research is subject to a paradox: If its findings are valid (i.e., biases and errors exist), then its findings are, to some degree, subject to biases and errors. At the same time, if its findings are *not* valid (i.e., biases and errors do not exist), then its findings are still in error. Either way, biases and errors are likely to be present. This paradox is similar in some respects to Austrian logician Kurt Gödel's Incompleteness Theorem, which states that any complete, mathematically powerful, and formalized system of logic must be internally inconsistent.

Of course, biases and errors need not undermine decision research any more than they undermine other research enterprises. The point is merely that, however reluctantly, decision researchers must include themselves when they speak of human fallibility. The purpose of these final remarks is to take a step in this direction, even if only in the manner described by B. F. Skinner (1980):

> I used to represent the behaviorist's attitude toward himself by describing a lecturer who explains human behavior, including the behavior of other lecturers, and leaves the stage. Then he sticks his head out from the wings and says, "And I'm like that too!"

"Now, _that's_ a welcome sight! I was just beginning to miss decision-making."

FURTHER READING

If you want to read more about the psychology of judgment and decision making, there are several books I highly recommend. For general overviews that emphasize decision making in managerial and business settings, see:

- Russo, J. E., & Schoemaker, P. J. H. (1989). *Decision traps: Ten barriers to brilliant decision making and how to overcome them*. New York: Simon & Schuster.
- Bazerman, M. H. (1990). *Judgment in managerial decision making* (2nd ed.). New York: John Wiley & Sons.
- Hogarth, R. (1987). *Judgement and choice* (2nd ed.). New York: John Wiley and Sons.

If you want a nontechnical overview that does *not* focus on business applications, try:

- Dawes, R. M. (1988). *Rational choice in an uncertain world*. San Diego: Harcourt Brace Jovanovich.
- Nisbett, R. E., & Ross, L. (1980). *Human inference: Strategies and shortcomings of social judgment*. Englewood Cliffs, NJ: Prentice-Hall.
- Gilovich, T. (1991). *How we know what ain't so*. New York: Free Press.

For more advanced material, Cambridge University Press has published three superb anthologies, the first of which is widely regarded as a modern-day classic:

- Kahneman, D., Slovic, P., & Tversky, A. (Eds.). (1982). *Judgment under uncertainty: Heuristics and biases*. Cambridge, England: Cambridge University Press.
- Arkes, H. R., & Hammond, K. R. (Eds.). (1986). *Judgment and decision making: An interdisciplinary reader*. Cambridge, England: Cambridge University Press.
- Bell, D. E., Raiffa, H., & Tversky, A. (Eds.). (1988). *Decision making: Descriptive, normative, and prescriptive interactions*. Cambridge, England: Cambridge University Press.

The University of Chicago has also published a very good collection of talks given at a symposium in memory of decision researcher Hillel Einhorn:

- Hogarth, R. M. (Ed.). (1990). *Insights in decision making: A tribute to Hillel J. Einhorn.* Chicago: University of Chicago Press.

If you want to read more about the effects of question wording, see:

- Schuman, H., & Presser, S. (1981). *Questions and answers in attitude surveys: Experiments on question form, wording, and context.* Orlando, FL: Academic Press.
- Hogarth, R. (Ed.). (1982). *New directions for methodology of social and behavioral science: Question framing and response consistency.* San Francisco: Jossey-Bass.
- Sudman, S., & Bradburn, N. M. (1982). *Asking questions: A practical guide to questionnaire design.* San Francisco: Jossey-Bass.

Finally, if you want to know more about the social-psychological dimensions of judgment and decision making, I recommend:

- Aronson, E. (1991). *The social animal* (6th rev. ed.). San Francisco: W. H. Freeman and Company.
- Zimbardo, P. G., & Leippe, M. (1991). *The psychology of attitude change and social influence.* New York: McGraw-Hill.
- Cialdini, R. B. (1988). *Influence: Science and practice* (2nd ed.). Glenview, IL: Scott, Foresman.

REFERENCES

Abramson, L. Y., Seligman, M. E. P., & Teasdale, J. D. (1978). Learned helplessness in humans: Critique and reformulation. *Journal of Abnormal Psychology, 87,* 49–74.

Ajzen, I. (1977). Intuitive theories of events and the effects of base-rate information on prediction. *Journal of Personality and Social Psychology, 35,* 303–314.

Ajzen, I., & Fishbein, M. (1977). Attitude-behavior relations: A theoretical analysis and review of empirical research. *Psychological Bulletin, 84,* 888–918.

Allais, P. M. (1953). The behavior of rational man in risk situations—A critique of the axioms and postulates of the American School. *Econometrica, 21,* 503–546.

Allison, S. T., & Messick, D. M. (1985). The group attribution error. *Journal of Experimental Social Psychology, 21,* 563–579.

Alloy, L. B., & Tabachnik, N. (1984). Assessment of covariation by humans and animals: The joint influence of prior expectations and current situational information. *Psychological Review, 91,* 112–149.

Allport, G. W. (1954). The historical background of modern social psychology. In G. Lindzey (Ed.), *The handbook of social psychology* (Vol. 1). Reading, MA: Addison-Wesley.

Alvarez, L. W. (1965). A pseudo experience in parapsychology. *Science, 148,* 1541.

American Psychological Association. (1989). Ethical principles of psychologists. *American Psychologist, 45,* 390–395.

Amir, T. (1984). The Asch conformity effect: A study in Kuwait. *Social Behavior and Personality, 12,* 187–190.

Anderson, C. A. (1982). Inoculation and counterexplanation: Debiasing techniques in the perseverance of social theories. *Social Cognition, 1,* 126–139.

Anderson, C. A. (1983). Imagination and expectation: The effect of imagining behavioral scripts on personal intentions. *Journal of Personality and Social Psychology, 45,* 293–305.

Anderson, N. H. (1965). Primacy effects in personality impression formation using a generalized order effect paradigm. *Journal of Personality and Social Psychology, 2,* 1–9.

Argote, L., Seabright, M. A., & Dyer, L. (1986). Individual versus group use of base-rate and individuating information. *Organizational Behavior and Human Decision Processes, 38,* 65–75.

Arkes, H. R., & Blumer, C. (1985). The psychology of sunk cost. *Organizational Behavior and Human Decision Processes, 35,* 124–140.

Arkes, H. R., Christensen, C., Lai, C., & Blumer, C. (1987). Two methods of reducing overconfidence. *Organizational Behavior and Human Decision Processes, 39,* 133–144.

Arkes, H. R., & Harkness, A. R. (1983). Estimates of contingency between two dichotomous variables. *Journal of Experimental Psychology: General, 112,* 117–135.

Arkes, H. R., Wortmann, R. L., Saville, P. D., & Harkness, A. R. (1981). Hindsight bias among physicians weighing the likelihood of diagnoses. *Journal of Applied Psychology, 66,* 252–254.

Aronson, E. (1969). The theory of cognitive dissonance: A current perspective. In L. Berkowitz (Ed.), *Advances in experimental social psychology* (Vol. 4, pp. 1–34). New York: Academic Press.

Aronson, E. (1972). *The social animal.* San Francisco: W. H. Freeman and Company.

Aronson, E., & Mills, J. (1959). The effect of severity of initiation on liking for a group. *Journal of Abnormal and Social Psychology, 59,* 177–181.

Asch, S. E. (1946). Forming impressions of personality. *Journal of Abnormal and Social Psychology, 41,* 258–290.

Asch, S. E. (1951). Effects of group pressure upon the modification and distortion of judgment. In H. Guetzkow (Ed.), *Groups, leadership and men.* Pittsburgh: Carnegie Press.

Asch, S. E. (1955, November). Opinions and social pressure. *Scientific American,* pp. 31–35.

Asch, S. E. (1956). Studies of independence and conformity: A minority of one against a unanimous majority. *Psychological Monographs, 70* (9, Whole No. 416).

Ausubel, N. (Ed.). (1948). *A treasury of Jewish folklore: Stories, traditions, legends, humor, wisdom and folk songs of the Jewish people.* New York: Crown Publishers.

Ayton, P., Hunt, A. J., & Wright, G. (1989). Psychological conceptions of randomness. *Journal of Behavioral Decision Making, 2,* 221–238.

Bakan, P. (1960). Response tendencies in attempts to generate random binary series. *American Journal of Psychology, 73,* 127–131.

Bandura, A. (1982). Self-efficacy: Mechanism in human agency. *American Psychologist, 37,* 122–147.

Bandura, A. (1986). *Social foundations of thought and action: A social cognitive theory.* Englewood Cliffs, NJ: Prentice-Hall.

Barclay, S., & Beach, L. R. (1972). Combinatorial properties of personal probabilities. *Organizational Behavior and Human Performance, 8,* 176–183.

Bar-Hillel, M. (1973). On the subjective probability of compound events. *Organizational Behavior and Human Performance, 9,* 396–406.

Bar-Hillel, M. (1980). The base-rate fallacy in probability judgments. *Acta Psychologica, 44,* 211–233.

Bar-Hillel, M. (1990). Back to base rates. In R. M. Hogarth (Ed.), *Insights in decision making: A tribute to Hillel J. Einhorn.* Chicago: University of Chicago Press.

Batson, C. D. (1975). Attribution as a mediator of bias in helping. *Journal of Personality and Social Psychology, 32,* 455–466.

Batson, C. D., & Marz, B. (1979). Dispositional bias in trained therapists' diagnoses: Does it exist? *Journal of Applied Social Psychology, 9,* 476–489.

Baxter, T. L., & Goldberg, L. R. (1987). Perceived behavioral consistency underlying trait attributions to oneself and another: An extension of the actor-observer effect. *Personality and Social Psychology Bulletin, 13,* 437–447.

Bazerman, M. H., Giuliano, T., & Appelman, A. (1984). Escalation of commitment in individual and group decision making. *Organizational Behavior and Human Performance, 33,* 141–152.

Bedau, H. A., & Radelet, M. L. (1987). Miscarriages of justice in potentially capital cases. *Stanford Law Review, 40,* 21–179.

Bell, D. E. (1982). Regret in decision making under uncertainty. *Operations Research, 30,* 961–981.

Bell, D. E. (1985). Disappointment in decision making under uncertainty. *Operations Research, 33,* 1–27.

Bem, D. J. (1972). Self-perception theory. In L. Berkowitz (Ed.), *Advances in experimental social psychology* (Vol. 6). New York: Academic Press.

Ben Zur, H., & Breznitz, S. J. (1981). The effects of time pressure on risky choice behavior. *Acta Psychologica, 47,* 89–104.

Bernoulli, D. (1738/1954). Exposition of a new theory on the measurement of risk, translated by Louise Sommer. *Econometrica, 22,* 22–36.

Beyth-Marom, M. (1982). Perception of correlation reexamined. *Memory & Cognition, 10,* 511–519.

Bierbrauer, G. (1973). *Effect of set, perspective, and temporal factors in attribution.* Unpublished doctoral dissertation, Stanford University.

Bishop, G. F., Oldendick, R. W., Tuchfarber, A. J., & Bennett, S. E. (1980). Pseudo-opinions on public affairs. *Public Opinion Quarterly, 44,* 198–209.

Blascovich, J., Ginsburg, G. P., & Howe, R. C. (1975). Blackjack and the risky shift, II: Monetary stakes. *Journal of Experimental Social Psychology, 11,* 224–232.

Block, J. R., & Yuker, H. E. (1989). *Can you believe your eyes?* New York: Gardner Press.

Blodgett, R. (1983, November). Against all odds. *Games,* pp. 14–18.

Bond, C. F., Jr., & Titus, L. J. (1983). Social facilitation: A meta-analysis of 241 studies. *Psychological Bulletin, 94,* 265–292.

Borgida, E., & Nisbett, R. E. (1977). The differential impact of abstract vs. concrete information on decisions. *Journal of Applied Social Psychology, 7,* 258–271.

Borrelli, S., Lockerbie, B., & Niemi, R. G. (1987). Why the Democrat-Republican partisanship gap varies from poll to poll. *Public Opinion Quarterly, 51,* 115–119.

Bostic, R., Herrnstein, R. J., & Luce, R. D. (1990). The effect on the preference-reversal phenomenon of using choice indifferences. *Journal of Economic Behavior and Organization, 13,* 193–212.

Bourne, L. E., Jr., & Guy, D. E. (1968). Learning conceptual rules: II. The role of positive and negative instances. *Journal of Experimental Psychology, 77,* 488–494.

Bransford, J. D., & Franks, J. J. (1971). The abstraction of linguistic ideas. *Cognitive Psychology, 2,* 331–350.

Brickman, P., Coates, D., & Janoff-Bulman, R. (1978). Lottery winners and accident victims: Is happiness relative? *Journal of Personality and Social Psychology, 36,* 917–927.

Brockner, J., & Rubin, J. Z. (1985). *Entrapment in escalating conflicts: A social psychological analysis.* New York: Springer-Verlag.

Brockner, J., Rubin, J. Z., & Lang, E. (1981). Face-saving and entrapment. *Journal of Experimental Social Psychology, 17,* 68–79.

Brockner, J., Shaw, M. C., & Rubin, J. Z. (1979). Factors affecting withdrawal from an escalating conflict: Quitting before it's too late. *Journal of Experimental Social Psychology, 15,* 492–503.

Brophy, J. E. (1983). Research on the self-fulfilling prophecy and teacher expectations. *Journal of Educational Psychology, 75,* 631–661.

Brown, E., Deffenbacher, K., & Sturgill, W. (1977). Memory for faces and the circumstances of encounter. *Journal of Applied Psychology, 62,* 311–318.

Bruner, J. S., & Postman, L. J. (1949). On the perception of incongruity: A paradigm. *Journal of Personality, 18,* 206–223.

Budiansky, S. (1988, July 11). The numbers racket: How polls and statistics lie. *U.S. News & World Report,* pp. 44–47.

Campbell, J. D., & Tesser, A. (1983). Motivational interpretations of hindsight bias: An individual difference analysis. *Journal of Personality, 51,* 605–620.

Cantril, H. (1940). Experiments in the wording of questions. *Public Opinion Quarterly, 4,* 330–332.

Carden, G. (1990, September 25). Strangers, but they share unbelievable mirror-image lives. *National Enquirer,* p. 19.

Carroll, J. S. (1978). The effect of imagining an event on expectations for the event: An interpretation in terms of the availability heuristic. *Journal of Experimental Social Psychology, 14,* 88–96.

Centor, R. M., Dalton, H. P., & Yates, J. F. (1984). *Are physicians' probability estimates better or worse than regression model estimates?* Paper presented at the Sixth Annual Meeting of the Society for Medical Decision Making, Bethesda, MD.

Cervone, D., & Peake, P. K. (1986). Anchoring, efficacy, and action: The influence of judgmental heuristics on self-efficacy judgments. *Journal of Personality and Social Psychology, 50,* 492–501.

Chandler, T. A., Shama, D. D., Wolf, F. M., & Planchard, S. K. (1981). Multiattributional causality: A five cross-national samples study. *Journal of Cross-Cultural Psychology, 12,* 207–221.

Chapman, L. J. (1967). Illusory correlation in observational report. *Journal of Verbal Learning and Behavior, 6,* 151–155.

Chapman, L. J., & Chapman, J. P. (1967). Genesis of popular but erroneous psychodiagnostic observations. *Journal of Abnormal Psychology, 72,* 193–204.

Chapman, L. J., & Chapman, J. P. (1969). Illusory correlation as an obstacle to the use of valid psychodiagnostic signs. *Journal of Abnormal Psychology, 74,* 271–280.

Chapman, L. J., & Chapman, J. P. (1971, November). Test results are what you think they are. *Psychology Today,* pp. 18–22, 106–110.

Cheng, P. W., & Novick, L. R. (1990). A probabilistic contrast model of causal induction. *Journal of Personality and Social Psychology, 58,* 545–567.

Christensen, D., & Rosenthal, R. (1982). Gender and nonverbal decoding skill as determinants of interpersonal expectancy effects. *Journal of Personality and Social Psychology, 42,* 75–87.

Christensen-Szalanski, J. J. J., & Beach, L. R. (1984). The citation bias: Fad and fashion in the judgment and decision literature. *American Psychologist, 39,* 75–78.

Christensen-Szalanski, J. J. J., Beck, D. E., Christensen-Szalanski, C. M., & Koepsell, T. D. (1983). Effects of expertise and experience on risk judgments. *Journal of Applied Psychology, 68,* 278–284.

Christensen-Szalanski, J. J. J., & Bushyhead, J. B. (1981). Physicians' use of probabilistic information in a real clinical setting. *Journal of Experimental Psychology: Human Perception and Performance, 7,* 928–935.

Christensen-Szalanski, J. J. J., & Willham, C. F. (1991). The hindsight bias: A meta-analysis. *Organizational Behavior and Human Decision Processes, 48,* 147–168.

Clifford, B. R., & Scott, J. (1978). Individual and situational factors in eyewitness testimony. *Journal of Applied Psychology, 63,* 352–359.

Clymer, A. (1982, May 6). Nuclear issue yields run on pollsters. *New York Times,* p. B14.

Cohen, B. L., & Lee, I. (1979). A catalog of risks. *Health Physics, 36,* 707–722.

Cohen, J., Chesnick, E. I., & Haran, D. (1971). Evaluation of compound probabilities in sequential choice. *Nature, 232,* 414–416.

Combs, B., & Slovic, P. (1979). Newspaper coverage of causes of death. *Journalism Quarterly, 56,* 837–843, 849.

Converse, P. E., & Schuman, H. (1970, June). "Silent majorities" and the Vietnam war. *Scientific American,* pp. 17–25.

Coombs, C. H. (1975). Portfolio theory and the measurement of risk. In M. F. Kaplan & S. Schwartz (Eds.), *Human judgment and decision processes.* New York: Academic Press.

Cooper, W. H. (1981). Ubiquitous halo. *Psychological Bulletin, 90,* 218–244.

Coren, S., & Miller, J. (1974). Size contrast as a function of figural similarity. *Perception and Psychophysics, 16*, 355–357.

Corey, S. M. (1937). Professed attitudes and actual behavior. *Journal of Educational Psychology, 28*, 271–280.

Costanza, R. (1984). Review essay: The nuclear arms race and the theory of social traps. *Journal of Peace Research, 21*, 79–86.

Craig, K. D., & Prkachin, K. M. (1978). Social modeling influences on sensory decision theory and psychophysiological indexes of pain. *Journal of Personality and Social Psychology, 36*, 805–815.

Crandall, V. J., Solomon, D., & Kellaway, R. (1955). Expectancy statements and decision times as functions of objective probabilities and reinforcement values. *Journal of Personality, 24*, 192–203.

Crocker, J. (1981). Judgment of covariation by social perceivers. *Psychological Bulletin, 90*, 272–292.

Crocker, J. (1982). Biased questions in judgment of covariation studies. *Personality and Social Psychology Bulletin, 8*, 214–220.

Cross, J. G., & Guyer, M. J. (1980). *Social traps.* Ann Arbor: University of Michigan Press.

Darley, J. M., & Batson, C. D. (1973). "From Jerusalem to Jericho": A study of situational and dispositional variables in helping behavior. *Journal of Personality and Social Psychology, 27*, 100–108.

Darley, J. M., & Fazio, R. H. (1980). Expectancy confirmation processes arising in the social interaction sequence. *American Psychologist, 35*, 867–881.

Darley, J. M., & Latané, B. (1968). Bystander intervention in emergencies: Diffusion of responsibility. *Journal of Personality and Social Psychology, 8*, 377–383.

Davis, J. H. (1973). Group decision and social interaction: A theory of social decision schemes. *Psychological Review, 80*, 97–125.

Dawes, R. M. (1975). The mind, the model, and the task. In F. Restle, R. M. Shiffrin, N. J. Castellan, H. R. Lindman, & D. B. Pisoni (Eds.), *Cognitive theory* (Vol. 1). Hillsdale, NJ: Erlbaum.

Dawes, R. M. (1980). Social dilemmas. *Annual Review of Psychology, 31*, 169–193.

Dawes, R. M., Faust, D., & Meehl, P. E. (1989). Clinical versus actuarial judgment. *Science, 243*, 1668–1674.

"Death Odds." (1990, September 24). *Newsweek*, p. 10.

Deci, E. L. (1975). *Intrinsic motivation.* New York: Plenum Press.

Deffenbacher, K. A. (1980). Eyewitness accuracy and confidence. *Law and Human Behavior, 4*, 243–260.

Diener, D., & Thompson, W. B. (1985). Recognizing randomness. *American Journal of Psychology, 98*, 433–447.

Dion, K., Berscheid, E., & Walster, E. (1972). What is beautiful is good. *Journal of Personality and Social Psychology, 24*, 285–290.

Doob, A. N., Carlsmith, J. M., Freedman, J. L., Landauer, T. K., & Tom, S., Jr.

(1969). Effect of initial selling price on subsequent sales. *Journal of Personality and Social Psychology, 11,* 345–350.

Dubé-Rioux, L., & Russo, J. E. (1988). An availability bias in professional judgment. *Journal of Behavioral Decision Making, 1,* 223–237.

Duncan, B. L. (1976). Differential social perception and attribution of intergroup violence: Testing the lower limits of stereotyping blacks. *Journal of Personality and Social Psychology, 43,* 590–598.

Dunning, D., Griffin, D. W., Milojkovic, J. D., & Ross, L. (1990). The overconfidence effect in social prediction. *Journal of Personality and Social Psychology, 58,* 568–581.

Dunning, D., & Parpal, M. (1989). Mental addition versus subtraction in counterfactual reasoning: On assessing the impact of personal actions and life events. *Journal of Personality and Social Psychology, 57,* 5–15.

Duval, S., & Wicklund, S. A. (1973). Effects of objective self–awareness on attribution of causality. *Journal of Experimental Social Psychology, 9,* 17–31.

Ebbesen, E. B., & Konečni, V. J. (1975). Decision making and information integration in the courts: The setting of bail. *Journal of Personality and Social Psychology, 32,* 805–821.

Edeal, G. H. (1950, March 27). Why the choir was late. *Life,* p. 19.

Eddy, D. (1982). Probabilistic reasoning in clinical medicine: Problems and opportunities. In D. Kahneman, P. Slovic, & A. Tversky (Eds.), *Judgment under uncertainty: Heuristics and biases.* Cambridge, England: Cambridge University Press.

Edwards, W. (1968). Conservatism in human information processing. In B. Kleinmuntz (Ed.), *Formal representation of human judgment.* New York: John Wiley and Sons.

Einhorn, H. J., & Hogarth, R. M. (1981). Behavioral decision theory: Processes of judgment and choice. *Annual Review of Psychology, 32,* 53–88.

Einhorn, H. J., & Hogarth, R. J. (1986). Backward and forward thinking in decision making. *Selected Paper No. 62.* Chicago: Graduate School of Business, University of Chicago.

Ellsberg, D. (1961). Risk, ambiguity, and the Savage axioms. *Quarterly Journal of Economics, 75,* 643–669.

Esser, J. K., & Lindoerfer, J. S. (1989). Groupthink and the space shuttle Challenger accident: Toward a quantitative case analysis. *Journal of Behavioral Decision Making, 2,* 167–177.

Fama, E. F. (1965). Random walks in stock market prices. *Financial Analysts Journal, 21,* 55–60.

Feldman, J. M. (1986). A note on the statistical correction of halo error. *Journal of Applied Psychology, 71,* 173–176.

Feldman, R. S., & Prohaska, T. (1979). The student as Pygmalion: Effect of student expectation on the teacher. *Journal of Educational Psychology, 71,* 485–493.

Feldman, R. S., & Theiss, A. J. (1982). The teacher and the student as Pygmalions: Joint effects of teacher and student expectations. *Journal of Educational Psychology, 74*, 217–223.

Festinger, L. (1954). A theory of social comparison processes. *Human Relations, 7*, 117–140.

Festinger, L. (1957). *A theory of cognitive dissonance.* Evanston, IL: Row, Peterson.

Festinger, L., & Carlsmith, J. M. (1959). Cognitive consequences of forced compliance. *Journal of Abnormal and Social Psychology, 58*, 203–210.

Feynman, R. P. (1988, February). An outsider's inside view of the Challenger inquiry. *Physics Today*, 26–37.

Fiedler, K. (1988). The dependence of the conjunction fallacy on subtle linguistic factors. *Psychological Research, 50*, 123–129.

Fischhoff, B. (1977). Perceived informativeness of facts. *Journal of Experimental Psychology: Human Perception and Performance, 3*, 349–358.

Fischhoff, B. (1991). Value elicitation: Is there anything in there? *American Psychologist, 46*, 835–847.

Fischhoff, B., & Bar-Hillel, M. (1984). Diagnosticity and the base-rate effect. *Memory & Cognition, 12*, 402–410.

Fischhoff, B., & Beyth, R. (1975). "I knew it would happen": Remembered probabilities of once-future things. *Organizational Behavior and Human Performance, 13*, 1–16.

Fischhoff, B., & Beyth-Marom, R. (1983). Hypothesis evaluation from a Bayesian perspective. *Psychological Review, 90*, 239–260.

Fischhoff, B., Lichtenstein, S., Slovic, P., Derby, S. L., & Keeney, R. L. (1981). *Acceptable risk.* Cambridge, England: Cambridge University Press.

Fischhoff, B., & Slovic, P. (1980). A little learning . . . : Confidence in multicue judgment tasks. In R. Nickerson (Ed.), *Attention and performance, VIII.* Hillsdale, NJ: Erlbaum.

Fischhoff, B., Slovic, P., & Lichtenstein, S. (1977). Knowing with certainty: The appropriateness of extreme confidence. *Journal of Experimental Psychology: Human Perception and Performance, 3*, 552–564.

Fishburn, P. C. (1984). SSB utility theory and decision making under uncertainty. *Mathematical Social Sciences, 8*, 253–285.

Fiske, S. T., & Taylor, S. E. (1991). *Social cognition* (2nd ed.). New York: McGraw-Hill.

Fletcher, G. J. O., & Ward, W. (1988). Attribution theory and processes: A cross-cultural perspective. In M. H. Bond (Ed.), *The cross-cultural challenge to social psychology.* Newbury Park, CA: Sage Publications.

Försterling, F. (1989). Models of covariation and attribution: How do they relate to the analogy of analysis of variance? *Journal of Personality and Social Psychology, 57*, 615–625.

Frenkel, O. J., & Doob, A. N. (1976). Post-decision dissonance at the polling booth. *Canadian Journal of Behavioural Science, 8*, 347–350.

Frieze, I. H., Bar-Tal, D., & Carroll, J. S. (Eds.). (1979). *New approaches to social problems.* San Francisco: Jossey-Bass.

Galper, R. E. (1976). Turning observers into actors: Differential causal attributions as a function of "empathy." *Journal of Research in Personality, 10,* 328–335.

Gansberg, M. (1964, March 27). 37 who saw murder didn't call the police. *New York Times,* pp. 1, 38.

Gill, S. (1947, March 14). How do you stand on sin? *Tide,* p. 72.

Gilovich, T., Vallone, R., & Tversky, A. (1985). The hot hand in basketball: On the misperception of random sequences. *Journal of Personality and Social Psychology, 17,* 295–314.

Gliksman, A. (1986, February 13). Behind Moscow's fear of "Star Wars." *New York Times,* p. 27.

Gmelch, G. (1978, August). Baseball magic. *Human Nature,* pp. 32–39.

Goldberg, L. R. (1959). The effectiveness of clinicians' judgments: The diagnosis of organic brain damage from the Bender-Gestalt test. *Journal of Consulting Psychology, 23,* 25–33.

Golding, S. L., & Rorer, L. G. (1972). Illusory correlation and subjective judgment. *Journal of Personality and Social Psychology, 80,* 249–260.

Graham, T. W., & Kramer, B. M. (1986). The polls: ABM and Star Wars: Attitudes toward nuclear defense, 1945–1985. *Public Opinion Quarterly, 50,* 125–134.

Greenberg, J., Williams, K. D., & O'Brien, M. K. (1986). Considering the harshest verdict first: Biasing effects on mock juror verdicts. *Personality and Social Psychology Bulletin, 12,* 41–50.

Gregory, W. L., Cialdini, R. B., & Carpenter, K. B. (1982). Self-relevant scenarios as mediators of likelihood and compliance: Does imagining make it so? *Journal of Personality and Social Psychology, 43,* 89–99.

Grether, D. M., & Plott, C. R. (1979). Economic theory of choice and the preference reversal phenomenon. *American Economic Review, 69,* 623–638.

Griffin, D. W., Dunning, D., & Ross, L. (1990). The role of construal processes in overconfident predictions about the self and others. *Journal of Personality and Social Psychology, 59,* 1128–1139.

Griggs, R. A., & Cox, J. R. (1982). The elusive thematic-materials effect in Wason's selection task. *British Journal of Psychology, 73,* 407–420.

Gross, E. J. (1964). The effect of question sequence on measures of buying interest. *Journal of Advertising Research, 4,* 40–41.

Haberman, C. (1990, July 19). A child's nightmare in Italy is now the nation's shame. *New York Times,* pp. A1, A11.

Hagafors, R., & Brehmer, B. (1983). Does having to justify one's judgments change the nature of the judgment process? *Organizational Behavior and Human Performance, 31,* 223–232.

Hake, H. W., & Hyman, R. (1953). Perception of the statistical structure of a random series of binary symbols. *Journal of Experimental Psychology, 45,* 64–74.

Hamilton, D. L., & Rose, T. L. (1980). Illusory correlation and the maintenance of stereotypic beliefs. *Journal of Personality and Social Psychology, 39,* 832–845.

Hardin, G. (1968). The tragedy of the commons. *Science, 162,* 1243–1248.

"Harper's Index." (1986, October). *Harper's,* p. 11.

Harris, R. J. (1973). Answering questions containing marked and unmarked adjectives and adverbs. *Journal of Experimental Psychology, 97,* 399–401.

Hartley, E. (1946). *Problems in prejudice.* New York: King's Crown Press.

Harvey, J. H., Town, J. P., & Yarkin, K. L. (1981). How fundamental is the "fundamental attribution error"? *Journal of Personality and Social Psychology, 40,* 346–349.

Hastie, R. (1986). Review essay: Experimental evidence on group accuracy. In B. Grofman and G. Owen (Eds.), *Information pooling and group decision making: Proceedings of the Second University of California, Irvine, Conference on Political Economy.* Greenwich, CT: Jai Press.

Hastorf, A. H., & Cantril, H. (1954). They saw a game: A case study. *Journal of Abnormal and Social Psychology, 49,* 129–134.

Hawkins, S. A., & Hastie, R. (1990). Hindsight: Biased judgments of past events after the outcomes are known. *Psychological Bulletin, 107,* 311–327.

Heider, F. (1958). *The psychology of interpersonal relations.* New York: Wiley.

Henchy, T., & Glass, D. C. (1968). Evaluation apprehension and the social facilitation of dominant and subordinate responses. *Journal of Personality and Social Psychology, 10,* 446–454.

Henslin, J. M. (1967). Craps and magic. *American Journal of Sociology, 73,* 316–330.

Hershey, J. C., & Schoemaker, P. J. H. (1980). Risk taking and problem context in the domain of losses: An expected utility analysis. *Journal of Risk and Insurance, 47,* 111–132.

Hewstone, M. R. C., & Jaspars, J. M. F. (1987). Covariation and causal attribution: A logical model for the intuitive analysis of variance. *Journal of Personality and Social Psychology, 53,* 663–672.

Hill, G. W. (1982). Group versus individual performance: Are $N + 1$ heads better than one? *Psychological Bulletin, 91,* 517–539.

Hilton, D. J., & Slugoski, B. R. (1986). Knowledge–based causal attribution: The abnormal conditions focus model. *Psychological Review, 93,* 75–88.

Hilts, P. J. (1990, September 26). Major gains are cited for smokers who quit. *New York Times,* p. B4.

Hintzman, D. L. (1969). Apparent frequency as a function of frequency and the spacing of repetitions. *Journal of Experimental Psychology, 80,* 139–145.

Hippler, H., & Schwarz, N. (1986). Not forbidding isn't allowing: The cognitive basis of the forbid–allow asymmetry. *Public Opinion Quarterly, 50,* 87–96.

Hoch, S. J. (1984). Availability and interference in predictive judgment. *Journal of Experimental Psychology: Learning, Memory, and Cognition, 10,* 649–662.

Hoch, S. J. (1985). Counterfactual reasoning and accuracy in predicting personal events. *Journal of Experimental Psychology: Learning, Memory, and Cognition, 11,* 719–731.

Hofstadter, D. R. (1985). *Metamagical themas: Questing for the essence of mind and pattern.* New York: Basic Books.

Hogarth, R. M. (1975). Cognitive processes and the assessment of subjective probability distributions. *Journal of the American Statistical Association, 70,* 271–289.

Hogarth, R. (1987). *Judgement and choice* (2nd ed.). New York: John Wiley and Sons.

Hooke, R. (1983). *How to tell the liars from the statisticians.* New York: Marcel Dekker.

Hornstein, H. A., Fisch, E., & Holmes, M. (1968). Influence of a model's feeling about his behavior and his relevance as a comparison other on observers' helping behavior. *Journal of Personality and Social Psychology, 10,* 222–226.

Hunter, I. M. L. (1964). *Memory.* Middlesex, England: Penguin Books.

Ingham, A. G., Levinger, G., Graves, J., & Peckham, V. (1974). The Ringelmann effect: Studies of group size and group performance. *Journal of Experimental Social Psychology, 10,* 371–384.

Irwin, F. W. (1953). Stated expectations as functions of probability and desirability of outcomes. *Journal of Personality, 21,* 329–335.

Irwin, F. W., & Metzger, J. (1966). Effects of probabilistic independent outcomes upon predictions. *Psychonomic Science, 5,* 79–80.

Irwin, F. W., & Snodgrass, J. G. (1966). Effects of independent and dependent outcome values upon bets. *Journal of Experimental Psychology, 71,* 282–285.

Isen, A. M., Daubman, K. A., & Nowicki, G. P. (1987). Positive affect facilitates creative problem solving. *Journal of Personality and Social Psychology, 52,* 1122–1131.

Isen, A. M., & Geva, N. (1987). The influence of positive affect on acceptable level of risk: The person with a large canoe has a large worry. *Organizational Behavior and Human Decision Processes, 39,* 145–154.

Isen, A. M., & Patrick, R. (1983). The effect of positive feelings on risk taking: When the chips are down. *Organizational Behavior and Human Performance, 31,* 194–202.

Ives, G. (1970). *A history of penal methods: Criminals, witches, lunatics.* Montclair, NJ: Patterson Smith.

Janis, I. L. (1982). *Groupthink: Psychological studies of policy decisions and fiascoes* (2nd ed.). Boston: Houghton Mifflin.

Jenkins, H. M., & Ward, W. C. (1965). The judgment of contingency between responses and outcomes. *Psychological Monographs, 79* (Whole No. 594).

Jenkins, J. J. (1981). Can we have a fruitful cognitive psychology? In J. H. Flowers (Ed.), *Nebraska symposium on motivation, 1980.* Lincoln: University of Nebraska Press.

Jennings, D. L., Amabile, T. M., & Ross, L. (1982). Informal covariation assessment: Data-based versus theory based judgments. In D. Kahneman, P. Slovic, & A. Tversky (Eds.), *Judgment under uncertainty: Heuristics and biases.* Cambridge, England: Cambridge University Press.

Johnson, E. J., & Tversky, A. (1983). Affect, generalization, and the perception of risk. *Journal of Personality and Social Psychology, 45,* 20–31.

Jones, E. E. (1979). The rocky road from acts to dispositions. *American Psychologist, 34,* 107–117.

Jones, E. E., & Davis, K. E. (1965). From acts to dispositions: The attribution process in person perception. In L. Berkowitz (Ed.), *Advances in experimental social psychology* (Vol. 2, pp. 219–266). New York: Academic Press.

Jones, E. E., & Harris, V. A. (1967). The attribution of attitudes. *Journal of Experimental Social Psychology, 3,* 1–24.

Jones, E. E., & Nisbett, R. E. (1971). The actor and the observer: Divergent perceptions of the causes of behavior. In E. E. Jones et al. (Eds.), *Attribution: Perceiving the causes of behavior.* Morristown, NJ: General Learning Press.

Jones, E. E., Wood, G. C., & Quattrone, G. A. (1981). Perceived variability of personal characteristics in in-groups and out-groups: The role of knowledge and evaluation. *Personality and Social Psychology Bulletin, 7,* 523–528.

Jones, R. T. (1971). Tetrahydrocannabinol and the marijuana-induced social "high," or the effects of the mind on marijuana. *Annals of the New York Academy of Sciences, 191,* 155–165.

Jussim, L. (1986). Self-fulfilling prophecies: A theoretical and integrative review. *Psychological Review, 93,* 429–445.

Kahneman, D. (1991). Judgment and decision making: A personal view. *Psychological Science, 2,* 142–145.

Kahneman, D., Knetsch, J. L., & Thaler, R. H. (1990). Experimental tests of the endowment effect and the Coase theorem. *Journal of Political Economy, 98,* 1325–1348.

Kahneman, D., & Tversky, A. (1972). Subjective probability: A judgment of representativeness. *Cognitive Psychology, 3,* 430–454.

Kahneman, D., & Tversky, A. (1973). On the psychology of prediction. *Psychological Review, 80,* 237–251.

Kahneman, D., & Tversky, A. (1979). Prospect theory: An analysis of decision under risk. *Econometrica, 47,* 263–291.

Kammer, D. (1982). Differences in trait ascriptions to self and friend: Unconfounding intensity from variability. *Psychological Reports, 51,* 99–102.

Kantola, S. J., Syme, G. J., & Campbell, N. A. (1984). Cognitive dissonance and energy conservation. *Journal of Applied Psychology, 69,* 416–421.

Karmarkar, U. (1978). Subjectively weighted utility: A descriptive extension of the expected utility model. *Organizational Behavior and Human Performance, 21,* 61–72.

Kassin, S. M. (1979). Consensus information, prediction, and causal attribution: A review of the literature and issues. *Journal of Personality and Social Psychology, 37,* 1966–1981.

Kelley, H. H. (1950). The warm-cold variable in first impressions of persons. *Journal of Personality, 18,* 431–439.

Kelley, H. H. (1967). Attribution theory in social psychology. In D. Levine

(Ed.), *Nebraska symposium on motivation, 1967*. Lincoln: University of Nebraska Press.

Kelley, H. H. (1973). The processes of causal attribution. *American Psychologist, 28*, 107–128.

Kelley, H. H., & Michela, J. L. (1980). Attribution theory and research. *Annual Review of Psychology, 31*, 457–501.

Keren, G. (1987). Facing uncertainty in the game of bridge: A calibration study. *Organizational Behavior and Human Decision Processes, 39*, 98–114.

Klayman, J., & Ha, Y. (1987). Confirmation, disconfirmation, and information in hypothesis testing. *Psychological Review, 94*, 211–228.

Kleinmuntz, D. N. (1985). Cognitive heuristics and feedback in a dynamic decision environment. *Management Science, 31*, 680–702.

Knetsch, J. L., & Sinden, J. A. (1984). Willingness to pay and compensation demanded: Experimental evidence of an unexpected disparity in measures of value. *Quarterly Journal of Economics, 99*, 507–521.

Knox, R. E., & Inkster, J. A. (1968). Postdecision dissonance at post time. *Journal of Personality and Social Psychology, 8*, 319–323.

Kogan, N., & Wallach, M. A. (1964). *Risk taking: A study in cognition and personality*. New York: Holt, Rinehart and Winston.

Koriat, A., Lichtenstein, S., & Fischhoff, B. (1980). Reasons for confidence. *Journal of Experimental Psychology: Human Learning and Memory, 6*, 107–118.

Kristiansen, C. M. (1983). Newspaper coverage of diseases and actual mortality statistics. *European Journal of Social Psychology, 13*, 193–194.

Lamal, P. A. (1979, October). College student common beliefs about psychology. *Teaching of Psychology*, pp. 155–158.

Landy, D., & Sigall, H. (1974). Beauty is talent: Task evaluation as a function of the performer's physical attractiveness. *Journal of Personality and Social Psychology, 29*, 299–304.

Langer, E. J. (1975). The illusion of control. *Journal of Personality and Social Psychology, 32*, 311–328.

Langer, E. J., & Rodin, J. (1976). The effects of choice and enhanced personal responsibility for the aged: A field experiment in an institutional setting. *Journal of Personality and Social Psychology, 34*, 191–198.

Langer, E. J., & Roth, J. (1975). Heads I win, tails it's chance: The illusion of control as a function of the sequence of outcomes in a purely chance task. *Journal of Personality and Social Psychology, 32*, 951–955.

LaPiere, R. T. (1934). Attitudes vs. actions. *Social Forces, 13*, 230–237.

Lasky, J. J., Hover, G. L., Smith, P. A., Bostian, D. W., Duffendack, S. C., & Nord, C. L. (1959). Post-hospital adjustment as predicted by psychiatric patients and by their staff. *Journal of Consulting Psychology, 23*, 213–218.

Latané, B., & Dabbs, J. M., Jr. (1975). Sex, group size and helping in three cities. *Sociometry, 38*, 180–194.

Latané, B., & Darley, J. M. (1969). Bystander "apathy." *American Scientist, 57*, 244–268.

Latané, B., & Darley, J. M. (1970). *The unresponsive bystander: Why doesn't he help?* Englewood Cliffs, NJ: Prentice-Hall.

Latané, B., & Nida, S. (1981). Ten years of research on group size and helping. *Psychological Bulletin, 89,* 308–324.

Latané, B., Williams, K., & Harkins, S. (1979). Many hands make light the work: The causes and consequences of social loafing. *Journal of Personality and Social Psychology, 37,* 822–832.

Latané, B., & Wolf, S. (1981). The social impact of majorities and minorities. *Psychological Review, 88,* 438–453.

Leary, M. R. (1981). The distorted nature of hindsight. *Journal of Social Psychology, 115,* 25–29.

Leary, M. R. (1982). Hindsight distortion and the 1980 presidential election. *Personality and Social Psychology Bulletin, 8,* 257–263.

Leddo, J., Abelson, R. P., & Gross, P. H. (1984). Conjunctive explanations: When two reasons are better than one. *Journal of Personality and Social Psychology, 47,* 933–943.

Lefcourt, H. M. (1982). *Locus of control: Current trends in theory and research.* Hillsdale, NJ: Erlbaum.

Leippe, M. R., Wells, G. L., & Ostrom, T. M. (1978). Crime seriousness as a determinant of accuracy in eyewitness identification. *Journal of Applied Psychology, 63,* 345–351.

Lelyveld, J. (1986, October 5). Britain heads for nuclear war at polls. *New York Times,* p. E2.

Levi, A. S., & Pryor, J. B. (1987). Use of the availability heuristic in probability estimates of future events: The effects of imagining outcomes versus imagining reasons. *Organizational Behavior and Human Decision Processes, 40,* 219–234.

Lichtenstein, S., & Fischhoff, B. (1977). Do those who know more also know more about how much they know? *Organizational Behavior and Human Performance, 20,* 159–183.

Lichtenstein, S., & Fischhoff, B. (1980). Training for calibration. *Organizational Behavior and Human Performance, 26,* 149–171.

Lichtenstein, S., Fischhoff, B., & Phillips, L. D. (1982). Calibration of probabilities: The state of the art to 1980. In D. Kahneman, P. Slovic, & A. Tversky (Eds.), *Judgment under uncertainty: Heuristics and biases.* Cambridge, England: Cambridge University Press.

Lichtenstein, S., & Slovic, P. (1971). Reversals of preference between bids and choices in gambling decisions. *Journal of Experimental Psychology, 89,* 46–55.

Lichtenstein, S., & Slovic, P. (1973). Response-induced reversals of preference in gambling: An extended replication in Las Vegas. *Journal of Experimental Psychology, 101,* 16–20.

Loftus, E. F. (1975). Leading questions and the eyewitness report. *Cognitive Psychology, 7,* 560–572.

Loftus, E. F. (1979) *Eyewitness testimony.* Cambridge, MA: Harvard University Press.

Loftus, E. (1980). *Memory: Surprising new insights into how we remember and why we forget*. New York: Ardsley House.

Loftus, E. F., & Palmer, J. C. (1974). Reconstruction of automobile destruction: An example of the interaction between language and memory. *Journal of Verbal Learning and Verbal Behavior, 13,* 585–589.

Loomes, G., & Sugden, R. (1982). Regret theory: An alternative theory of rational choice under uncertainty. *Economic Journal, 92,* 805–824.

Loomes, G., & Sugden, R. (1983). A rationale for preference reversal. *American Economic Review, 73,* 428–432.

Loomes, G., & Sugden, R. (1987). Some implications of a more general form of regret theory. *Journal of Economic Theory, 41,* 270–287.

Lopes, L. L. (1981). Decision making in the short run. *Journal of Experimental Psychology: Human Learning and Memory, 7,* 377–385.

Lopes, L. L. (1982). Doing the impossible: A note on induction and the experience of randomness. *Journal of Experimental Psychology: Learning, Memory, and Cognition, 8,* 626–636.

Lopes, L. L. (1991). The rhetoric of irrationality. *Theory & Psychology, 1,* 65–82.

Lopes, L. L., & Oden, G. C. (1987). Distinguishing between random and nonrandom events. *Journal of Experimental Psychology: Learning, Memory, and Cognition, 13,* 392–400.

Lord, C. G., Lepper, M. R., & Preston, E. (1984). Considering the opposite: A corrective strategy for social judgment. *Journal of Personality and Social Psychology, 47,* 1231–1243.

Lord, C. G., Ross, L., & Lepper, M. R. (1979). Biased assimilation and attitude polarization: The effects of prior theories on subsequently considered evidence. *Journal of Personality and Social Psychology, 37,* 2098–2109.

Loy, J. W., & Andrews, D. S. (1981). They also saw a game: A replication of a case study. *Replications in Social Psychology, 1,* 45–49.

Luce, R. D. (1959). *Individual choice behavior*. New York: Wiley.

Luce, R. D. (1990). Rational versus plausible accounting equivalences in preference judgments. *Psychological Science, 1,* 225–234.

Luck, R. F., van den Bosch, R., & Garcia, R. (1977). Chemical insect control—A troubled pest management strategy. *BioScience,* 606–611.

Maass, A., & Clark, R. D., III. (1984). Hidden impact of minorities: Fifteen years of minority research. *Psychological Bulletin, 95,* 428–450.

Mackie, D. M., & Allison, S. T. (1987). Group attribution errors and the illusion of group attitude change. *Journal of Experimental Social Psychology, 23,* 460–480.

Maier, N. R. F., & Solem, A. R. (1952). The contribution of a discussion leader to the quality of group thinking: The effective use of minority opinions. *Human Relations, 5,* 277–288.

Malkiel, B. G. (1985). *A random walk down Wall Street* (4th ed.). New York: W. W. Norton & Co.

Malone, B. (1990, September 9). Double trouble: Lives of two Frank William

Boumas bedeviled by strange coincidences. *Grand Rapids Press,* pp. B1–B2.

Marks, R. W. (1951). The effect of probability, desirability, and "privilege" on the stated expectations of children. *Journal of Personality, 19,* 332–351.

Matsuda, N. (1985). Strong, quasi-, and weak conformity among Japanese in the modified Asch procedure. *Journal of Cross Cultural Psychology, 16,* 83–97.

Mazur, A. (1981). Three Mile Island and the scientific community. In T. H. Moss & D. L. Sills (Eds.), The Three Mile Island nuclear accident: Lessons and implications. *Annals of the New York Academy of Sciences* (Vol. 365, pp. 216–221). New York: The New York Academy of Sciences.

McArthur, L. A. (1972). The how and what of why: Some determinants and consequences of causal attribution. *Journal of Personality and Social Psychology, 22,* 171–193.

McArthur, L. Z. (1980). Illusory causation and illusory correlation: Two epistemological accounts. *Personality and Social Psychology Bulletin, 6,* 507–519.

McArthur, L. Z., & Post, D. L. (1977). Figural emphasis and person perception. *Journal of Experimental Social Psychology, 13,* 520–535.

McMillen, D., Smith, S., & Wells-Parker, E. (1989). The effects of alcohol, expectancy, and sensation seeking on driving risk taking. *Addictive Behaviors, 14,* 477–483.

McNeil, B. J., Pauker, S. G., Sox, H. C., Jr., & Tversky, A. (1982). On the elicitation of preferences for alternative therapies. *New England Journal of Medicine, 306,* 1259–1262.

Merton, R. K. (1948). The self-fulfilling prophecy. *Antioch Review, 8,* 193–210.

Meyerowitz, B. E., & Chaiken, S. (1987). The effect of message framing on breast self-examination attitudes, intentions, and behavior. *Journal of Personality and Social Psychology, 52,* 500–510.

Michaels, J. W., Blommel, J. M., Brocato, R. M., Linkous, R. A., & Rowe, J. S. (1982). Social facilitation and inhibition in a natural setting. *Replications in Social Psychology, 2,* 21–24.

Milgram, S. (1963). Behavioral study of obedience. *Journal of Abnormal and Social Psychology, 67,* 371–378.

Miller, A. G., Gillen, B., Schenker, C., & Radlove, S. (1973). Perception of obedience to authority. *Proceedings of the 81st Annual Convention of the American Psychological Association, 8,* 127–128.

Miller, D. T. (1976). Ego involvement and attribution for success and failure. *Journal of Personality and Social Psychology, 34,* 901–906.

Miller, D. T., & Ross, M. (1975). Self-serving biases in the attribution of causality: Fact or fiction? *Psychological Bulletin, 82,* 213–225.

Miller, D. T., & Turnbull, W. (1986). Expectancies and interpersonal processes. *Annual Review of Psychology, 37,* 233–256.

Miller, J. G. (1984). Culture and the development of everyday social explanation. *Journal of Personality and Social Psychology, 46,* 961–978.

Miller, N., & Campbell, D. T. (1959). Recency and primacy in persuasion as a function of the timing of speeches and measurements. *Journal of Abnormal and Social Psychology, 59,* 1–9.

Mitchell, R. C. (1982). Public response to a major failure of a controversial technology. In D. L. Sills, C. P. Wolf, & V. B. Shelanski (Eds.), *Accident at Three Mile Island: The human dimensions* (pp. 21–38). Boulder, CO: Westview Press.

Moede, W. (1927). Die Richtlinien der Leistungs-Psychologie. *Industrielle Psychotechnik, 4,* 193–207.

Morier, D. M., & Borgida, E. (1984). The conjunction fallacy: A task specific phenomenon? *Personality and Social Psychology Bulletin, 10,* 243–252.

Moscovici, S., Lage, E., & Naffrechoux, M. (1969). Influence of a consistent minority on the responses of a majority in a color perception task. *Sociometry, 32,* 365–380.

Moscovici, S., & Zavalloni, M. (1969). The group as a polarizer of attitudes. *Journal of Personality and Social Psychology, 12,* 125–135.

Mullen, B., & Hu, L. (1989). Perceptions of ingroup and outgroup variability: A meta-analytic integration. *Basic and Applied Social Psychology, 10,* 233–252.

Mullen, B., & Johnson, C. (1990). Distinctiveness-based illusory correlations and stereotyping: A meta-analytic integration. *British Journal of Social Psychology, 29,* 11–28.

Mullen, B., & Riordan, C. A. (1988). Self-serving attributions for performance in naturalistic settings: A meta-analytic review. *Journal of Applied Social Psychology, 18,* 3–22.

Murphy, A. H., & Brown, B. G. (1984). A comparative evaluation of objective and subjective weather forecasts in the United States. *Journal of Forecasting, 3,* 369–393.

Murphy, A. H., & Winkler, R. L. (1984). Probability forecasting in meteorology. *Journal of the American Statistical Association, 79,* 489–500.

Myers, D. G. (1975). Discussion-induced attitude polarization. *Human Relations, 28,* 699–714.

Myers, D. G. (1982). Polarizing effects of social interaction. In H. Brandstatter, J. H. Davis, & G. Stocker-Kreichgauer (Eds.), *Group decision making.* London: Academic Press.

Myers, D. G. (1990). *Social psychology* (2nd ed.). McGraw-Hill: New York.

Myers, D. G., & Bishop, G. D. (1970). Discussion effects on racial attitudes. *Science, 169,* 778–779.

Myers, D. G., & Kaplan, M. F. (1976). Group-induced polarization in simulated juries. *Personality and Social Psychology Bulletin, 2,* 63–66.

Myers, D. G., & Lamm, H. (1976). The group polarization phenomenon. *Psychological Bulletin, 83,* 602–627.

Mynatt, C. R., Doherty, M. E., & Tweney, R. D. (1977). Confirmation bias in a simulated research environment: An experimental study of scientific inference. *Quarterly Journal of Experimental Psychology, 29,* 85–95.

Mynatt, C. R., Doherty, M. E., & Tweney, R. D. (1978). Consequences of confirmation and disconfirmation in a simulated research environment. *Quarterly Journal of Experimental Psychology, 30,* 395–406.

Nahinsky, I. D., & Slaymaker, F. L. (1970). Use of negative instances in conjunctive identification. *Journal of Experimental Psychology, 84,* 64–84.

Nathanson, S., Brockner, J., Brenner, D., Samuelson, C., Countryman, M., Lloyd, M., & Rubin, J. Z. (1982). Toward the reduction of entrapment. *Journal of Applied Social Psychology, 12,* 193–208.

Nemeth, C. (1986). Differential contributions of majority and minority influence. *Psychological Review, 93,* 1–10.

Nemeth, C., & Chiles, C. (1988). Modelling courage: The role of dissent in fostering independence. *European Journal of Social Psychology, 18,* 275–280.

Neuringer, A. (1986). Can people behave "randomly"?: The role of feedback. *Journal of Experimental Psychology: General, 115,* 62–75.

Nisbett, R. E., & Borgida, E. (1975). Attribution and the psychology of prediction. *Journal of Personality and Social Psychology, 32,* 932–943.

Nisbett, R. E., Borgida, E., Crandall, R., & Reed, H. (1976). Popular induction: Information is not always informative. In J. S. Carroll & J. W. Payne (Eds.), *Cognition and social behavior* (Vol. 2, pp. 227–236). Hillsdale, NJ: Lawrence Erlbaum Associates.

Nisbett, R. E., Caputo, C., Legant, P., & Marecek, J. (1973). Behavior as seen by the actor and as seen by the observer. *Journal of Personality and Social Psychology, 27,* 154–165.

Nisbett, R. E., & Ross, L. (1980). *Human inference: Strategies and shortcomings of social judgment.* Englewood Cliffs, NJ: Prentice–Hall.

Nisbett, R. E., & Schachter, S. (1966). Cognitive manipulation of pain. *Journal of Experimental Social Psychology, 2,* 227–236.

Northcraft, G. B., & Neale, M. A. (1987). Experts, amateurs, and real estate: An anchoring-and-adjustment perspective on property pricing decisions. *Organizational Behavior and Human Decision Processes, 39,* 84–97.

Orvis, B. R., Cunningham, J. D., & Kelley, H. H. (1975). A closer examination of causal inference: The roles of consensus, distinctiveness, and consistency information. *Journal of Personality and Social Psychology, 32,* 605–616.

Osberg, T. M., & Shrauger, J. S. (1986). Self-prediction: Exploring the parameters of accuracy. *Journal of Personality and Social Psychology, 51,* 1044–1057.

Oskamp, S. (1965). Overconfidence in case study judgments. *Journal of Consulting Psychology, 29,* 261–265.

Paese, P. W., & Sniezek, J. A. (1991). Influences on the appropriateness of confidence in judgment: Practice, effort, information, and decision-making. *Organizational Behavior and Human Decision Processes, 48,* 100–130.

Park, B., & Rothbart, M. (1982). Perception of out-group homogeneity and levels of social categorization: Memory for the subordinate attributes of in-group and out-group members. *Journal of Personality and Social Psychology, 42,* 1051–1068.

Paulos, J. A. (1986, November 24). Orders of magnitude. *Newsweek*, pp. 12–13.

Paulos, J. A. (1988). *Innumeracy: Mathematical illiteracy and its consequences*. New York: Vintage Books.

Payne, J. W. (1973). Alternative approaches to decision making under risk: Moments versus risk dimensions. *Psychological Bulletin, 80*, 439–453.

Payne, J. W. (1982). Contingent decision behavior. *Psychological Bulletin, 92*, 382–402.

Pennington, D. C., Rutter, D. R., McKenna, K., & Morley, I. E. (1980). Estimating the outcome of a pregnancy test: Women's judgments in foresight and hindsight. *British Journal of Social and Clinical Psychology, 19*, 317–324.

Peter, L. J. (1977). *Peter's quotations: Ideas for our time*. New York: Bantam Books.

Peterson, C. (1980). Recognition of noncontingency. *Journal of Personality and Social Psychology, 38*, 727–734.

Peterson, C., Semmel, A., von Baeyer, C., Abramson, L. Y., Metalsky, G. I., & Seligman, M. E. P. (1982). The Attributional Style Questionnaire. *Cognitive Therapy and Research, 6*, 287–300.

Pettigrew, T. F. (1979). The ultimate attribution error: Extending Allport's cognitive analysis of prejudice. *Personality and Social Psychology Bulletin, 5*, 461–476.

Phillips, L. D., & Edwards, W. (1966). Conservatism in a simple probability inference task. *Journal of Experimental Psychology, 72*, 346–354.

Pietromonaco, P. R., & Nisbett, R. E. (1982). Swimming upstream against the fundamental attribution error: Subjects' weak generalizations from the Darley and Batson study. *Social Behavior and Personality, 10*, 1–4.

Platt, J. (1973). Social traps. *American Psychologist, 28*, 641–651.

Plous, S. (1989). Thinking the unthinkable: The effects of anchoring on likelihood estimates of nuclear war. *Journal of Applied Social Psychology, 19*, 67–91.

Plous, S. (1989, March). Political illiteracy: A threat to international security. *Swords and Ploughshares*, pp. 9–10.

Plous, S. (1991). Biases in the assimilation of technological breakdowns: Do accidents make us safer? *Journal of Applied Social Psychology, 21*, 1058–1082.

Plous, S., & Zimbardo, P. G. (1984, November). The looking glass war. *Psychology Today*, pp. 48–59.

Plous, S., & Zimbardo, P. G. (1986). Attributional biases among clinicians: A comparison of psychoanalysts and behavior therapists. *Journal of Consulting and Clinical Psychology, 54*, 568–570.

Pool, R. (1988). The Allais Paradox. *Science, 242*, 512.

Prothro, J. W., & Grigg, C. M. (1960). Fundamental principles of democracy: Bases of agreement and disagreement. *Journal of Politics, 22*, 276–294.

Pruitt, D. G., & Hoge, R. D. (1965). Strength of the relationship between the value of an event and its subjective probability as a function of method of measurement. *Journal of Personality and Social Psychology, 69*, 483–489.

Pryor, J. B., & Kriss, N. (1977). The cognitive dynamics of salience in the attribution process. *Journal of Personality and Social Psychology, 35*, 49–55.

Quattrone, G. A. (1982). Overattribution and unit formation: When behavior engulfs the person. *Journal of Personality and Social Psychology, 42*, 593–607.

Quattrone, G. A., Lawrence, C. P., Warren, D. L., Souza-Silva, K., Finkel, S. E., & Andrus, D. E. (1984). *Explorations in anchoring: The effects of prior range, anchor extremity, and suggestive hints.* Unpublished manuscript, Stanford University, Stanford.

Quattrone, G. A., & Tversky, A. (1988). Contrasting rational and psychological analyses of political choice. *American Political Science Review, 82*, 719–736.

Reeder, G. D. (1982). Let's give the fundamental attribution error another chance. *Journal of Personality and Social Psychology, 43*, 341–344.

Regan, D. T., Straus, E., & Fazio, R. (1974). Liking and the attribution process. *Journal of Experimental Social Psychology, 10*, 385–397.

Regan, D. T., & Totten, J. (1975). Empathy and attribution: Turning observers into actors. *Journal of Personality and Social Psychology, 32*, 850–856.

Reichenbach, H. (1949). *The theory of probability.* Berkeley: University of California Press.

Reyes, R. M., Thompson, W. C., & Bower, G. H. (1980). Judgmental biases resulting from differing availabilities of arguments. *Journal of Personality and Social Psychology, 39*, 2–12.

Robbins, J. (1987). *Diet for a new America.* Walpole, NH: Stillpoint Publishing.

Rodin, J. (1986). Aging and health: Effects of the sense of control. *Science, 233*, 1271–1276.

Ronis, D. L., & Yates, J. F. (1987). Components of probability judgment accuracy: Individual consistency and effects of subject matter and assessment method. *Organizational Behavior and Human Decision Processes, 40*, 193–218.

Rosenhan, D. L., & Messick, S. (1966). Affect and expectation. *Journal of Personality and Social Psychology, 3*, 38–44.

Rosenthal, R. (1976). *Experimenter effects in behavioral research* (enlarged ed.). New York: Irvington.

Rosenthal, R. (1987, December). *Pygmalion* effects: Existence, magnitude, and social importance. *Educational Researcher*, pp. 37–41.

Rosenthal, R., & Fode, K. L. (1963). The effect of experimenter bias on the performance of the albino rat. *Behavioral Science, 8*, 183–189.

Rosenthal, R., & Jacobson, L. (1968). *Pygmalion in the classroom: Teacher expectation and pupils' intellectual development.* New York: Holt, Rinehart & Winston.

Ross, L. (1977). The intuitive psychologist and his shortcomings: Distortions in the attribution process. In L. Berkowitz (Ed.), *Advances in experimental social psychology* (Vol. 10). New York: Academic Press.

Ross, L., Lepper, M., & Hubbard, M. (1975). Perseverance in self perception and social perception: Biased attributional processes in the debriefing paradigm. *Journal of Personality and Social Psychology, 32,* 880–892.

Ross, L., Lepper, M., Strack, F., & Steinmetz, J. (1977). Social explanation and social expectation: Effects of real and hypothetical explanations on subjective likelihood. *Journal of Personality and Social Psychology, 37,* 817–829.

Ross, L., Rodin, J., & Zimbardo, P. G. (1969). Toward an attribution therapy: The reduction of fear through induced cognitive-emotional misattribution. *Journal of Personality and Social Psychology, 12,* 279–288.

Ross, M., & Sicoly, F. (1979). Egocentric biases in availability and attribution. *Journal of Personality and Social Psychology, 37,* 322–336.

Rothbart, M. (1970). Assessing the likelihood of a threatening event: English Canadians' evaluation of the Quebec separatist movement. *Journal of Personality and Social Psychology, 15,* 109–117.

Rothstein, H. G. (1986). The effects of time pressure on judgment in multiple cue probability learning. *Organizational Behavior and Human Decision Processes, 37,* 83–92.

Rubin, D. M. (1981). What the president's commission learned about the media. In T. H. Moss & D. L. Sills (Eds.), The Three Mile Island nuclear accident: Lessons and implications. *Annals of the New York Academy of Sciences* (Vol. 365, pp. 95–106). New York: The New York Academy of Sciences.

Rubin, J. Z., Brockner, J., Small-Weil, S., & Nathanson, S. (1980). Factors affecting entry into psychological traps. *Journal of Conflict Resolution, 24,* 405–426.

Ruble, D. N., & Feldman, N. S. (1976). Order of consensus, distinctiveness, and consistency information and causal attributions. *Journal of Personality and Social Psychology, 34,* 930–937.

Rugg, D. (1941). Experiments in wording questions: II. *Public Opinion Quarterly, 5,* 91–92.

Rusbult, C. E. (1980). Commitment and satisfaction in romantic associations: A test of the investment model. *Journal of Experimental Social Psychology, 16,* 172–186.

Russo, J. E. (1977). The value of unit price information. *Journal of Marketing Research, 14,* 193–201.

Russo, J. E., & Schoemaker, P. J. H. (1989). *Decision traps: Ten barriers to brilliant decision making and how to overcome them.* New York: Simon & Schuster.

Ryback, D. (1967). Confidence and accuracy as a function of experience in judgment-making in the absence of systematic feedback. *Perceptual and Motor Skills, 24,* 331–334.

Rylsky, M. (1986, February). A town born of the atom. *Soviet Life,* pp. 8–15.

Salovey, P., & Birnbaum, D. (1989). Influence of mood on health-relevant cognitions. *Journal of Personality and Social Psychology, 57,* 539–551.

Sande, G. N., Goethals, G. R., & Radloff, C. E. (1988). Perceiving one's own traits and others': The multifaceted self. *Journal of Personality and Social Psychology, 54,* 13–20.

Savage, L. J. (1954). *The foundations of statistics.* New York: Wiley.

Schelling, T. (1971). The ecology of micromotives. *Public Interest, 25,* 61–98.

Schelling, T. C. (1981). Economic reasoning and the ethics of policy. *Public Interest, 63,* 37–61.

Schkade, D. A., & Johnson, E. J. (1989). Cognitive processes in preference reversals. *Organizational Behavior and Human Decision Processes, 44,* 203–231.

Schlenker, B. R., & Miller, R. S. (1977). Egocentrism in groups: Self-serving biases or logical information processing? *Journal of Personality and Social Psychology, 35,* 755–764.

Schmemann, S. (1985, March 3). The emergence of Gorbachev. *New York Times Magazine,* pp. 40, 44–46, 55–57.

Schoemaker, P. J. H. (1982). The expected utility model: Its variants, purposes, evidence and limitations. *Journal of Economic Literature, 20,* 529–563.

Schum, D. (1990). Discussion. In R. M. Hogarth (Ed.), *Insights in decision making: A tribute to Hillel J. Einhorn.* Chicago: University of Chicago Press.

Schuman, H., & Presser, S. (1981). *Questions and answers in attitude surveys: Experiments on question form, wording, and context.* Orlando, FL: Academic Press.

Schuman, H., & Scott, J. (1987). Problems in the use of survey questions to measure public opinion. *Science, 236,* 957–959.

Schwarz, N., Hippler, H., Deutsch, B., & Strack, S. (1985). Response scales: Effects of category range on reported behavior and comparative judgments. *Public Opinion Quarterly, 49,* 388–395.

Seligman, M. E. P., Abramson, L. Y., Semmel, A., & von Baeyer, C. (1979). Depressive attributional style. *Journal of Abnormal Psychology, 88,* 242–247.

Selvin, S. (1975, February). A problem in probability. *American Statistician,* p. 67.

Shaklee, H., & Fischhoff, B. (1990). The psychology of contraceptive surprises: Cumulative risk and contraceptive effectiveness. *Journal of Applied Social Psychology, 20,* 385–403.

Shaklee, H., & Mims, M. (1982). Sources of error in judging event covariations: Effects of memory demands. *Journal of Experimental Psychology: Learning, Memory, and Cognition, 8,* 208–224.

Shaklee, H., & Tucker, D. (1980). A rule analysis of judgments of covariation between events. *Memory & Cognition, 8,* 459–467.

Shenkel, R. J., Snyder, C. R., Batson, C. D., & Clark, G. M. (1979). Effects of prior diagnostic information on clinicians' causal attributions of a client's problems. *Journal of Consulting and Clinical Psychology, 47,* 404–406.

Sherif, M., Taub, D., & Hovland, C. I. (1958). Assimilation and contrast effects of anchoring stimuli on judgments. *Journal of Experimental Psychology, 55,* 150–155.

Sherman, S. J., Cialdini, R. B., Schwartzman, D. F., & Reynolds, K. D. (1985). Imagining can heighten or lower the perceived likelihood of contracting a disease: The mediating effect of ease of imagery. *Personality and Social Psychology Bulletin, 11,* 118–127.

Sherman, S. J., & Gorkin, L. (1980). Attitude bolstering when behavior is inconsistent with central attitudes. *Journal of Experimental Social Psychology, 16,* 388–403.

Sherman, S. J., Zehner, K. S., Johnson, J., & Hirt, E. R. (1983). Social explanation: The role of timing, set and recall on subjective likelihood estimates. *Journal of Personality and Social Psychology, 44,* 1127–1143.

Shubik, M. (1971). The Dollar Auction game: A paradox in noncooperative behavior and escalation. *Journal of Conflict Resolution, 15,* 109–111.

Sieber, J. E. (1974). Effects of decision importance on ability to generate warranted subjective uncertainty. *Journal of Personality and Social Psychology, 30,* 688–694.

Simon, H. A. (1956). Rational choice and the structure of the environment. *Psychological Review, 63,* 129–138.

Skinner, B. F. (1980). *Notebooks.* Englewood Cliffs, NJ: Prentice-Hall.

Slovic, P. (1975). Choice between equally valued alternatives. *Journal of Experimental Psychology: Human Perception and Performance, 1,* 280–287.

Slovic, P. (1987). Perception of risk. *Science, 236,* 280–285.

Slovic, P., & Fischhoff, B. (1977). On the psychology of experimental surprises. *Journal of Experimental Psychology: Human Perception and Performance, 3,* 544–551.

Slovic, P., Fischhoff, B., & Lichtenstein, S. (1979, April). Rating the risks. *Environment,* pp. 14–20, 36–39.

Slovic, P., Fischhoff, B., & Lichtenstein, S. (1982a). Facts versus fears: Understanding perceived risk. In D. Kahneman, P. Slovic, & A. Tversky (Eds.), *Judgment under uncertainty: Heuristics and biases.* Cambridge, England: Cambridge University Press.

Slovic, P., Fischhoff, B., & Lichtenstein, S. (1982b). Response mode, framing, and information-processing effects in risk assessment. In R. M. Hogarth (Ed.), *New directions for methodology of social and behavioral science: Question framing and response consistency* (No. 11). San Francisco: Jossey-Bass.

Slovic, P., Griffin, D., & Tversky, A. (1990). Compatibility effects in judgment and choice. In R. M. Hogarth (Ed.), *Insights in decision making: A tribute to Hillel J. Einhorn.* Chicago: University of Chicago Press.

Slovic, P., & Lichtenstein, S. (1983). Preference reversals: A broader perspective. *American Economic Review, 73,* 596–605.

Smedslund, J. (1963). The concept of correlation in adults. *Scandinavian Journal of Psychology, 4,* 165–173.

Smith, J. F., & Kida, T. (1991). Heuristics and biases: Expertise and task realism in auditing. *Psychological Bulletin, 109,* 472–489.

Smith, T. W. (1984). Nonattitudes: A review and evaluation. In C. F. Turner & E. Martin (Eds.), *Surveying subjective phenomena* (Vol. 2). New York: Russell Sage Foundation.

Sniezek, J. A. (1989). An examination of group process in judgmental forecasting. *International Journal of Forecasting, 5,* 171–178.

Sniezek, J. A., & Henry, R. A. (1989). Accuracy and confidence in group judgment. *Organizational Behavior and Human Decision Processes, 43,* 1–28.

Sniezek, J. A., & Henry, R. A. (1990). Revision, weighting, and commitment in consensus group judgment. *Organizational Behavior and Human Decision Processes, 45,* 66–84.

Sniezek, J. A., Paese, P. W., & Switzer, F. S., III. (1990). The effect of choosing on confidence and choice. *Organizational Behavior and Human Decision Processes, 46,* 264–282.

Snyder, C. R. (1977). "A patient by any other name" revisited: Maladjustment or attributional locus of problem? *Journal of Consulting and Clinical Psychology, 45,* 101–103.

Snyder, M. (1984). When belief creates reality. In L. Berkowitz (Ed.), *Advances in experimental social psychology* (Vol. 18, pp. 247–305). New York: Academic Press.

Snyder, M. (in press). Motivational foundations of behavioral confirmation. In M. P. Zanna (Ed.), *Advances in experimental social psychology* (Vol. 25). New York: Academic Press.

Snyder, M., Campbell, B. H., & Preston, E. (1982). Testing hypotheses about human nature: Assessing the accuracy of social stereotypes. *Social Cognition, 1,* 256–272.

Snyder, M., & Cantor, N. (1979). Testing hypotheses about other people: The use of historical knowledge. *Journal of Experimental Social Psychology, 15,* 330–342.

Snyder, M., & Jones, E. E. (1974). Attitude attribution when behavior is constrained. *Journal of Experimental Social Psychology, 10,* 585–600.

Snyder, M., & Swann, W. B., Jr. (1978). Hypothesis-testing processes in social interaction. *Journal of Personality and Social Psychology, 36,* 1202–1212.

Snyder, M., Tanke, E. D., & Berscheid, E. (1977). Social perception and interpersonal behavior: On the self-fulfilling nature of social stereotypes. *Journal of Personality and Social Psychology, 35,* 656–666.

Snyder, M., & Uranowitz, S. W. (1978). Reconstructing the past: Some cognitive consequences of person perception. *Journal of Personality and Social Psychology, 36,* 941–950.

Starr, C. (1969). Social benefit versus technological risk. *Science, 165,* 1232–1238.

Staw, B. M. (1976). Knee-deep in the big muddy: A study of escalating commitment to a chosen course of action. *Organizational Behavior and Human Performance, 16,* 27–44.

Staw, B. M. (1981). The escalation of commitment to a course of action. *Academy of Management Review, 6,* 577–587.

Staw, B. M., & Ross, J. (1987). Behavior in escalation situations: Antecedents, prototypes, and solutions. *Research in Organizational Behavior, 9,* 39–78.

Staw, B. M., & Ross, J. (1987, March-April). Knowing when to pull the plug. *Harvard Business Review,* pp. 68–74.

Stone, E. R., & Yates, J. F. (1991). *Communications about low-probability risks: Effects of alternative displays.* Unpublished manuscript, University of Michigan, Ann Arbor.

Stoner, J. A. F. (1961). *A comparison of individual and group decisions involving risk.* Unpublished master's thesis, Massachusetts Institute of Technology.

Stoner, J. A. F. (1968). Risky and cautious shifts in group decisions: The influence of widely held values. *Journal of Experimental Social Psychology, 4,* 442–459.

Storms, M. D. (1973). Videotape and the attribution process: Reversing actors' and observers' points of view. *Journal of Personality and Social Psychology, 27,* 165–175.

Sullivan, K. (1990, October 5). Chip rivals in comedy of errors. *San Francisco Examiner,* pp. B1, B4.

Suls, J. M., & Miller, R. L. (Eds.). (1977). *Social comparison processes: Theoretical and empirical perspectives.* Washington, DC: Hemisphere Publishing Corporation.

Sweeney, P. D., Anderson, K., & Bailey, S. (1986). Attributional style in depression: A meta-analytic review. *Journal of Personality and Social Psychology, 50,* 974–991.

Synodinos, N. E. (1986). Hindsight distortion: "I knew-it-all along and I was sure about it." *Journal of Applied Social Psychology, 16,* 107–117.

Taylor, D. M., & Doria, J. R. (1981). Self-serving and group-serving bias in attribution. *Journal of Social Psychology, 113,* 201–211.

Taylor, D. M., & Jaggi, V. (1974). Ethnocentrism and causal attribution in a South Indian context. *Journal of Cross Cultural Psychology, 5,* 162–171.

Taylor, S. E., & Brown, J. D. (1988). Illusion and well-being: A social-psychological perspective on mental health. *Psychological Bulletin, 103,* 193–210.

Taylor, S. E., & Fiske, S. T. (1975). Point of view and perceptions of causality. *Journal of Personality and Social Psychology, 32,* 439–445.

Taylor, S. E., & Fiske, S. (1978). Salience, attention, and attribution: Top of the head phenomena. In L. Berkowitz (Ed.), *Advances in experimental social psychology* (Vol. 11, pp. 249–288). New York: Academic Press.

Taylor, S. E., Fiske, S. T., Close, M., Anderson, C., & Ruderman, A. (1977).

Solo status as a psychological variable: The power of being distinctive. Unpublished manuscript, Harvard University, Cambridge, MA.

Taylor, S. E., & Koivumaki, J. H. (1976). The perception of self and others: Acquaintanceship, affect, and actor-observer differences. *Journal of Personality and Social Psychology, 33,* 403–408.

Taylor, S. E., & Thompson, S. C. (1982). Stalking the elusive "vividness" effect. *Psychological Review, 89,* 155–181.

Teger, A. I. (1980). *Too much invested to quit.* New York: Pergamon Press.

Tetlock, P. E. (1983). Accountability and complexity of thought. *Journal of Personality and Social Psychology, 45,* 74–83.

Tetlock, P. E. (1985a). Accountability: A social check on the fundamental attribution error. *Social Psychology Quarterly, 48,* 227–236.

Tetlock, P. E. (1985b). Accountability: The neglected social context of judgment and choice. *Research in Organizational Behavior, 7,* 297–332.

Tetlock, P. E., & Kim, J. I. (1987). Accountability and judgment processes in a personality prediction task. *Journal of Personality and Social Psychology, 52,* 700–709.

Tetlock, P. E., Skitka, L., & Boettger, R. (1989). Social and cognitive strategies for coping with accountability: Conformity, complexity, and bolstering. *Journal of Personality and Social Psychology, 57,* 632–640.

Thaler, R. (1980). Toward a positive theory of consumer choice. *Journal of Economic Behavior and Organization, 1,* 39–60.

Thaler, R. (1985). Mental accounting and consumer choice. *Marketing Science, 4,* 199–214.

Thomas, E. J., & Fink, C. F. (1961). Models of group problem solving. *Journal of Abnormal and Social Psychology, 63,* 53–63.

Thompson, S. C., & Kelley, H. H. (1981). Judgments of responsibility for activities in close relationships. *Journal of Personality and Social Psychology, 41,* 469–477.

Thorndike, E. L. (1920). A constant error in psychological ratings. *Journal of Applied Psychology, 4,* 25–29.

Thorngate, W. (1980). Efficient decision heuristics. *Behavioral Science, 25,* 219–225.

Tindale, R. S. (1989). Group vs individual information processing: The effects of outcome feedback on decision making. *Organizational Behavior and Human Decision Processes, 44,* 454–473.

Tindale, R. S., Sheffey, S., & Filkins, J. (1990). *Conjunction errors by individuals and groups.* Paper presented at the annual meeting of the Society for Judgment and Decision Making, New Orleans, LA.

Tversky, A. (1969). Intransitivity of preferences. *Psychological Review, 76,* 31–48.

Tversky, A. (1972). Elimination by aspects: A theory of choice. *Psychological Review, 79,* 281–299.

Tversky, A., & Kahneman, D. (1971). Belief in the law of small numbers. *Psychological Bulletin, 76,* 105–110.

Tversky, A., & Kahneman, D. (1973). Availability: A heuristic for judging frequency and probability. *Cognitive Psychology, 5,* 207–232.

Tversky, A., & Kahneman, D. (1974). Judgment under uncertainty: Heuristics and biases. *Science, 185,* 1124–1130.

Tversky, A., & Kahneman, D. (1981). The framing of decisions and the psychology of choice. *Science, 211,* 453–458.

Tversky, A., & Kahneman, D. (1982). Judgments of and by representativeness. In D. Kahneman, P. Slovic, & A. Tversky (Eds.), *Judgment under uncertainty: Heuristics and biases.* Cambridge, England: Cambridge University Press.

Tversky, A., & Kahneman, D. (1983). Extensional versus intuitive reasoning: The conjunction fallacy in probability judgment. *Psychological Review, 90,* 293–315.

Tversky, A., & Kahneman, D. (1986). Rational choice and the framing of decisions. *Journal of Business, 59,* S251–S278.

Tversky, A., Sattath, S., & Slovic, P. (1988). Contingent weighting in judgment and choice. *Psychological Review, 95,* 371–384.

Tversky, A., Slovic, P., & Kahneman, D. (1990). The causes of preference reversal. *American Economic Review, 80,* 204–217.

U.S. Congress: House, Subcommittee of the Committee on Government Operations. (1981, May 19–20). *Failures of the North American Aerospace Defense Command's (NORAD) Attack Warning System.* 97th Congress, First Session, Washington, DC: U.S. Government Printing Office.

Valins, S., & Nisbett, R. E. (1971). Attribution processes in the development and treatment of emotional disorders. In E. E. Jones et al. (Eds.), *Attribution: Perceiving the causes of behavior.* Morristown, NJ: General Learning Press.

Vallone, R. P., Griffin, D. W., Lin, S., & Ross, L. (1990). Overconfident prediction of future actions and outcomes by self and others. *Journal of Personality and Social Psychology, 58,* 582–592.

Vallone, R. P., Ross, L., & Lepper, M. R. (1985). The hostile media phenomenon: Biased perception and perceptions of media bias in coverage of the Beirut massacre. *Journal of Personality and Social Psychology, 49,* 577–585.

Verplanken, B., & Pieters, R. G. M. (1988). Individual differences in reverse hindsight bias: I never thought something like Chernobyl would happen, did I? *Journal of Behavioral Decision Making, 1,* 131–147.

⇒ von Neumann, J., & Morgenstern, O. (1947). *Theory of games and economic behavior.* Princeton, NJ: Princeton University Press.

vos Savant, M. (1990, September 9). Ask Marilyn. *Parade,* p. 13.

Wagenaar, W. A. (1970a). Appreciation of conditional probabilities in binary sequences. *Acta Psychologica, 34,* 348–356.

Wagenaar, W. A. (1970b). Subjective randomness and the capacity to generate information. *Acta Psychologica, 33,* 233–242.

Wagenaar, W. A. (1972). Generation of random sequences by human subjects: A critical survey of the literature. *Psychological Bulletin, 77,* 65–72.

Wallsten, T. S. (1981). Physician and medical student bias in evaluating diagnostic information. *Medical Decision Making, 1,* 145–164.

Walster, E. (1967). Second-guessing important events. *Human Relations, 20,* 239–249.

Ward, W. C., & Jenkins, H. M. (1965). The display of information and the judgment of contingency. *Canadian Journal of Psychology, 19,* 231–241.

Warwick, D. P. (1975, February). Social scientists ought to stop lying. *Psychology Today,* pp. 38, 40, 105, 106.

Wason, P. C. (1960). On the failure to eliminate hypotheses in a conceptual task. *Quarterly Journal of Experimental Psychology, 12,* 129–140.

Wason, P. C., & Johnson-Laird, P. N. (1972). *Psychology of reasoning: Structure and content.* Cambridge, MA: Harvard University Press.

Watson, D. (1982). The actor and the observer: How are their perceptions of causality divergent? *Psychological Bulletin, 92,* 682–700.

Weaver, W. (1982). *Lady luck: The theory of probability.* New York: Dover Publications.

Weinberg, A. M. (1981). Three Mile Island in perspective: Keynote address. In T. H. Moss & D. L. Sills (Eds.), The Three Mile Island nuclear accident: Lessons and implications. *Annals of the New York Academy of Sciences* (Vol. 365, pp. 1–12). New York: The New York Academy of Sciences.

Weinstein, N. D. (1980). Unrealistic optimism about future life events. *Journal of Personality and Social Psychology, 39,* 806–820.

Weirich, P. (1984). The St. Petersburg gamble and risk. *Theory and Decision, 17,* 193–202.

Weldon, E., & Gargano, G. M. (1985). Cognitive effort in additive task groups: The effects of shared responsibility on the quality of multiattribute judgments. *Organizational Behavior and Human Decision Processes, 36,* 348–361.

Weldon, E., & Gargano, G. M. (1988). Cognitive loafing: The effects of accountability and shared responsibility on cognitive effort. *Personality and Social Psychology Bulletin, 14,* 159–171.

Wells, G. L., & Harvey, J. H. (1977). Do people use consensus information in making causal attributions? *Journal of Personality and Social Psychology, 35,* 279–293.

White, P. A., & Younger, D. P. (1988). Differences in the ascription of transient internal states to self and other. *Journal of Experimental Social Psychology, 24,* 292–309.

Wicker, A. W. (1969). Attitudes versus actions: The relationship of verbal and overt behavioral responses to attitude objects. *Journal of Social Issues, 25,* 41–78.

Wicker, A. W. (1971). An examination of the "other variables" explanation of attitude-behavior inconsistency. *Journal of Personality and Social Psychology, 19,* 18–30.

Williams, L. (1990, February 14). Decisions, decisions, decisions: Enough! *New York Times,* pp. B1, B5.

Wilson, D. K., Kaplan, R. M., & Schneiderman, L. J. (1987). Framing of decisions and selections of alternatives in health care. *Social Behaviour, 2,* 51–59.

Wilson, G. T., & Abrams, D. (1977). Effects of alcohol on social anxiety and physiological arousal: Cognitive versus pharmacological processes. *Cognitive Research and Therapy, 1,* 195–210.

Wilson, R. (1979, February). Analyzing the daily risks of life. *Technology Review,* pp. 41–46.

Word, C. O., Zanna, M. P., & Cooper, J. (1974). The nonverbal mediation of self-fulfilling prophecies in interracial interaction. *Journal of Experimental Social Psychology, 10,* 109–120.

Wortman, C. B. (1975). Some determinants of perceived control. *Journal of Personality and Social Psychology, 31,* 282–294.

Wright, G. N., Phillips, L. D., Whalley, P. C., Choo, G. T., Ng, K., & Tan, I. (1978). Cultural differences in probabilistic thinking. *Journal of Cross Cultural Psychology, 9,* 285–299.

Wright, J. C. (1962). Consistency and complexity of response sequences as a function of schedules of noncontingent reward. *Journal of Experimental Psychology, 63,* 601–609.

Wright, P. (1974). The harassed decision maker: Time pressures, distractions, and the use of evidence. *Journal of Applied Psychology, 59,* 555–561.

Wright, W. F., & Anderson, U. (1989). Effects of situation familiarity and financial incentives on use of the anchoring and adjustment heuristic for probability assessment. *Organizational Behavior and Human Decision Processes, 44,* 68–82.

Wright, W. F., & Bower, G. H. (1992). Mood effects on subjective probability assessment. *Organizational Behavior and Human Decision Processes, 52,* 276–291.

Wyer, R. S., Jr. (1976). An investigation of the relations among probability estimates. *Organizational Behavior and Human Performance, 15,* 1–18.

Yates, J. F. (1990). *Judgment and decision making.* Englewood Cliffs, NJ: Prentice Hall.

Yates, J. F., Zhu, Y., Ronis, D. L., Wang, D., Shinotsuka, H., & Toda, M. (1989). Probability judgment accuracy: China, Japan, and the United States. *Organizational Behavior and Human Decision Processes, 43,* 145–171.

Zajonc, R. B. (1965). Social facilitation. *Science, 149,* 269–274.

CREDITS

renewed 1992 by Michael A. Wallach and Nathan Kogan, reprinted by permission of the publisher.

19.1: From S. Oskamp, "Overconfidence in Case Study Judgments," *Journal of Consulting Psychology*, vol. 29. Copyright 1965 by the American Psychological Association. Reprinted by permission.

19.3: From *Decision Traps* by J. Edward Russo and Paul J. H. Schoemaker. Copyright © 1989 by J. Edward Russo and Paul J. H. Schoemaker. Used by permission of Doubleday, a division of Bantam Doubleday Dell Publishing Group, Inc. Reprinted in the British Commonwealth, except Canada, by permission of Judy Piatkus (Publishers) Ltd.

19.4: *Calvin and Hobbes* copyright 1990 Watterson. Dist. by Universal Press Syndicate. Reprinted with permission. All rights reserved.

21.2: From Barry Staw, "Knee-deep in Big Muddy: A Study of Escalating Commitment to a Chosen Course of Action," *Organizational Behavior and Human Performance*. Copyright © 1976 by Academic Press. Used by permission of publisher and author.

A-2: Drawing by Jonik, 1981. The New Yorker Magazine, Inc.

TABLES

3.1, 3.2: From E. Loftus and J. Palmer, "Reconstruction of Automobile Destruction: An Example of the Interaction Between Language and Memory," *Journal of Verbal Learning and Verbal Behavior*, vol. 13. Copyright © 1974 by Academic Press. Used by permission of publisher and author.

5.1: From John Hershey and Paul Schoemaker, "Risk Taking and Problem Context Expected Utility Analysis," *Journal of Risk and Insurance*, vol. 47. Copyright American Risk and Insurance Association. Used with permission. All rights reserved.

6.1: From Howard Schuman, "Problems in the Use of Survey Questions to Measure Public Opinion," *Science*, vol. 235, p. 957ff. Copyright 1987 by the AAAS. Used by permission of the AAAS and the author.

6.2: Top 2 pairs of questions from Elizabeth Loftus, "Leading Questions and the Eyewitness Report," *Cognitive Psychology*, vol. 7. Copyright © 1975 by Academic Press. Used by permission of the publisher and author.

11.1: Adapted from Eugene Borgida and Richard Nisbett, "The Differential Impact of Abstract vs. Concrete Information on Decisions," *Journal of Applied Social Psychology*, vol. 7. Copyright © 1977. Used by permission of V. H. Winston & Son, Inc.

12.1: Adapted from S. Selvin, "A Problem in Probability," *American Statistician*, Feb. 1975. Copyright © 1975. Used by permission of American Statistical Association.

13.1: Adapted from Gregory Northcraft and Margaret Neale, "Experts, Amateurs, and Real Estate," *Organizational Behavior and Human Decision Processes*, vol. 39. Copyright © 1987 by Academic Press. Used by permission of the publisher and Prof. Northcraft.

TEXT

Pp. 69ff: From Amos Tversky and Daniel Kahneman, "The Framing of Decisions and the Psychology of Choice," *Science*, vol. 211, p. 453ff. Copyright 1981 by the AAAS. Used by permission of the AAAS and Prof. Tversky.

P. 131: From Marilyn vos Savant, *Ask Marilyn*. Copyright © 1992 by Marilyn vos Savant. Reprinted with permission from St. Martin's Press, Inc., New York, NY. Reprinted with permission from Parade, copyright © 1990.

Pp. 245–246: B. F. Skinner, *Notebooks* (Englewood Cliffs: Prentice Hall), p. 150f. Copyright © 1980. Used by permission of the B. F. Skinner Foundation.

AUTHOR INDEX

SUBJECT INDEX